LEGAL ASPECTS
OF BUSINESS TRANSACTIONS
AND INVESTMENT
IN THE FAR EAST

Legal Aspects of Business Transactions and Investment in the Far East

Editors

Dennis Campbell

Director
Center for International Legal Studies
Salzburg, Austria

Of Counsel
Brown, Rudnick, Freed & Gesmer
Boston, Massachusetts

Partner
Rau, von Pander & Campbell
Brussels, Belgium

Counsellor at Law
Rau, von Pander & Partner
Munich, Germany

and

Arthur Wolff

Law Offices of Arthur Wolff
Vienna, Austria

Kluwer Law and Taxation Publishers
P.O. Box 23
7400 GA Deventer
The Netherlands

Tel.:   31–5700–47261
Telex: 49295
Fax: 31–5700–22244

Library of Congress Cataloging-in-Publication Data

Legal aspects of business transactions and investment
  in the Far East.

  1. Investments, Foreign – Law and legislation –
East Asia.   2. Business enterprises, Foreign – East
Asia.   I. Wolff, Arthur.   II. Campbell, Dennis.
LAW   346.6'07   88-27186
ISBN 90-6544-315-0   345.067

Cover design: Eset

ISBN 90 6544 315 0

Table of Contents

Foreword vii
    Arthur Wolff

Chapter 1. Legal Aspects of Entering the Japanese Market – A
             Western Perspective 1
    Mark Abell

Chapter 2. Parallel Imports in Japan 37
    Yukukazu Hanamizu

Chapter 3. Termination of Distributor Agreements in Japan 45
    Yukukazu Hanamizu

Chapter 4. Technology Transfer, Cooperation and Joint Venture
             Agreements with Korea 53
    Duck Soon Chang

Chapter 5. Legal Aspects of Trade and Investment in Singapore and
             Malaysia 65
    Robert D.A. Pick

Chapter 6. Legal Considerations for Investment in Taiwan 89
    Jui-Ming Huang

Chapter 7. Current Regulations on Foreign Investment in
             Indonesia 113
    Amin Azeharie

Chapter 8. Legal Aspects of Trade and Investment in Thailand 141
    Srisanit Anek

Chapter 9. Hong Kong at the Crossroads: the People's Republic of
             China – Hong Kong Nexus and Its Impact on
             Business Transactions 187
    Cole R. Capener and David B. Kay

Chapter 10. The Forms of Foreign Investment in the People's
Republic of China 219
Owen D. Nee

Chapter 11. Technology Transfer to the People's Republic
of China 249
Arthur Wolff

Chapter 12. Negotiation and Establishment of Joint Ventures in the
People's Republic of China 281
Stefan Messmann

Foreword

The economies of the Asian and Pacific Rim countries are among the fastest growing in the world:

China, as the country with by far the largest population, has been the focus of interest of foreign businessmen and investors since the 'open-door' policy started in the late 1970s, leading to a host of legislative acts to regulate and encourage foreign investment.

Hong Kong has for many years been a place attracting foreign business and investment, a development that has gained momentum with the 'open-door' policy of China, as many companies use Hong Kong to their advantage as a stepping stone to do business in China.

Indonesia, confronting the nation's worst economic crisis in two decades, has since 1986 been moving boldly to redirect the economy's whole thrust and taken a series of steps to improve and enliven the investment climate to ensure foreign business can thrive there.

Japan is now one of a handful of major players in the international business arena and one of the largest foreign investors. Yet, it offers also to the foreign businessman and investor significant opportunities for doing business and investing in Japan.

Korea is predicted by some to be likely to become the leader of what is sometimes called the 'Pacific Age', a plausible prediction if past economic achievements are an indication of future events.

Malaysia is one of the high-growth countries of southeast Asia, amply endowed with land and other natural resoures. The present policy agenda includes attractive industrial incentives, foreign equity participation rules as well as foreign investment guarantees.

Singapore, because of its successful economic policy, is sometimes termed as the 'Business Centre of Asia', and aims at becoming the 'Total Business Centre of Asia', *inter alia* by taking maximum advantage of the business opportunities presented by the 'open-door' policy in China.

Taiwan has become the model for many Asian countries because of its remarkable economic achievements over the past three decades. The 'Taiwan economic miracle' has attracted and is continuing to attract considerable foreign investments.

Thailand is on its way to being the next Asian newly industrialized country. More politically stable than many of its Southeast Asian neighbors, it has become a magnet for foreign investment, foreign investment being a major factor in Thailand's rise.

The region as defined here by the above list of countries is already a major economic force and will become even more important in the remainder of the twentieth century. Some observers believe it will soon dominate the world economy, making the 21st century 'The Pacific Century'. Doomsayers even see calamity for the West.

A closer look, however, reveals new opportunities for foreign business-men and investors in that region. Foreign companies are more and more aware of this increasingly interesting market for their merchandise, techno-logy and high-technology products and also interested in investing there. There is, therefore, a great need for information on the legal framework for trading with, licensing to and investing in the countries of that area, the more so as there are marked differences between the socio-economic back-ground in these countries and Western countries, which influence the legal situation in the various countries.

There was, therefore, organized in spring 1988 in Austria a conference on 'Legal Aspects of Business Transactions and Investment in Asia and the Pacific', which I had the honor to chair. The papers presented at that conference have been expanded and – where this proved necessary in view of recent legislation – updated and are presented in this book to give the interested businessman/investor some initial information.

I am very grateful to the authors not only for having undertaken to speak at the conference, but also to prepare papers of publishable quality, which, as they are all busy practitioners, involved not only much work, but also a sacrifice of otherwise free time.

November 1988   Dr. Arthur Wolff

Chapter 1

Legal Aspects of Entering the Japanese Market – A Western Perspective

by Mark Abell

Field Fisher & Martineau
London, England

Legal Environment

Japan is a unique country. Its people, its government, its laws, its industry and its commerce all show a peculiar mixture of insularity and the ability to absorb and 'Nipponise' foreign influences.

The first thing that any businessman entering the Japanese market must appreciate is that not only the language but also the whole system of doing things is vastly different from that in Europe and the United States. This is not the place to give a dissertation on such matters, but it is important that the legal environment and the way that it will affect a foreign businessman seeking to enter the Japanese market, is at least partly understood.

ROLE OF GOVERNMENT

Japan is a unique mixture of the free market and government regulation of the economy. This government influence comes mostly from the Ministry of International Trade and Industry (MITI – known as Tsusansho in Japan-

1

ese). MITI uses non-legal weapons to organise and direct Japanese business towards what the government believes to be in the nation's economic interest.

There is a very close link between the leaders of big business, and the upper levels of government agencies such as MITI, due in part to the fact that many senior businessmen will have started their careers in the civil service having graduated usually from Japan's most prestigious university, *Todai* (Tokyo University). After twenty years or so in the civil service, those who do not achieve the most senior positions in the civil service take early retirement and start a new career in industry. This *Amakudari* (meaning fall from heaven in Japanese) ensures that senior management and senior bureaucrats have much in common. These common attitudes, coupled with the all important personal connections (*Conne* in Japanese) that exist from student days enable administrative guidance, as it is so called, to be extremely effective.

Such administrative guidance can be promotional (advising enterprises in their own interests), adjudicatory (helping industry, resolve disputes instead of the courts), regulatory (especially MITI issues recommendations which must be followed by business).

Failure to follow such administrative guidance, while not unknown, is extremely rare, and the foreigner must not fall into the trap of believing that lack of any apparent compulsion, or coercive measure to ensure that a particular piece of guidance is followed means that it can be ignored with impunity. Even such industrial giants as Sumitomo Metal Mining Company have been brought to heel in the past.

ROLE OF LAW

The Japanese idea of the Role of Law in both Commerce and Society differs markedly from that of the West. Its regulatory function is extremely important as it helps the government to retain a good deal of control over the economy. However, the 'dispute resolution' function of law is markedly less important and law is seen very much as a tool of last resort. Indeed, a party that has to exercise its 'legal' rights is often perceived as having to do so due to its own shortcomings, its inability to find an acceptable compromise by using the appropriate, social, commercial and political pressures.

REGISTRATION REQUIREMENTS

Anti-trust law

Before World War II, there were four big *Zaibatsu* (cartels). These were Mitsubishi, Mitsui, Sumitomo and Yasuda. These effectively controlled the larger part of the Japanese economy and were actively supported by Government and bureaucracy.

2

During the American occupation, SCAP (Supreme Commander for the Allied Powers) aimed to destroy these. Part of this plan was the introduction of the 1947 law relating to Prohibition of Private Monopoly and Methods of Preserving Fair Trade (the Anti-Monopoly Law) (Law No. 54, 14 April 1947). This can be compared to the Sherman, Clayton and Federal Trade Commission Acts in the US.

Since 1947, the Act has been altered several times and arguably greatly weakened. To enforce the law, the Fair Trade Commission (FTC) was created. This has both administrative and quasi judicial functions. It is independent of all Government Ministries and administratively is responsible direct to the Prime Minister. The members of the FTC are selected by the Prime Minister with consent of both houses of the Diet (Parliament).

Jurisdiction

The FTC has primary jurisdiction in anti-trust matters. As the FTC head does not have cabinet rank, the FTC is not regarded as being as powerful as Ministries charged with economic regulations such as MITI. Decisions of the FTC are appealable to the Tokyo High Court in the first instance (this appeal is called 'Koso').

The provisions of the Anti-Monopoly Act provide for private anti-trust action and criminal prosecutions in addition to actions by FTC. Article 709 of the Civil Code also provides that the parties may bring an action in Tort for damages where there is no final action taken by the FTC. (If the FTC identifies a violation, the injured party does not have to prove intention or negligence in such Civil action.) But, these provisions are ineffective and nearly all suits are taken out by the FTC. The reason for this is that the damages in Tort are low (there are no treble damages as in the US). There are also no class actions in Japan, discovery is limited, there is a heavy burden of proof in private actions, costs are high and the process is slow.

Procedure

Fines for violating the Anti Monopoly Act are approximately 5-million Yen. Investigations by the FTC originate in one of three ways:

(a) a follow-up of an individual complaint;
(b) a follow-up of a violation report from the Procurator General;
(c) independent investigation by FTC staff.

A case may be settled in several ways:

(a) the issue of a recommendation finding, indicating that voluntary measures are needed to remedy the violation;
(b) if the recommendation is not followed, formal proceedings can be instituted in which the FTC is the adjudicating tribunal and also hands down a decision after hearing oral argument.
(c) the defendants may accept a consent decree before the formal decision is actually handed down.

3

Most FTC rulings are either recommendations or consent decrees.

Anti-Monopoly Law generally prohibits the following:

(a)   private monopolization;
(b)   unreasonable restraint of trade;
(c)   unfair business practices.

The approach adopted by the FTC is similar to the 'Rule of Reason' adopted in the US; that is to say, few activities are illegal per se and most activities are permitted if justifiable on sound business grounds.

International contracts (kokusaiteki Keiyakusho)

Japan has few natural resources and relies upon international trade for its prosperity. It is, therefore, not surprising that the government closely controls such trade and that legislation provides the machinery necessary for it.

Article 6(1) of the Anti-Monopoly Act is of great relevance to foreigners carrying out business in Japan. It provides that:

(1)   no entrepreneur shall enter into an international agreement or an international contract that contains matters that constitute an unreasonable restraint of trade or an unfair business practise;
(2)   an entrepreneur who has entered into an international agreement or an international contract shall in accordance with the Rules of the Fair Trade Commission, file a report thereof with the Commission, accompanied by a copy of said agreement or contract (in the case of an oral agreement or contract, a document describing its contents), within thirty days from its execution.

The significant point to note is that this Article applies to both parties to the agreement, and so allows the FTC to monitor and 'control' international agreements by directing its alteration to the Japanese party even if it is the one who has accepted the unfair business practices rather than imposed them.

In 1968, at the same time that foreign technology procedures were liberalized, the FTC issued two sets of guidelines for international agreements. The purpose of these guidelines is to indicate the principal type of contract terms that the FTC deem not to be permissible under Article 6. It is worthwhile noting that the exercise of ordinary intellectual property rights are not considered to be unfair and many types of contracts are also specifically exempted under guidelines.

The most definitive statement of what agreement need to be registered is contained in the FTC rules which provide that the following agreements must be registered under Article 6(2).

(i)   Agreements or contracts between a domestic entrepreneur and a foreign entrepreneur involving transfer of patent rights, utility model right, or other rights on technology, or licensing of these rights, or technical guidance on management for a period of over one year (excluding those which come under paragraph (iii).

(ii)   Agreements or contracts between a domestic entrepreneur and a foreign entrepreneur involving sales transactions (limited to only those which aim to resell to the third party what the purchaser purchased) to be conducted under paragraphs (i) or (iii).

(iii) Agreements or contracts between a domestic entrepreneur and a foreign entrepreneur involving joint management of business through holding stocks or shares of a company to be conducted for a period of over one year.

(iv)   Agreements or contracts between a domestic entrepreneur and a foreign entrepreneur involving transfer of rights on a trademark or copyrights (including neighbouring rights), or licensing of these rights for a period of over one year (excluding those which come under paragraphs (i), (ii) or (iii).

(v)   Other agreements or contracts than those prescribed in any one of the preceeding paragraphs, which come under any one of the following subparagraphs.

(a)   Agreements or contracts between domestic entrepreneurs who are in a competing relationship with one another and a foreign entrepreneur involving sales transaction to be conducted continuously for a period of over one year; or

(b)   Agreements or contracts between a domestic entrepreneur and a foreign entrepreneur (limited to only those who are in a competing relationship) involving continuous restriction on business activities relating to export or import such as restricting prices, quantities or areas in export or import trading.

Need for compliance

The FTC may take action against the Japanese party to enforce the law, even though the Japanese party is freely consenting to it. This means that the non-Japanese party must ensure that the agreement is registered, if appropriate.

The consequences of entering into an international contract with a Japanese party that provides for unfair business practices and not registering it (as well as the legal approach of the Japanese Courts to such questions), is well illustrated by the Novo case (*Novo Industri SA* v. *FTC*, 29(10) Minshu 1592 (Supreme Court (1975))). In this case, the plaintiff, Novo, was a Danish pharmaceutical company which had licensed Amano, a Japanese pharmaceutical company, to distribute certain enzymatic products of Novo in Japan. Amano, however, failed to register the Distribution agreement with the FTC. Three years later in 1969, Novo terminated the distributorship agreement and Amano submitted the agreement to the FTC. The FTC declared that three provisions of the agreement infringed the statutory prohibition of unfair business practices and so on 16 December 1969, the

5

FTC ordered Amano to abandon the offending provisions. Amano duly agreed as this meant that it could now violate all of the restrictions in the distributorship agreement. Novo appealed the decision to the Tokyo High Court, but it was held that it had no locus standii. This clearly shows that unless exempted under Article 6(3) of the Anti Monopoly Act, the foreign party must ensure that the Japanese party registers the agreement. One approach is to make the effective date of the agreement when the Japanese party has filed the agreement. The Japanese party may be reluctant to accept this, but it is wise to insist.

Foreign investment

Until the early 1970s, establishment of a subsidiary in Japan was quite difficult.

On 1 December 1980, the Foreign Exchange and Foreign Trade Control Law (FEFTCL) became effective (Law No. 228, 1949, as amended). This abolished the previous need to obtain approval or validation and replaced it with a reporting requirement.

Areas of concern
The FEFTCL's reporting requirements are triggered off by:

(a)   portfolio investment;
(b)   direct domestic investment;
(c)   takeovers: takeovers include a foreign investor proposing to acquire any shares of, or other equitable interest in, an unlisted Japanese company, or shares in a listed company which will result in the foreign investor, together with all of the corporations it controls owning ten per cent or more of the outstanding shares of such a Japanese listed company.

Procedure
Within three months before the date of the transaction, the foreign investor must submit a report to the Government (Ministry of Finance (MOF) and any other relevant Ministry having jurisdiction over the industry involved). The notice must include, *inter alia*:

(a)   name, address, nationality and occupation of the investor or the prin-cipal office, type of business and the capital of the organization, if a corporate entity;
(b)   the purpose of the business relating to the investment;
(c)   the time for completion of the investment;
(d)   reasons for the investments.

The investor cannot progress with the investment for 30 days after giving such notice. This period may be reduced in ordinary cases to fifteen days and under current Ministerial ordinances it has been reduced to a same day consent procedure in most cases.

The MOF and other relevant Ministry examine the proposal in the light of four criteria:

(a) potential threat to the public;
(b) it may adversely effect Japanese enterprises, or the Japanese economy;
(c) there is no trade treaty granting reciprocal agreement to Japanese with the relevant country;
(d) it should be modified/suspended as the MOF has decided to protect the balance of payment, the Japanese Yen, or finance/capital market in Japan requiring Government permission for that kind of capital transfer.

The MOF and other relevant Ministry can extend the fifteen days period to four months and then upon a showing of need by the Foreign Exchange Council, for one further month, although this is not usual.

If one of the four criteria exists, the MOF must recommend reference to the Foreign Exchange Enquiry Council appointed by the MOF. If the FEEC are of the opinion that one of the four criteria exists, it can 'suggest' changes in the agreement or suspension or cancellation. An appeal is possible.

Introduction of technology

All introduction of technology agreements between Japanese and non-residents are also subject to these notification requirements.

There are some minor differences between the introduction of technology and inward investment reporting requirements, the more important of which are that while direct inward investment must be reported by only the foreign investor, technology introductions must be dealt with by both the foreign and the Japanese resident parties involved and that the 'non-performance' period for introduction of technology can be totally eliminated.

Despite the above, no cases of foreign investment or technology transfers have to date been terminated.

Miscellaneous reporting requirements

There are several transactions concerning dealing in foreign currency and the export or import of Japanese Yen that require approval of the Japanese government but these are too specific to deal with in this paper. Licenses should also be registered, and these are discussed below. The need to register a physical presence in Japan is discussed below as well.

Legal Mediums

The alternative mediums through which a foreign businessman can enter the Japanese market are now considered.

DISTRIBUTOR

The simplest method of entering the Japanese market is for the European manufacturer to find and appoint a Japanese company to buy, import and distribute its products in Japan. This has the advantage of relatively risk-free distribution of products at low financial cost, but may result in only smaller amounts of products being sold.

Restrictions

There are a number of legal restrictions and procedures on exporting products to Japan, some of which are briefly described below:

(a) certain types of products are prohibited or subject to prior notification procedures. Examples include some agricultural products (e.g., fruit juices, beef, fuels, tobacco, chemicals, etc.). The list needs to be checked in each case. Most manufactured products are not included;
(b) if a special method of payment for the products is to be used, particularly more than one years credit or by reciprocal set off between accounts, the approval of the Bank of Japan will be needed which may be difficult to obtain unless the importer is a large trading company;
(c) import taxes are payable according to the classification of the products. Rates vary but are often low by international standards. International categories are used but negotiations with the customs may well be desirable in advance;
(d) imports which are related to technology licensing or transfer may require prior notification under the Foreign Transaction Control Law. This only applies to certain types of products such as aircraft, vaccines, oil and leather products, etc.;
(e) the distribution of imported products is of course subject to the Anti Monopoly Act, and must be registered with the FTC as detailed above. For distribution (compare Licensing), the restrictions are not too severe. Examples of permitted restrictions would be exclusivity to the importer (but not necessarily reciprocally), and a requirement for minimum level of sales: Resale price maintenance and competitive restrictions may not be permitted. The consequences of not registering can be severed, as evidenced by the Amano case (*see* above);
(f) if a distribution contract is also a licensing or inward investment, other registration may be required (*see* above and below).

Form of agreement

Traditionally, distribution agreements have been short and general in form, to reflect the philosophy that once the parties have committed themselves to a relationship, they have also accepted the obligations to negotiate changes to the agreement as the markets and products change. In recent years, the much more detailed US style of agreement has become increasingly popular, but the approach of the Japanese party to its operation remains much the same.

Choice of distributor

This is basically between a general trading company (*Sogo-Shosha*), and a company in the relevant industry. A general trading company may not have the detailed knowledge of the products any may only be willing to deal with larger businesses, but it does have great financial resources it could choose to promote the products. A more specialized company may have greater knowledge and contacts, but may not have (or be reluctant to use) financial support. This can lead it to preferring to sell fewer products at higher prices.

In both cases, there can also be pressure from the distributor to manufacture part or all of the products under license.

Finally, the manufacturer should be aware that successful imported products which can easily be copied, can lead to the development of competitive or alternative products by the distributor or others. New product development by the manufacturer is particularly important. Another solution is to license their manufacture in Japan as an alternative to distribution.

LICENSEE

A common form of doing business in Japan is to license the Japanese company (either unrelated or a subsidiary of the manufacturer) to produce all or part of the products under license. This is still a fairly simple method of doing business with relatively few restrictions on the manufacturer.

License agreement

This is more normally in the US form than a distribution agreement. There are several different styles of agreement ranging from simple and general Japanese form, to much more detailed US and European styles.

Taxes

Withholding taxes on royalties are set out under the applicable Double Tax Treaties with Japan. In addition the manufacturer may well be able to claim a tax credit in its own country for any withholding tax suffered in Japan.

Sourcing of products

There are restrictions under the Export and Import Transactions Law on the import of certain products including components from non-European countries (particularly Hong Kong and Taiwan) which may limit the sourcing of components for the licensed products in Japan. The re-valuation of the Yen has made this quite a common pattern. This may need to be discussed with the licensee.

Notice requirements

Registration of the license of the Patent office can be vital and is discussed below. A licensing agreement constitutes an international contract, and must therefore be notified to the FTC (*see* above). Such an agreement will probably also amount to an introduction of technology and must therefore be notified to the MOF and any other relevant ministry, under FEFTCL.

REPRESENTATIVE OFFICE

A representative office can be established without the requirement to notify the Japanese government, since there are no provisions concerning representative offices in the FEFTCL. However, when a foreign bank or securities firm established a representative office, there is a reporting requirement under the Bank Law or the Foreign Securities Firm Law.

Activities of a representative office are limited to those such as gathering information, researching the market and serving as a liaison office for the overseas Head Office. Its operations are usually not subject to Japanese corporate tax (*see* below).

BRANCH OFFICE

A foreign company can establish a Branch office under Part 2, Chapter 6, of the Japanese Commercial Code. A foreign company can also include foreign partnership. Foreign is defined as 'any company not created under Japanese law'.

Management

The representative appointed need not be a director or manager of the foreign company, and there can be more than one representative if so desired. The representative has the power to perform any act with regard to the business operations of the foreign company concerned (Article 479, paragraph 4, Article 78).

Registration

It is necessary to apply for registration of the branch, and make a public announcement within three weeks of the creation of the place of business. The procedure to be followed is the same as the creation of the place of business by a Japanese company of the same form (which in the case of the foreign limited company would usually be *Kabushiki Kaisha*, *see* below), with an additional mention in the registration of the law under which the company was formed and the full name and address of the representative in Japan.

Any change in the representative, or in the company itself, must be registered within three weeks of such change.

A foreign company cannot commence business in Japan until registration has been completed, and failure to do so results in the individual offender and the company becoming jointly responsible for any offence committed in this respect in the form of business transactions.

The application for registration for the place of business must be made by the representative person in Japan personally, or by proxy, at the public registration office covering the locality of the intended place of business. Postal applications are not accepted.

The application must be accompanied by the following documentation:

(a) document evidencing the existence of the head office (e.g. Memorandum and Articles of Association);
(b) document evidencing the qualifications of the representative in Japan (e.g. letter of appointment, contract, affidavit of the representative himself);
(c) Memorandum and Articles of Association, or other documentation showing the nature of the foreign company.

Each of the above documents must be verified by the appropriate government agencies in the company's country of origin, or by the relevant embassy in Japan. The documents in a foreign language must be accompanied by a Japanese translation.

Notice requirements

The branch office will constitute a direct inward investment. This requires reporting under the FEFTCL mentioned above. Any contracts between the branch and Japanese companies will amount to international agreements, and therefore are reportable to the FTC under the Anti Monopoly Act (*see* above). Ang introduction of technology by the branch must also be reported under the FEFTCL (*see* above).

Other formalities

In addition to these notification requirements, the simple procedure stipulated in the Commercial Code for the *Yugen Kaisha* should be followed in establishing a branch office of a company. This does not require the consent of the Court, and there are only certain filing requirements. Anyone setting up in Japan should be aware that there is also specific legislation governing particular businesses.

JAPANESE SUBSIDIARY

There are four forms of company in Japan. They are as follows:

(a) *Kabushiki Kaisha*
   A joint-owned company, which consists of shareholders whose liabilities to creditors of the company are limited to the amount of stock paid to the company.
(b) *Gomei Kaisha*
   A joint-owned company, which consists of partners whose liabilities to creditors of the company are unlimited.
(c) *Goshi Kaisha*
   A joint-fund company, which consists of limited and unlimited partners. The limited partners' liability to the creditors of the company are limited to the amount of their contribution to the company.
(d) *Yugen Kaisha*
   A limited liability company, which is a form of simplified joint stock company. There are certain restrictions, for example the number of shareholders is limited to 50, and executive procedures are much easier.

The need for limited liability and management participation mean that the *Kabushiki Kaisha* is the most usual form for foreign enterprises establishing an operation in Japan. There is no distinction between public and private companies.

Establishment of a Kabushiki Kaisha

There are two main methods of establishing a *Kabushiki Kaisha*. One is promotive incorporation whereby the total number of shares initially issued are taken up solely by the promoter. The other method is the subscriptive incorporation where the promoter takes up part of the shares and the remainder are offered for subscription. The foreign investor usually chooses the subscriptive method as it is much quicker. Promotive incorporation requires the appointment of an outside examiner and therefore it may take considerable time before the incorporation of the company.

The following steps should be taken to set up a *Kabushiki Kaisha*:

(a) the Articles of Incorporation of the *Kabushiki Kaisha* should be prepared;
(b) a report on the acquisition of shares should be filed with the Minister of Finance and other Ministers in accordance with the FEFTCL, as described above;
(c) the Articles of Incorporation should be notarized;
(d) the shares should be paid up by the promoters and subscribers;
(e) a constituent general meeting must be held to elect directors and statutory auditors. The directors elect a representative director in the directors' meeting;

(f) the formation of the *Kabushiki Kaisha* must be registered with the local office of the Legal Affairs Bureau of the Ministry of Justice within two weeks after the constituent general meeting. The documents to be attached to the application for registration are as follows:

    (i) the notarized Articles of Incorporation;
    (ii) acceptance of the shares prepared by each promoter;
    (iii) application for subscription of the shares prepared by each subscriber;
    (iv) certificate of payment of the initial share capital issued by a commercial bank;
    (v) minutes of the constituent general meeting;
    (vi) minutes of the Directors' meeting;
    (vii) application for registration of the official seal of the company's representative director (in Japan it is customary that the representative director of the company uses the seal instead of providing his personal signature).

The items to be registered are as follows:

    (i) the trade name and address of offices of the company;
    (ii) objects;
    (iii) total number of shares authorised to be issued;
    (iv) the par value of the shares;
    (v) the number of shares issued and the amount of paid in capital;
    (iv) names of directors and statutory auditor;
    (vii) name and address of the representative director;
    (viii) method of public notice of the company.

The date of registration and formation is regarded as the date of incorporation of a *Kabushiki Kaisha*. This whole process may take some three or four weeks.

Legal requirements for a Kabushiki Kaisha

The main provisions of the Commercial Code regarding a *Kabushiki Kaisha* are as follows:

(a) *Shareholders*

    (i) At least seven promoters are required.
    (ii) Each promoter must subscribe for at least one share of the company to be established.
    (iii) Theoretically, the promoters may be individuals or legal entities, resident or non-resident, Japanese or foreign citizens. However, as all the promoters must affix their seals (*Hanko*) to the Articles of Incorporation and attach the identification of their *Hanko* when the Articles of Incorporation are notarized the promoters should in practice be resi-

13

dent Japanese individuals. The *Hanko* has usually been registered with the local governmental office in the area where the person lives. The registered personal *Hanko* is usually used for important documents, together with the identification issued by the local government office. If a signature is used by a foreign national in certain legal documents which must be submitted to the registration authorities, such signature must be notarized.

(iv) The shares not subscribed for by the promoters may be subscribed by a foreign investor. Immediately after the formation of a Kabushiki Kaisha, the shares subscribed by the promoters may be transferred to the foreign investor.

(b) *Share capital*

(i) The Commercial Code does not stipulate a minimum paid-in capital requirement. It does require, however, a minimum of seven promoters as mentioned above, each holding at least one share. Since the lowest par value allowed is 50,000 Yen, the minimum effective capital requirement is therefore 350,000 Yen.

(ii) The share capital issued must be fully paid at the time of incorporation.

(iii) The total number of shares authorised to be issued should be stated in the Articles of Incorporation. In order to accomplish the incorporation, at least 25 per cent of the total number of authorised shares must be issued and paid up.

(c) *Management*

(i) Shareholders must elect at least three directors. Their terms of office cannot exceed two years (one year for those who are elected at the Constituent General Meeting). Any director may be re-elected. The Commercial Code places only one restriction on the residence or nationality of directors; that is, at least one representative director must be a resident of Japan.

(ii) Board Meetings may be held either inside or outside Japan. At least one week's prior notice is required, unless the Articles specify otherwise. All of the directors constitute a quorum, and unless otherwise stated in the Articles, a majority vote of those present at the meeting is sufficient to pass a resolution.

(iii) Directors may be held jointly and severally liable to both the corporation and the shareholders for acts of bad faith and may be removed from office at any time by a two-thirds vote of shareholders present at a General Meeting.

(iv) Directors are vested with full managerial authority, but the Commercial Code requires that one or two directors be specially designated to represent the company in dealing with third parties.

Naturally, a technical assistance agreement between a foreign Parent and Japanese subsidiary will be reportable under the FEFTCL, as will any international contract under the Anti-Monopoly law (*see* above).

However, any subsequent contract between the Japanese subsidiary and Japanese third parties are not reportable. A Japanese subsidiary thus has the advantage of reducing the reporting requirements imposed by the Japanese Government on foreign parties.

Japanese subsidiaries used not to be particularly popular amongst foreign investors, due mostly to a 'fear of the unknown' and a lack of willingness to be so completely committed to and subject to the political, economic and legal, systems of Japan.

JOINT VENTURE

Choosing a joint venture partner in any country is always a problem and when setting up a joint venture operation with a Japanese corporation in Japan, apart from the usual problems of 'suitability' and the need for complementary managerial styles, it is essential also to find out what Japanese industrial group or *Keiretsu* it comes from. Examples of these groups are Sumitomo, Mitsui, Dai-Ichii Kangyo, Sanwa and Mitsubishi. Each group has at least one major bank, trading company, insurance company, shipping company together with a host of manufacturing companies. It is essential when asking Japanese companies for advice or attempting to woo a potential partner, they are all members of the same Keiretsu or have other intimate links. Failure to ensure this may well result in a lack of cooperation from the parties involved.

It is also necessary to appreciate that the Japanese attitude to joint ventures is quite different to that of most European or US Corporations and many potentially successful joint ventures have failed due to the Japanese partners' reluctance to pay out dividends after the first two or three years. A joint venture may also help to solve the problem of recruiting Japanese managers, since the 'life time employment' systems often makes this difficult.

The joint venture company should be set up as a *Kubishiki Kaisha* (*see* above).

Naturally, the joint venture agreement requires registration at the FTC as an International Agreement and a report under the FEFTCL must also be made on the basis of direct inward investment and possibly due to the introduction of technology (*see* above). Alternatively, it is possible for the foreign investor to buy an existing *Kabushki Kaisha*, in which case there are further reporting requirements under the FEFTCL as such a purchase would, of course, constitute a takeover (*see* above).

15

Kumiai

This is similar to a partnership in England and merely requires two or more people with a 'mutual intent' to cooperate together. This is permitted under Chapter 12, Article 667, of the Japanese Commercial Code.

It is easy to create and there is no requirement for a detailed Agreement which thus ensures that there are few complications upon termination.

Kumiai are very popular in Japan among, for example, construction companies. Such a partnership was established for the duration of the Osaka Airport project.

For a foreign company to take part in a *Kumiai* it is, of course, necessary for it first to establish itself as a Japanese resident company by forming a *Kabushiki Kaisha*, as described above.

Franchising

Japan is the world's third largest franchise market, following the US and Canada, boasting 5,654 outlets of American franchises alone in 1984.

The various retailer laws enacted to protect small retail businesses are reasonably favourable franchising approach and the only disclosure requirements necessary to take advantage of them are those which the Japan Franchising Associations has agreed with MITI. These are far less strenuous than those encountered in most parts of the US.

Many foreign franchisors appoint one of the large *Sogoshosha*, such as C. Hoh and Mitsui, as area developers for Japan. This has the benefit of lessening the franchisor commitment but also greatly reduces its potential profits.

Intellectual Property Law

Patent

Substantive requirements for patent (Tokkyoken)

Under the Patent Law (Law No. 121, 1959) the invention (*hatsumei*) must meet the requirements of patentability. Article 29 lays down three tests of novelty, utility and inventiveness or non-obviousness.

In addition to satisfying these three criteria, the application must be annexed with a note of the invention title, a brief explanation of the drawing if also attached and a detailed explanation of the invention to a standard, whereby a person with ordinary knowledge in the invention field could easily work it.

Patent application and examination procedure

Application
The Patent Office (*Tokkyocho*) is an agent of MITI and administers the Japanese intellectual property law under the Director General (*Chokan*). The Office deals with applications, appeals, trials, interpretation of the technical scope, patent and inventions, publications, and determination for patent attorneys (*Benrishi*). A patent is granted to the first applicant for the invention in question. The Patent application must be in a form specified by the Patent Law Enforcement Regulations and filed with the Director General.

Filing application
After the application has been filed, the first examination department looks at the formalities, i.e. documents, fees, etc. Any deficiencies can be cured. If the application passes the examination it is submitted to successive Examination Departments for examination as to substance.

Public disclosure of applications
Every application is disclosed to the public (*kokui*) within eighteen months of the date of filing. Early publication (*kokoku*) encourages early challenging and prevents duplication and therefore wasted investment. The disclosure is made by publication in the *Official Patent Gazette*. A system of examination upon demand is incorporated into the processing of patent applications to streamline the assessment and granting procedure.

Examination of applications
The examination of applications is generally carried out by an Examiner in order of demand. If examination is not demanded within seven years the application is treated as abandoned. The examiner must notify the applicant of the reasons for refusal and give a reasonable time, fixed by the examiner for a counter statement to the notice. The applicant may amend his application to overcome the grounds of the refusal. In other cases, the application may be changed, but not so as to alter the identity of the invention, i.e. the gist of the specification. The statement of claim for patent is deemed not to be the gist. Amendment can normally be made within fifteen months from filing. If the examiner finds no reason for refusing the patent he will make a decision (*Kettei*) to publish the application. (*Shutsugan Kokoku*). The Director General will then arrange the publication in the *Official Patent Gazette* (*Tokkyo Koho*). The application and accompanying materials are deposited for two months at the Patent Office for public inspection. Publication is to invite opposition and opinion. If opposition (*tokkyoigimoshitatesho*) is received in the required form a copy is served on the applicant and a reasonable time allowed for a reply (*Hobensho*). A final decision (*Satei*) is reached after a search is made by the examiner. A transcript of the final decision is served on the applicant by the Director General. The publication of an

application confers the right to work the invention on the applicant. The protection is provisional until full patent is granted. In the event of refusal by the examiner, the applicant has 30 days to demand a trial (*shimpan*).

The validity and scope of patent rights

A patent right (*Tokkyoken*) comes into existence through registration and the payment of Patent fees for the first to third years must be within 30 days of the final decision when registration is made after which it is published in the *Official Gazette*. The duration of a patent right is fifteen years from the date of publication of the application, but not exceeding twenty years from application.

The patentee enjoys an exclusive right to work (*Jisshi*) the patented invention as a business (Article 68). It does not extend to the working of the invention for experimental or research purposes.

Compulsory licenses

These are granted if the protected invention has not been worked continuously in Japan for more than three years, or there is a strong need for exploiting a patented invention for public interest (Article 93). This remedy is rarely sought.

Infringement of patent and available remedies

Wilful or negligent infringement leads to compensation in damages.

There are both civil and criminal remedies for infringement: the civil remedies include an Injunction (Article 100) (*Karishobun*), Damages (Article 102), and Measures to restore business goodwill of the patentee (Article 106).

Licensing of patents

Both exclusive (*senyojisshiken*) and non-exclusive (*tsujojisshiken*) licenses can be granted of patent rights. In the case of exclusive licenses, it does not take effect as against third parties unless registered.

Senyojisshiken

To register a license with the Director-General of the Patent Office, the applicant must provide the Patent number of Patent to be licensed, the name of Patented invention, the ground for registration and date of Contract, the scope of license, the Details of Consideration and Registration tax (£5,000). The application must be signed by owner and licensee and be accompanied by a Proforma Senyojisshiken Agreement, and a copy of the original agreement.

Tsujojisshiken

The procedure to register is the same as for *Senyojisshiken*.

18

UTILITY MODEL (JITSUYOSHINAN)

The Utility Model Law is designed to protect small inventions (*koan*) by Japanese nationals, that do not qualify for patent protection. The law provides ten years protection and is based on the German law. Applications are made to the Patent Office for full examination. The Patent Law was enacted in 1959 (Law No. 123) and lays down a system of patent application and administration.

Devices eligible for utility model registration

Article 1 sets out the purpose of the law: 'to promote the protection and utilisation of devices relating to the configuration or structure or combination or both, of goods, with a view to encouraging the creation of such devices and thereby to contribute to the development of industry'. A device is defined in Article 2 as 'the creation of technical ideas utilising natural laws', whereas patent law is for highly advanced technical ideas. Utility model registration only applies to products and not to processes (Article 3) and further is limited to those which have shape and structure, e.g. not used for materials such as glass and alloys.

Registration, application and examination

This is basically the same as the patent law system, but the Fees are lower, the period for demanding examination is shorter, the public disclosure is simpler, the period for conversion from a patent application to a utility application is shorter, and there is no equivalent to additional patent.

Exclusive right of owner of registered utility model

Establishment of utility model rights is on registration and payment of fees. The first fees are paid for the first second and third year and registration is published in the Official Utility Model Gazette. Fees must be paid in 30 days of notice of the final decision. Protection is for ten years from the date of publication of application, but not longer than fifteen years from the date of the application. The utility model right owner has the exclusive right to work his registered utility model as a business. The exclusive right is limited in the same way as the patent law.

TRADE MARK LAW

Trade marks (*shohyo*) affixed to goods are only afforded protection under this law. There is no service mark protection. Trade mark protection is based on registration and prior use is of little consequence.

Substantive requirements for trade mark registration.

A trade mark, like a design, comes into existence upon registration of its establishment at the Patent Office. The right obtained on registration extends to the designated goods (Article 25). The protection of the trade mark is for ten years following registration.

A trade mark is defined as 'characters, letters, figures or signs or any combination of these and colours (hyosho), which a person who, as a business, produces, processes, certifies or assigns goods on such goods'. Configurations of goods and signs, service marks and trade names are not included (*see* Unfair Competition Law). Trade marks can be obtained for any goods to be used for one's own business. The applicant does not have to prove use, but it must have a distinctive quality.

Generally, trade mark registration can be obtained for any trade mark to be used for goods relating to one's own business. There are unregisterable trade marks set out in the law as being so, since they lack distinctiveness, e.g. a trade mark indicating a generic name, common use, trade mark customary use for such goods, simple and common mark.

Unregisterable trade marks

These include marks which are similar to well-known trade marks of stock, etc., contrary to public order/good morals, trade marks adopting portrait/ name of person, trade marks similar to well-known Trade Mark, similar to trade mark of earlier application, identical to defensive trade mark of same class, likely to cause confusion, or likely to mislead public as to quality of goods.

Trade marks identical to the Red Cross or the symbol of some other international organisation are unregisterable on the ground of public interest.

Application and examination procedure for trade mark registration

Priority is given to the first applicant for trade mark registration and where there are similar applications submitted on the same day then negotiations must take place between the applicants to decide who will obtain registration. Trade mark law provides six months for the registration of a trade mark attached to the goods after goods are displayed at a Government exhibition, Patent Office exhibition, etc. in accord with the Paris Convention.

Application procedure
An application for trade mark registration must be filed with the Director General of the Patent Office in the form specified by regulation (the method of application is broadly the same as patent applications).

Registration of associated trade marks
The registration of associated Trade Marks (*rengoshohyo*) and defensive trade marks (*bogohyosho*) are modelled on British trade mark Law. By registering the same trade mark for similar goods, similar trade marks for the same goods or a similar trade mark for similar goods the owner is given an assurance that he has an exclusive right not only within the scope of his original trade mark, but also in the surrounding area confusing similarity with respect to the goods. This prevents confusing trade marks being registered. There are currently 34 classes of goods under Trade Mark Law Enforcement Order (Cabinet Order No. 19, 1960).

Examination of applications
The examination of applications on receipt, their publication, the registration of any opposition and registration procedure follow the principles of patent law. The grounds for refusal in connection with trade marks include broadly lacking distinctiveness, unregisterability, misleadingness and prior registration, and where applicant or alien without qualification for registration, i.e. not resident, not Paris Convention National, not other Agreed Country national.

If trade mark is unregisterable, the applicant can file counter statement (*ikensho*) within a reasonable time. The Application is available for public inspection for two months, within which period anyone can file opposition (*igimoshitatesho*) giving reason for objections. A copy is served on the applicant who has a right of reply (*tobensho*) within a reasonable time fixed by examiner.

Rights acquired upon registration
Registration is again effected upon payment of the registration fee for each mark (c Y44,000). When registration is made, the name and domicile of trade mark owner (*shohyokensha*) the registration number and date of registration are published in the *Official Trade Mark Journal*. A trade mark owner has exclusive right to use his registered trade mark for the designated goods (*shiteishohin*). The duration of trade mark protection is ten years from registration which is renewable unless the mark has become unregisterable. If for three years before filing renewal (*koshin*) there is non-user, then renewal is only granted if there is a justifiable reason for a non-user shown. Generally 'use' is the attaching of marks to goods or sale material. The scope of the trade mark is determined from the description in the document attached to the application. An interested person may demand the Patent Office for an interpretation of the effect of the trade mark right. There is the right of prior user and there is a restriction on the use of a registered trade mark that conflicts with a design right or a copyright of another. The exclusive right of an owner of a registered trade mark is subject to the right to continuously use an identical/similar trade mark of one who used it before the owner registered his application if it is bona fide and well-known.

Infringement of registered trade marks

Infringement is deemed to occur when an unauthorised third party uses an identical or similar trade mark on identical or similar goods. Acts of infringement against the owner or exclusive licensee (*Senyoshiyokensha*) are set out in the Act in Article 37. These are very broadly the use of a registered Trade Mark or one similar to on identical or similar goods, possessing goods so marked or things so marked for marking goods and manufacturing or importing goods so marked or things so marked. An infringer is presumed to have been negligent in such act of infringement and the general principle of tort is applicable in infringement actions.

Defenses

The defenses in trade mark infringement actions are usually the assertion of dissimilarity. The Courts determine similarity with the viewpoint of the public. The defense of prior use to registration can also be alleged as a defense. The assertion of design/copyright registration which supersedes the trade mark registration is also a defense, but the filing of copyright or design application must be shown to be before the plaintiff's trade mark application. Other defenses are the assertion that the alleged infringing mark is not a trade mark for the purposes of indication of source of products or the assertion that the plaintiff's trade mark has become generic.

Remedies

The remedies for trade mark infringement are those available for infringement of patent rights i.e. injunction, damages, measures to restore business reparation of Plaintiff.

Trade mark notice

As for patent law, the trade mark law encourages trade mark notices (*Shohyotorokuhyoji*) to be attached in a form set down by MITI ordinance to the goods, i.e. the letters *Torokushohyo* and the registration number does not affect recovery of damages in infringement actions.

Exclusion of goods from import

Exclusion of infringing goods from importation under the tariff law is also seen where goods bearing counterfeit trade marks are imported. Tariff law prohibits the import of goods which infringe patent rights, utility model rights, design rights, trade marks and copyright.

Defensive mark registration (bogohyosho)

Defensive mark registration is possible where a registered trade mark has become well known and there is a risk that a third party will use the trade mark for goods different to the designated goods and hence cause confusion as to source.

Assignment and licensing of trade marks

The licensing of Trade Marks can be exclusive (*Senyoshiyoken*) or non exclusive (*Tsujoshiyoken*). As with patents, the licenses must be registered.

Under trade mark law, trade marks are regarded as property distinct of business or goodwill and can be assigned without the accompaniment of business or goodwill. There are some restrictions on assignment.

DESIGNS

Designs (*Isho*) are protected by the Copyright or Design Law or both (Berne Convention). It is up to each member country of the Berne Union, whether to protect works of applied art as artistic works or industrial design. Design Law No. 125 1959 adopts the Patent Law approach.

Artistic works are as defined in copyright law to include 'articles of artistic craftsmanship' but it was intended not to extend copyright protection to works for use as models or designs of mass produced articles. These were meant to be afforded protection under the design or other industrial property law.

The Design Law was revised in 1979 and today's Design Law was enacted in 1959. The exclusive right of an owner of registered design is that of use as a business.

Subject matter design protection

Article 1 of the Design Law sets out the purpose of the law 'to promote the protection and utilisation of designs with a view to encouraging creation of designs and thereby contributing to the development and industry'.

The word 'Design' (*Isho*) is defined as the shape, pattern, color or combination of these in an article which through the sense of sight arouses an aesthetic sensation. Aesthetic sensation is a unique feature of Japanese law (N.B. color is included in the concept of design). The design law adopts the patent law concept of novelty, utility and non-obviousness as requirements for registration (Article 3). Designs not in the public interest, are unregisterable.

Application of determination procedure for design registration

As with patent law, priority is given to the first application and any person who has created a design may apply for Design registration. The right to obtain Design registration is assignable and employees and aliens are in the same position as they are in patent law. Registration of a Design is by application to the Director General of the Patent Office in a form specified in the Design law (MITI Ordinance). Basically, the same particulars that are required in patent applications are required in design applications.

Amendments and joint applications can also be made. The article must be stated to which the design is applied and if there is a set of customary designs sold as a set and used simultaneously such as, e.g., coffee cups and pot, the set can be registered as one design. An application by an owner for a similar design must be marked *Ruijiisho Toroku Negai* and the registration number of the principal design stated.

The examination of applications and review of the examiner's refusal are the same as in patent law procedure, unlike with Patents and Utility Models, there is a secret design system adopted in design law, which requires the Patent Office to keep the established design secret for up to three years after registration. This is used in the fashion industry a great deal. Secrecy is demanded on the original application and marked in red ink *Himitsu Isho*. It also states the period of secrecy desired, which can be amended. There are exceptions to the secrecy of designs under seal in certain circumstances, e.g. when demanded by the Court.

Exclusive right of the owner of a registered design

A Design right (*Ishoken*) comes into existence on registration of its establishment, i.e. after payment of the fees. Registration of the fact is published in the *Official Design Gazette* (*Ishokoho*) with details. Publication will be delayed until expiration of the period of secrecy if this has been granted. Annual Fees are laid down by law and the first year's fees must be paid before the expiration of 30 days from notice of registration served on the applicant. The design right is for fifteen years from the registration and the owner of a design enjoys an exclusive right to work his registered design and similar designs as a business. 'Working' is defined as 'act of manufacturing, using, assigning, leasing, displaying for the purpose of assignment or lease or importing goods incorporating a design'.

The scope of the design is determined on the basis of a description and drawings/photographs/models submitted on application. As with patent law, interested persons may demand the Patent Office for interpretation of scope and the principle of prior user is the same. *Bona fide* prior user can be granted *Tsujo jisshiken*. (Prior user can be used as a defense to an infringement action.) Remedies for infringement include injunction, damages and measures to restore goodwill to plaintiff.

There are special principles for damages in design infringement which take account of any profits made by offender, any royalty owner would usually be able to receive and any extra damages deemed desirable. There is a presumption of negligence against the infringer.

Assignment/licensing

Patent law principles also prevail in design law for assignment and licensing of design rights. The transfer of design rights must be recorded in the *Design*

Register to be effective and notification to the Director General on inheritance or succession must be observed.

Design rights are freely assignable but all co-owners must consent to assignment, and the transfer is not effective unless recorded in *Design Register* (*Ishogensho*) at the Patent Office.

Licenses of Design Rights can be either *Senyojisshiken no settei* (exclusive) or *Tsujojisshihen no Kyodaku* (non exclusive).

COPYRIGHT LAW

The first modern copyright (*chosaku-ken*) law was enacted to incorporate the principles of the Berne convention for the protection of literary and artistic works. The protection of these principles enables Japan to join in the convention.

The present copyright law was established in 1970, and in 1975 Japan ratified the convention establishing the World Intellectual Property Organisation (WIPO).

Works of authorship protected by copyright

Article 1 states the purpose of the law as 'providing for the rights of authors and rights neighbouring thereto with respect to works of authorship as well as performances phonogram and broadcasts to secure protection of these rights, paying due regard to fair exploitation of these cultural products, and thereby to contribute to the development of culture'. The term 'works of authorship' is defined as 'productions in which thoughts or emotions are expressed in a creative way'.

The Court decides whether a matter is a work of authorship and Article 10 excludes works of authorship that merely communicate certain facts or news of events.

Protection is only afforded to those that come within:

(a) works of Japanese nationals;
(b) works first published in Japan or in 30 days of first publication;
(c) reciprocal protection under an international treaty.

Moral rights (Jinkakuken)

Authors, (*Chosakusha*), i.e. persons who create a work (can be an association which has a representative), have moral rights which are protected automatically under Articles 18(1), 19(1) and 20(1), i.e. the right to publish, to claim authorship and right to integrity of the works. These are personal to the author and inalienable. They cease to exist when the author dies, except in the case of a publisher who is bound to refrain from infringing the author's moral right during and after his life. After death his kin can bring an act of infringement.

25

Copyright (economic rights) of authors

The copyright law provides the exclusive right for authors to secure economic gains, i.e. a property right from which he can derive and control the use of his works. Copyright is a bundle of rights to use works of authorship in various different ways. When a derivative work is created from an original work, the original work author is entitled to the same rights as the derivative author. The duration of copyright is from the moment of creation to 50 years after the author's death. If the work is anonymous or pseudonymous, copyright is for 50 years after its publication, unless the name is well known, the author registered his own name or the author publishes work under his own name or well known pseudonym. For a juristic person copyright is for 50 years after publication, unless the real name/well known pseudonym was indicated when published.

The members of the Berne Convention that are afforded reciprocal protection in Japan are afforded such protection only for the period of protection enjoyed in the country of origin.

To balance economic gains of authors with the interests of the general public to enjoy and benefit from the author's cultural contributions, there are exemptions from copyright liability, which allows fair use when the copying is made for limited purposes, e.g. reproductions for examinations non profit performances, quotations, reproduction in braille, etc. Compulsory licenses are granted for reproduction for School textbooks, use of works in broadcasting school educational programmes and reproduction of examinations and tests concluded for profit. This does not affect the author's moral right. The reproduction must be fair in the circumstances and for non profit. It must not injure the interests of the copyright owner.

Assignment and licensing of copyright

Copyright is personal property, which is freely assignable or licensable in whole or in part (Article 61).

The granting of a right of publication is unique to Japanese law. It is called *Shuppanken*, which is one of the divisional rights of copyright. There are the same requirements for effectiveness as above, but on establishing *Shuppanken*, the copyright owner can no longer publish the work in its original form or include it in a collection or compilation of works. After three years have expired from the date of establishment of the *Shuppanken*, the author (himself only) can publish a collection or compilation including the work, unless the contract granting the right of publication states otherwise.

Article 81 provides compulsory terms that are imposed on the Shuppanken holder by law, e.g. publication within a time limit and notice of republication to the copyright owner.

The licensing of musical copyrights is through JASEAC, which is the Japanese Society of Rights of Authors and Composers. This body arranges collective licensing for all its members and ministers their copyrights.

Compulsory licenses

Compulsory licenses can also be granted under copyright law by arbitration (*satei*). These are granted by the Director General of the Cultural Affairs Agency, where the procedure for applying for compulsory license is similar to the patent law.

Infringement of moral right, copyright, publication right and neighbouring rights

Civil remedies are found in Articles 112 to 118. When infringement occurs or is likely to occur, the owner of the right can demand discontinuance or prevention of such infringement. Destruction of infringing material or objects connected herewith can also be demanded in accord with the above.

Injunctions and temporary injunctions can be obtained to prevent infringement. Damages are also available under the general tort provision in Article 709 of the Civil Code, where the defendant has willfully or negligently infringed.

Criminal sanctions in relation to infringement of copyright is either penal servitude with hard labor normally not exceeding three years or a fine.

PROTECTION OF UNPATENTED KNOW-NOW AND TRADE SECRETS

General tort principles are used in the protection of trade secrets, i.e. civil remedies under the Civil Code: 'A person who, wilfully or negligently has injured the right of another is bound to compensate him for the damage which has arisen therefrom.'. A strict interpretation of the aforementioned would only give someone a remedy if he could show he has a right and that right was injured.

An injunction may be a remedy if the claim is based on ownership or other exclusive rights, but there is no provision for this remedy in the Code therefore it is not available.

Employers trade secrets

These are safeguarded by binding employees by contract not to disclose for a period of time.

Protection of trade secrets under confidential relationships

Statutory provision imposes confidential obligations on persons in various positions or professions. The statutory provisions are in the Civil and Commercial Codes, e.g. directors that are bound by the duty of loyalty and non-competition with their corporation. There are no cases on either Code.

Protection for the owner of unpatented know-how under the patent law

The general principles in Part 2 Model Law for Developing Countries inventions [United International Bureau for the Protection of Intellectual Property (BIRPI) 1965] apply to Japan.

Protection under the patent law is afforded by these general principles of secrecy. As we have seen, novelty of invention is a condition for applying for a patent. An examiner is required to refuse approval to an applicant who is not the inventor or successor to the right to obtain a patent.

Criminal sanctions for unauthorised disclosure or misuse of trade secrets

There is no specific provision in the Criminal Code, but intimidation, obstruction of another's business, theft, fraud, breach of trust may be applied.

UNFAIR COMPETITION

The unfair competition law is provided in the Unfair Competition Prevention Law 1965 enacted to ratify the Hague revision of the Paris Convention for the protection of industrial property. The Japanese law does not provide for misappropriation of trade secrets or industrial espionage. All the Japanese Intellectual Property Law statutes contribute to the Unfair Competition Law, together with provisions in the Criminal Law and Civil Code. The Trade Mark law is the most important statute in the area of unfair competition, the latter being supplementary to the Trade Mark law as it provides protection for service marks and trade names otherwise unregisterable.

General provisions

The Unfair Competition Prevention Law is a short Act to enact the Hague Act of the Paris Convention. It provides for injunctions and damages as remedies for unfair competition, exempt geographical names that have become generic, states the situation of aliens, prevents the use of flags, emblems, symbols, etc., of nations or organisations and gives exemptions for exclusive rights under the Intellectual Property Laws in Japan.

The statutory provision for an Injunction is very important, as the general tort provision of the Civil Code does not provide for such a remedy.

To be entitled to an injunction under the Act, a person who is alleging the injury must establish that his Trade Mark, trade and location are well known and confusion is caused to his goods, business establishment or activities.

A person who injures the goodwill of another or disrupts the business of another is punishable under the criminal code or under the criminal sanctions of the Unfair Competition Prevention Law.

This statute sets out acts which are exempt from remedy under the Act and are generally those that constitute using customary use/no names for the circumstances/situations concerned or using the person's own name in good faith or prior use of the common place.

The remedies against unfair competition are injunction, damages, measures to restore business and goodwill of the plaintiff. For an injunction, objective elements such as confusion only have to be proved by the plaintiff. The exercise of industrial property rights is a defence to an unfair competition action.

Protection of trade names under the Commercial Code

Article 20 of the Commercial Code provides for an injunction for the owner of a trade name registered in the Commercial Register (*Shogyotokiho*) against the user of an identical or similar trade name for the purpose of unfair competition in the same geographical area of a trade name registered in the *Commercial Register* (administered by the Justice Minister).

Registration (*toki*) under the Commercial Code is separate from registration (*toroku*) under the Trade Mark Designs and Utility Model Laws. The Commercial Registration Law (Law No. 125, 1963 provides for the Commercial Register which comprises of seven separate registers, which are trade names (*Shogo*), Minors, guardians, manager (*Shihainin*), general partnerships (*Gomes Karsha*), limited partnership (*Goshi Kaisha*), stock companies (*Kabushiki Kaisha*), limited liability companies (*Yisgen Kaisha*), foreign corporations. The *Register* is kept at the District Office of the Justice Ministry.

Article 210 also prohibits use for dishonest purposes of a name likely to cause confusion with the business of another.

Repression of unfair competition under the Anti-Monopoly Law

The Unfair Competition Law of Japan is broadly defined and includes the Anti-Monopoly Law, which aims at promoting fair and free competition by prohibiting private monopolisation, unreasonable restraint of trade and unfair business practices. Unfair business practices (*fukosei na torihikihoho*) are defined in Article 19 of the Unfair Competition Prevention Law and is generally the unreasonable interference or restriction of another's business. Cease and desist orders can be granted under the Act, which can both give rise to penal servitude or a fine. The civil remedy of damages is available without the burden of proving intent or negligence on behalf of the defendant.

LICENSING

The *Horei*, which codifies private international agreements, allows the parties to an agreement to specify the jurisdiction to which it is subject. In Japanese Law, there are two basic types of license, which apply to patents, trade marks, utility marks, and designs. The possible scope of a license obviously depends on the law by which the right e.g. a patent, is created. For the sake of simplicity, this section refers only to patents, but the same principles apply to trade marks, utility marks, and designs equally.

Types of license

There are two basic types of license: *senyojisshiken*, which can roughly be termed an exclusive license and can be granted under Article 77(1), and *tsûjôjisshiken*, which can roughly be termed an ordinary license and can be granted under Article 78(1).

Both *senyojisshiken* and *tsujojisshiken* can be registered at the Patent Office, but the effect of registration is very different.

It is not compulsory to register either type of license (under Article 98) but there are great disadvantages in not doing so.

If a *senyojisshiken* is not registered it does not take effect against third parties, although it is still a valid license, as regards the licensor and licensee (Article 98(1)).

If a *tsûjôjisshiken* is not registered the *tsûjôjisshikensha* is not protected against subsequent assignee or *senyojisshikensha* (Article 98(3)). Transfer, alteration, extinction or restriction of disposition can't be enforced against a third party unless registered.

There is no compulsion to register unless the parties impose such a compulsion themselves, but it is essential that anyone granting a license in Japan inserts a provision in the license agreement to require the registration of the license, until a *senyojisshiken* is registered it is an unregistered *tsûjôjisshiken*.

Characteristics of senyojisshiken

Senyojisshiken is a right 'in rem' (*bukken*). Its characteristics are that:

(a) the patent right can be split with another *senyojisshikensha* geographically, time etc., but cannot overlap;
(b) the total right to the exclusion of the licensor, to practice the invention is granted to the licensee if less is granted it is not *senyojisshiken;*
(c) the license can be negotiated.

Article 77(2) provides that *senyojisshikensha* can 'within the scope provided by the act of its establishment exclusively have the right to work the patented invention as a business'.

Once the licensor has granted and registered a *senyojisshiken*, the effect is very similar to that of a transfer or, assignment and *senyojisshikensha* can take legal action in his own name against the infringer.

However, it has been held that a patentee can still bring an action against infringers even after granting a *senyojisshiken*.

It is important to note that *senyojisshikensha* cannot transfer their right to sub-licensee apart from 'the business which it is worked' unless it has consent of licensor. The right can, however, be transferred under the inheritance process. A sub-license can only granted with consent of licensor and even then any license should have a clause specifically permitting the grant of a sub-license if the licensee wishes to conduct his business in this way.

However, the licensee can sub-contract work to a third party unless there is a specific bar on it.

With respect to trade marks, however, a *senyojisshiken* cannot prevent parallel import of the genuine article.

Termination of senyo license

A *senyo* license can be terminated in six ways: (a) the expiration of patent (the patent can expire due to non-payment of annuities on patent); (b) expiration of the contract; (c) forfeiture of license (*Kaijo*); (d) government-imposed termination, e.g. for breach of anti-trust law; (e) surrender of a sub-license; (f) purchase of entire at by licensee.

If the licensor wishes to amend the patent licensed, he can only do so with the licensee's agreement.

Characteristics of tsujojisshiken

A *tsûjôjisshiken* granted by a patent license is different from a *senyôjisshiken*. It can be created by a license agreement alone, and registration is not required for its establishment. The only effect of registration of *tsûjôjisshiken* is that it 'shall take effect even against a person who has thereafter acquired the patent or *senyôjisshiken*' (Patent Law Article 99(1)). This insoever if the license properties to be a *senyojisshiken*, but has not been properly registered.

Tsüjôjisshiken is established within the scope set by a license agreement and the licensor can impose restrictions as to the content place or time and give *tsüjôjisshiken* of the same contents to a number of persons at the same time. In addition, the licensor can exploit the patent by himself even after the establishment of *tsüjôjisshiken* unless otherwise provided in the license agreement. From the standpoint of the licensee, a person who is granted *tsüjôjisshiken* under a license agreement can exploit the licensed patent within the scope established by the agreement. The licensee is not holding *jisshiken* (a right to exploit) exclusively, but has a right to demand the licensor a right of such nature, it does not have an inherent nature of exclusivity, and exclusivity is not necessary for the achievement of the purpose of the parties.

Registration of a *tsujojisshiken* acts as notice to third parties.

There are three main types of *tsûjôjisshiken*: *Kyodaku* (contractual), *Horei* (legal right), and *Satei* (granted due to government intervention). *Kyodaku tsûjôjisshiken* itself is divided into two very different categories. The first category, *Dokusenteki tsûjôjisshiken*, must be registered and prevents the licensor from granting a *tsûjôjisshiken* to a third party. It is a

31

'monopolistic ordinary license' the licensee to exclude an infringer and allows the second category. *Hi-Dokusenteki tsûjôjisshiken* takes effect without registration and allows the licensor to grant a *tsûjôjisshiken* to a third party. Even if registered, it does not allow the licensee to exclude anyone. An unregistered *senyojisshiken* is thus a *Dokusentekei tsûjôjisshiken*, although of course not all *Dokusentekei tsûjôjisshiken* are failed *senyojisshiken*.

Article 78(2) provides that *tsûjôjisshikensha* 'shall in accordance with the provisions of this law or within the scope provided by the act of its establishment, have a right to work the patented invention as a business'. The *tsûjôjisshikensha* cannot grant a sub-license or assign without consent of the licensor.

A *tsujojishikensha* has the right to export products manufactured under the license unless the agreement provided otherwise. It is, therefore, important to carefully define the territory of the license.

Tsûjôjisshikensha cannot sue for an injunction against an infringer, and so the licensor owes a duty to its *tsûjôjisshikensha* licensees to enjoin the infringer unless otherwise provided in the license agreements.

Registration of licenses

To register both a *senyojisshiken* and a *tsujojisshiken* license with the Director-General of Patent Office the applicant must provide the patent number of patent to be licensed; the name of patented invention; the ground for registration and date of contract; the scope of license; the details of consideration, and the registration tax (£5,000).

Application must be signed by owner and licensee and be accompanied by a proforma *senyojisshiken* agreement, and a copy of the original agreement. A copy must also be registered with the Bank of Japan under FECFT Law.

Taxation

When selecting a medium throught which to enter the Japanese market, naturally taxation will be a prime consideration.

Import and export duties will affect the importer regardless of whether it is a branch, Japanese subsidiary, or agent/distributor. These are frequently discussed in the news, as the cause of a good deal of trade friction between Japan and other countries.

CORPORATE TAX

Representative office

A representative office constitutes an office in Japan which does not amount to a branch and therefore is not subject to Japanese corporate income tax.

Branch

A branch must submit the following various documents to its district tax office within two months of its establishment, including copies of its Memorandum and Articles in both English and Japanese and is subject to Japanese tax in a similar way to a Japanese resident company with some small exceptions.

Japanese resident subsidiary

It is normal for a Japanese subsidiary of an overseas company to take the form of a *Kabushiki Kaisha* (*see* above). The company must submit various documents to its district tax office within two months of its establishment.

Forms of taxation

(a) Corporation tax – The normal rate of corporation tax from 1 April 1987 to 31 March 1988 is 43.3 per cent.
(b) Inhabitance tax – Inhabitance tax consists of both prefectural and municipal taxes and is a percentage of the corporation tax liability.
(c) Enterprise tax – Enterprise Tax is a local tax levied on domestic source income.

Work and Residence Permission

The comments below apply to British business persons entering Japan. It is likely that the procedure is similar for other European business persons but, before going to Japan, a check should be made with the local Japanese Consul.

VISITS

Generally, European business persons visiting Japan for less than six months do not require a visa from a Japanese Consul, and on entry to Japan, the Immigration Officer will normally allot the status of residence 4–1–16–1 CE carrying a period of stay of 180 days.

LONG-TERM STAY IN JAPAN

There are various categories which may be applicable for business persons wishing to enter Japan to work for an indefinite period. One of the common categories is 'long-term commercial entrant' which would, for example, apply to a banker going to work in Japan for a large British bank. Visa applications are made to the local Japanese Consul. The visa is normally valid for any number of entries to Japan within twelve months from the date of issue. The twelve-month validity of the visa is distinct from the period of residence to be permitted in Japan which is usually specified at the bottom of the visa.

ALIEN REGISTRATION

Under the Alien Registration Law, aliens intending to stay in Japan for more than 60 days must within that period register with the local authority, for example, the Ward Office. An Aliens Registration Certificate will be issued to the applicant. This certificate or card must be carried at all times for production on demand to the Police or other local officials.

Conclusion

A proper understanding of Japanese legal, commercial and bureaucratic practise is difficult to acquire due to both great cultural and linguistic differences with the West. However, in order to increase the chances of an investments success it is essential that the foreign lawyer at least understands the main principles involved so that he can help his client adopt the most appropriate approach to the Japanese Market and work knowledgeably with his Japanese legal counterpart.

Appendix

Basic Organization of the Ministry of International Trade and Industry

International Trade Policy Bureau	*International Trade Administration Bureau*	*Industrial Policy Bureau*
The American-Oceania	Exports	Research
West Europe-Africa-Middle East	Imports	Industrial Structure
South Asia-East Europe	Agricultural and Marine Products	Industrial Finance
North Asia	Foreign Exchange and Trade Finance	Business Behaviour
Trade Research	Export Insurance and Planning	International Enterprise
International Economic Affairs	Long-Term Export Insurance	Commercial Policy
Economic Co-operation	Short-Term Export Insurance	Commercial Affairs
		Price Policy

*Basic Industries
Bureau*

Iron and Steel
   Administration
Iron and Steel
   Production
Nonferrous Metals
Basic Chemical
   Products
Chemical Products
   Safety
Chemical Fertilizers
Alcohol Industry

Machinery and Information Industries Bureau	*Industrial Location and Environmental Protection Bureau*	*Consumer Goods Industries Bureau*
International Trade	Industrial Relocation	International Trade
Industrial Machinery	Industrial Location	Fiber and Spinning
Cast and Forged	Guidance	Textile Products
Products	Industrial Water	Paper and Pulp
Electronics Policy	Environmental	Industry
Data Processing	Protection Plan-	Household Goods
Electronics and	ning Guidance	Recreational Goods
Electrical Machinery	Environmental	Ceramics and
Automobiles	Protection Gui-	Construction
Aircraft and	dance	Materials
Ordnance	Industrial Safety	Housing Industry
Other Vehicles		Textile Inspection
Weights and		Administrator
Measures		
Machinery Credit		
Insurance		

Chapter 2
Parallel Imports in Japan

by Yukukazu Hanamizu

Yuasa & Hara
Tokyo, Japan

Introduction

'Parallel imports' are of great practical importance, in particular, for sole distributors because they are frequently forced to reduce their resale price in order to compete with parallel imports thereby decreasing their sales amount with a resulting loss in profits. Sole distributors are obligated to spend a substantial amount of money in advertising, sales promotion, maintenance of stocks, aftersale facilities, and similar business activities. Therefore, they normally set sales prices at a fairly high level in order to earn a high margin to cover such costs. However, parallel importers are not faced with such costs and can usually set sales prices at a level much lower than sole distributors are able to do.

If parallel imports of certain goods increase and gain a substantial share of the Japanese market, the price of such goods decreases. Sole distributors may be able to earn only a low margin in such a situation which may be insufficient for them to make a reasonable profit. As a result, they may be forced to request their manufacturers to supply the goods at a lower price, and will be discouraged from spending money for advertisement and other sales promotion activities, all of which may cause a loss of consumer loyalty to their preferred brand.

Moreover, since most sole distributorship contracts require the distributor to sell minimum amounts of prescribed goods, a distributor's inability to meet its quota may force it to seek a release from such minimum warranty to the manufacturer, or may event result in termination of the distributorship entirely. Even if the distributor is able to retain a margin sufficient to merely survive, the relationship between the manufacturer and distributor is adversely affected. In this sense, parallel imports are as important to a foreign manufacturer as they are to a domestic distributor, especially when the goods involved are of a high quality brand name since the parallel imports may denigrate such brand name and cause loss of consumer confidence in the brand.

The Parker Case

The general rule in Japan until 1970 provided that parallel imports would be enjoined to protect the owner of a trademark registered in Japan.

However, such rule was abrogated in February 1970 when the Osaka District Court rendered its judgment in the *Parker* case.[1] The relevant facts of the Parker case can be summarized as follows;

> Plaintiff was importing through Hong Kong Parker fountain pens manufactured in the United States. Defendant was a sole distributor appointed by Parker and had been granted an exclusive license to use the trademark 'Parker' in Japan. To prevent plaintiff's import of the goods from Hong Kong, the defendant filed an application with the Customs Office to stop the import of fountain pens with the trademark 'Parker'. The Customs Office admitted such application and denied the plaintiff's license to import Parker fountain pens in accordance with Article 21 of the Customs Tariff Act.[2]

---

1. Osaka District Court Case (Wa) No. 7003/1968 (*M.M.C. Co., Ltd.* v. *Shuryro Trading Co., Ltd.*)
2. Customs Tariff Act provides for in Article 21 that;
   (Import Prohibition)

   Article 21. Any goods specified in any of the following sub-Paragraphs shall not be imported:
   (1) opium, other narcotic drugs and utensils for opium smoking, excluding those imported by the Government or any person who has obtained an approval of the Government;
   (2) counterfeit, altered or imitated articles of coins, paper money, banknote or securities;
   (3) books, drawings, carvings and any other articles, to injure public security or morals; and
   (4) articles to infringe upon rights in patents, utility-models, designs, trade marks, or copyright or neighbouring right.

The plaintiff instituted a lawsuit before the Osaka District Court, demanding a declaratory judgment to the effect that the defendant was not entitled to enjoin the plaintiff from importing the Parker fountain pens. The court ruled that the importation by the plaintiff of the Parker fountain pens did not amount to an infringement of the trademark 'Parker' registered in Japan and, therefore, defendant would be unable to stop the importation by the plaintiff of the genuine products.

The reasoning of the court relied upon the fact that the products distributed by defendant and plaintiff were manufactured by the same manufacturer and had exactly the same quality. Moreover, the manufacturer exercised control over both plaintiff and defendant sufficient to protect the reputation of the trademark 'Parker'. However, the court did not adopt the 'doctrine of consumption' which means that, in a case where a person is a trademark owner both in Japan and foreign countries, the consumption of foreign trademark rights by the products with such trademark being duly placed in a market results in the consumption of the corresponding Japanese trademark right.

The Lacoste Case

The parallel imported goods in the *Parker* case were identical to those imported and distributed by the authorized distributor. In this respect, the *Lacoste*[3] case is distinguishable, but the Tokyo District Court nevertheless admitted the parallel import. In the latter case, the plaintiff was granted an exclusive license to use the trademark 'Lacoste' in Japan. Under such license, the plaintiff manufactured the goods and distributed them under the trademark. However, the trademark owner granted the same type of license to a US company within the territory of US, which also manufactured and

---

2. The Director-General of Customs shall be authorized to forfeit and abandon the goods provided for in sub-Paragraph (1), (2) or (4) of the preceding Paragraph, which are to be imported, or to order any importer to reship such goods.
3. In cases where there are any goods, with respect to which there are sufficient reasons to show that they correspond to any of the articles specified in sub-Paragraph (3) of Paragraph 1, among goods which are about to be imported in accordance with the provisions of Chapter VI of the Customs Law, the Director-General of Customs shall notify it to the person who intends to import such goods.
4. When any person who received the notification provided for in the preceding Paragraph has a complaint about it, he may file with the Director-General of Customs who made the notification the complaint in writing, stating the reason for his complaint, within one month from the date of this receipt of the notification.
5. Upon receipt of the complaint provided for in the preceding Paragraph, the Director-General of Customs shall make a decision concerning the complaint after referring it to the Council on Imported Motion Pictures, etc., as prescribed by a Cabinet Order, and shall notify the desision, in writing, to the person who filed the complaint.
3. Tokyo District Court Case (Wa) 8489/1984 *La Lacoste et al.* v. *Shin-shin Trading Co., Ltd.*

sold the goods under the same trademark. The defendant imported into Japan the marked goods made in the US. However, the goods were different from those distributed by the plaintiff. The plaintiff brought an action to enjoin the defendant from importing and distributing its marked goods based on its exclusive license (*Senyo-shiyoken*) to the registered trademark and based on alleged violations of the Unfair Competition Prevention Law.

The Tokyo District Court ruled that the plaintiff was not entitled to enjoin the defendant from importing and distributing its goods bearing the trademark 'Lacoste'. The judgment of the court was based on the fact that, although there was a difference in the quality between the goods, such difference was not so substantial as to adversely affect the trademark function provided for in Article 1 of the Trademark Law.[4] In determining that such difference was permissible, the Court examined in detail the high quality control exercised by the trademark owner over the goods manufactured by each licensee. As a result of such quality control and minor difference in quality in the goods sold by each license, the reputation of the trademark 'Lacoste' was adequately protected. The *Lacoste* case makes it clear that, even if a parallel import is not manufactured by the same maker who is supplying the goods to an authorized distributor, such parallel goods cannot be enjoined by the trademark registered in Japan provided the quality of goods are identical or virtually equivalent under the quality control exercised by the same trademark owner.

The Paris Convention

The Paris Convention provides in paragraph 3, Article 6, that a trademark registered in a member country shall be independent of one registered in another member country. In the case of a patent right, such patent right shall be independent. Under this rule, the importation of a licensed product into another member country would, unless the importer is licensed to do so, amount to an infringement of the patent right granted in that country, even if a licensed product has been lawfully put in a certain member country. This is a well established rule under the Japanese Patent Law. If the same rule were applicable to a trademark right, a parallel import would not be allowed and would amount to a trademark infringement, unless a parallel importer is granted a right by a holder of the trademark to do so.

In the *Parker* case, which is the leading case as to a parallel import, the

---

4. Trademark Act provides for in Article 1 as follows;
   'The purpose of this Law shall be to ensure the maintenance of the business reputation of persons using trademarks by protecting trademarks, and thereby to contribute to the development of industry and to protect the interests of consumers.'

defendant submitted such argument, but the court denied it on the following grounds:

(a) at the time when the Paris Convention was made, it was not foreseeable that a parallel import problem would take place. In other words, paragraph 3 of Article 6 did not intend to cover the issue of a parallel import;

(b) in the case of a trademark right, different from a patent right, there is no provision similar to Article 4-2-2[5] of the Paris Convention; and

(c) a trademark system is very concerned with protecting not only the trademark owner but also the public interest by allowing consumers to identify a manufacturer and to thereby warrant the quality of its goods. Applicability of paragraph 3, Article 6, should be limited to the extent that such public interest is protected.

Requirements for Lawful Parallel Import

Under Japanese laws, parallel imports will not constitute an infringement of trademark rights in Japan, unless the following requirements are satisfied:

- the trademark owner is the same both in Japan and the country from where the goods originated or, where the trademark owner in Japan and such country is different, there must exist a special relationship between them so they may be deemed the same. An illustration of the latter case occurs when an authorized distributor is the Japanese subsidiary company established by the trademark owner or when an authorized distributor has obtained the trademark from the maker or has registered it in his name with the consent of the maker; and
- the parallel imported goods have the same quality as the goods distri-

---

5. Article 4 [Patents; Independence of Patents Obtained for the Same Invention in Different Countries]

(1) Patents applied for in the various countries of the Union by nationals of countries of the Union shall be independent of patents obtained for the same invention in other countries, whether members of the Union or not.

(2) The foregoing provision is to be understood in an unrestricted sense, in particular, in the sense that patents applied for during the period of priority are independent, both as regards the grounds for nullity and forfeiture, and as regards their normal duration.

(3) The provision shall apply to all patents existing at the time when it comes into effect.

(4) Similarly, it shall apply, in the case of the accession of new countries, to patents in existence on either side at the time of accession.

(5) Patents obtained with the benefit of priority shall, in the various countries of the Union, have a duration equal to that which they would have, had they been applied for or granted without the benefit of priority.

buted by an authorized distributor or have so similar a quality as to not damage the purpose served by such trademark right.

Repacking

In this respect, we should draw our attention to the repacking of genuine goods which are imported in bulk form.

It is the established rule under Japanese law that it constitutes a trademark infringement to purchase the marked goods from an authorized party and after repacking sell them under the same trademark. This rule is also applicable to parallel imports.

For instance, in the *STP* case,[6] the Osaka District Court issued an injunctive order in favor of the trademark owner. The respondent imported an oil treatment drum from the applicant, a US corporation which was the owner of the trademark 'STP'. The drum was bearing the applicant's trademark 'STP'. The respondent repackaged the oil treatment imported from the applicant and sold it under the trademark 'STP'. In response to the application for a preliminary injunction, the respondent alleged the parallel import defense, and also contended that the applicant had impliedly granted a license to use the trademark for the repackaged goods because it knew that the goods in the drum would be repackaged for resale.

The court did not support either of the defenses raised by the respondent. The order unfortunately did not state in detail the reason why such repackaging of genuine goods amounted to a trademark infringement. It is likely that the Court mostly relied on the fact that, as a result of repackaging, the 'source' of goods become different. It is not prudent to conclude, however, that based upon the STP case any type of repackaging of genuine goods is prohibited by Japanese trademark rights since, if the *Lacoste* case applies, such repackaging will not adversely affect the purpose served by trademark protection as provided for in Article 1 of the Trademark Law.

Contribution of local distributor

The court stated in the *Parker* case that, since the reputation of the trademark had been established by the foreign maker and not by the authorized distributor, parallel imports in Japan would not damage the reputation of the foreign maker in the United States. However, where a trademark is not well known in Japan at the time an authorized distributor begins distributing the marked goods in Japan, and the distributor spends a substantial amount of money in building the reputation of the trademark in Japan, can such distributor enjoin another party from importing goods in order to protect the domestic reputation built by the local distributor? Since the distributor has only contributed to building a local reputation which is dependent upon

---

6. *Osaka District Court (Yo) 2469/1976 S.T.P. Corporation* v. *National Shoji Co., Ltd.*

high quality originally established by the manufacturer, the answer to this question may be negative. Therefore, this requirement will become an issue only in a very special case, for example, where an authorized distributor has built his own goodwill which is entirely independent from the reputation of the manufacturer.

Antimonopoly Aspect

Under the Japanese antimonopoly law,[7] any international contract which contains an unfair trade practice or unfair trade restriction is prohibited. The Fair Trade Commission should be notified of certain types of international contracts within thirty days after execution thereof and the Commission must screen such contracts for compliance. Most distributorship agreements fall within such category of international contracts. For the purpose of screening such contracts, the Fair Trade Commission on 22 November 1972 made public the guideline titled 'Antimonopoly Act Guideline For Sole Import Distributorship Agreement, etc.' which lists typical clauses which are likely to amount to an unfair trade practice within the meaning of the antimonopoly law.

The law does allow for a manufacturer to appoint an exclusive distributor and to agree not to sell the goods covered by the contract to any party other than the distributor within the territory. The guideline was drafted, however, taking into consideration the ruling of the *Parker* case and states in paragraph 4, Article 1, that it is likely an unfair trade practice to unduly hinder parallel importation of the goods covered by the contract. The Fair Trade Commission recently issued a report concerning parallel imports, which states that the following actions taken by a sole distributor are likely to constitute an unfair trade practice to unduly hinder parallel imports under the Anti-monopoly Law:

(a) to directly or through a manufacturer prevent a foreign dealer or distributor in its business with an authorized manufacturer from accepting a purchase order of genuine goods placed by a parallel importer;
(b) to conduct business with wholesalers or retailers on the condition they agree not to deal with parallel imports;
(c) to conduct business with wholesalers on the condition that they agree not to sell the goods to retailers who are dealing with parallel imports;
(d) to demand sellers dealing with parallel imports to stop selling them, or

---

7. Act Concerning Prohibition of Private Monopoly and Maintenance of Fair Trade. (Act No. 54 of 14 April 1947)
8. Fair Trade Commission Report issued on 17 April 1987. 'Opinion from the viewpoint of the Anti-monopoly Law concerning Unfair Hinderance of Parallel Imports.'

to threaten that the parallel imports are not genuine or are infringing the trademark right;
(e)   to corner parallel imports on the market; and
(f)   to refuse after-sale service of parallel imports.

This is illustrated in the *Old Par* case.[9] In order to hinder a parallel import, a Japanese sole distributor of the famous whisky 'Old Par' instructed its dealers not to sell the Old Par whisky to retailers who were selling a parallel imported Old Par whisky or who were selling it at a price less than the instructed price. The Fair Trade Commission stated that such instruction amounts to an unfair trade practice and recommended the distributor to withdraw such instruction given to the dealers.

Conclusion

Since Japan's markets place a high demand on finished products, the level of parallel imports into Japan is increasing quickly. Moreover, due to the high value of the Japanese yen, parallel imports level can be expected to continue to grow. Therefore, protection of domestic sole distributors from parallel importers is a significant concern. However, as shown, trademark rights can no longer be expected to protect sole distributors from such importers.

---

9.   Recommendation No. 3/1978 (Delivered on 23 March 1978).

Chapter 3
Termination of Distributorship Agreements in Japan

by Yukukazu Hanamizu

Yuasa & Hara
Tokyo, Japan

Introduction

This chapter is to give a brief explanation regarding the termination of distributorship agreements under Japanese law.

A distributorship agreement is an agreement in which a manufacturer appoints a person or company as its distributor in return for the purchase by the appointed distributor of goods from the manufacturer and sale thereof within a designated territory. Thus, it is a type of sales agreement and is, as a general rule, subject to contract law, which is specifically governed by the Japanese Civil Code.[1] One major difference from a normal sales agreement is the more extensive relationship created between the manufacturer and distributor which typically is continued for a fairly long period of time, and which places duties upon the distributor to spend a substantial amount of

---

1. It contains the rules of contract in Chapters 1 and 2 of Book III (Articles 399 to 696). Chapter 1 provides general rules commonly applicable to any type of contracts and Chapter 2 classifies contracts into several typical types of contract such as sale, exchange, etc. and provides the rules applicable to each type of contract.

money for advertisement, sales promotion, and so on. Such relationship establishes fudiciary duties between the parties. In determining whether or not a distributorship agreement has been lawfully terminated, Japanese courts take into consideration the destruction of fudiciary duties, damage suffered by a distributor due to the termination, etc.

Agreement Having No Express Terms

In cases where a formal contract has been prepared and executed, the duration of the contract should be expressly provided for in the contract.

Under applicable Japanese law, however, it is not required that a distributorship agreement must be reduced to writing. That is, an oral agreement is also valid and binding on the parties to an agreement. Since oral agreements do not usually involve express terms or conditions, such agreements also usually fail to specify the duration of the agreement.

In cases where a formal written contract fails to provide for its duration, it will be difficult to persuade a court that both parties have impliedly agreed to a certain duration. However, in the case of an oral agreement, a court will be more inclined to find an implied agreement as to its duration.

In reviewing past court cases, it is possible to summarize the grounds justifying a termination as follows:

BREACH OF CONTRACT

The fiduciary relationship has been destroyed due to acts of one of the parties in connection with the transaction. Such a case usually arises where one of the parties has failed to perform a duty or obligation essential to the contract. Where the duty or obligation which was breached is not essential but incidental to the contract, the terminating party must prove that the other party's breach is so serious as to bring the fiduciary relationship to an end.

CHANGE OF FUNDAMENTAL CIRCUMSTANCES OR CONDITIONS

Distributorship agreements can be terminated upon the occurrence of various circumstances or conditions, some of which may be specified in the contract. However, it is impossible to state beforehand in the contract all of the circumstances or conditions the occurrence of which may be grounds for termination. This is especially true in Japan where Japanese businessmen generally prefer a short contract rather than a long and detailed one. Indeed, some may ignore a written contract, and instead rely more upon a side oral agreement the terms or interpretation of which may be in apparent contradiction to the terms of the written contract. Most disputes are settled through consultation in accordance with the common sense of the businessmen, rather than based on the legal effect of the terms and conditions in the contract. In recognition of this business practice, Japanese courts have been giving substantial consideration to circumstances and conditions not expressly stated or disclosed in the contract.

In determining whether or not a change of circumstance or condition entitles a party to terminate a contract, the court will consider whether such change is essential or fundamental to the contract.

Sometimes, such change will be caused by one of the parties to the contract. Such a case exists where a distributor company has merged into the other company or has been assigned its business and the degree in change of management will be relevant to determining whether the change is substantial enough to constitute a ground for termination. For example, where a distributorship agreement is concluded in the name of a particular company and the manufacturer has heavily relied upon a strong personal connection with the management of such company but its management subsequently changed because of a merger, assignment of business, or similar change, a court might conclude the personal connection was an essential condition to the continuation of the distributorship relationship and, therefore, such change of management constituted a justifiable reason for the manufacturer to terminate the relationship. However, in the absence of such personal relationship, the manufacturer should not ordinarily be able to terminate the contract on the sole ground that the management of the distributor company has changed.

In one court case, a distributor was prosecuted under a criminal law for acts unrelated to its distributorship relationship. However, the reputation of the brand of the distributed goods was seriously damaged and its sales rapidly decreased. Although not specified in the contract, such an event would be sufficient to justify manufacturer's termination of the relationship.

Change of a fundamental circumstance or condition can also occur due to events beyond the control of either party to the contract. Suspension of the business by government decree, or drastic decrease in sales due to a change in the market are examples. The rule similar to the doctrine of frustration may be applicable in such situations. Where an agreement contains an express duration of the contract, the doctrine of frustration will be directly applicable without any change or modification. However, with agreements having no express duration, termination will be granted even though such change in circumstance or condition is not serious enough to frustrate the purpose of the contract.

REASONABLE NOTICE OF TERMINATION

Distributorship agreements which do not contain an express duration can be unilaterally terminated by giving the reasonable notice of termination to the other party. In determining whether notice of termination is reasonable or not, the nature of the transaction, each party's situation, and similar factors will be considered.

As a very general rule, notice should be given by a manufacturer at least one year prior to the termination date. In the case of a distributor six months prior notice is generally required. If the notice period is too short, pecuniary damages suffered during the period when notice was actually given and when it should have been given may be awarded.

Contract with Express Duration

BREACH OF CONTRACT

Japanese rules of contract provide that if one of the parties has breached a material term of the contract, the other party is entitled to rescind the contract. Its effect is to bring the contract to an end and both parties are thereafter discharged from any duties or obligations thereunder, but duties and obligations existing at the time of rescission are not affected and survive. However, if the breach has been of a minor term and is not essential to the contract, the injured party would not be entitled to terminate the contract. The party which allegedly breached the contract could contend that the termination would amount to an abuse of right under Article 1 of the Civil Code.[2] In order to avoid the issue of whether a failure to perform a certain duty or obligation is substantial or not, it is advisable to specify in the contract particular duties and obligations the breach of which entitles the other party to terminate the contract. Without examining in detail whether such failure is minor or not, the court will support the termination due to such failure specified in the contract on the premise that both parties have agreed that such duties or obligations are deemed to be essential to the contract. The breaching party could respond that, although a particular duty or obligation is provided for in the contract the breach of which amounts to the termination of the contract, the actual failure is minor and not substantial enough to go to the root or essence of the contract.

However, such party bears the burden of proof that the failure was minor, whereas the party terminating the contract bears the burden of proof that the breach is essential if the particular duty or obligation is not specified in the contract.

Most distributorship agreements provide for a termination clause, a typical one which might simply state that 'in the event that one of the parties has failed to perform any of the duties or obligations under this Agreement, the other party may terminate the contract........'.

The court will, however, interpret such a termination clause to confirmingly state the rule of contract and, therefore, such termination clause

---

2. Article 1 provides that:
   '1.   all private rights shall conform to the public welfare;
    2.   the exercise of rights and performance of duties shall be done in good faith and in accordance with the principles of trust;
    3.   it is not permissible to abuse rights.'

would not be effective. As mentioned above, most of the distributorship contracts do not specify the duties or obligation the breach of which will entitle the other party to terminate the contract. Therefore, it will be useful to explain what kinds of factors will be considered by the court in determining whether a failure in performing a certain duty or obligation is essential to the contract and justifies the termination. In the light of court precedents, the justifiable grounds for termination can be summarized as follows;

To stop shipment of the contracted goods

In the event that a manufacturer has stopped selling the contracted goods to a distributor in breach of the contract, the disbributor can terminate the contract. In a usual case, however, the manufacturer will not stop shipment of the goods to the distributor without any reason. One reason which may justify the stoppage of shipment is when a manufacturer has stopped shipment in order to collect from the distributor the money payable under the distribution agreement. Where there is a delay in shipment the court will determine whether such delay goes to the root of the contract by taking into consideration the delay period, amount of goods in delay, cause of delay, and so on. Except when delay has taken place so often and has seriously damaged the distributor's business, the court will usually not support a termination due to a delay of shipment.

Non-payment by distributor

Where a distributor has failed to make payment under a contract, the manufacturer must demand that it be paid within a certain period of time. If the distributor has failed to make payment within such period of time, the manufacturer is then entitled to terminate the contract. As a normal practice, such demand is made in writing.

Breach of non-competition clause

Under some exclusive distributorship contracts, a distributor is prohibited from dealing with goods which are competing with the contracted goods.

Distributorship agreements are based upon the long standing relationship between a manufacturer and distributor. In the case of exclusive distributorships, a manufacturer is solely relying upon the marketing by his exclusive distributor and has no second source in the agreed territory. Such reliance is essential to the contract. Therefore, loss of such reliance will go to the root of the contract and the termination will be supported.

CHANGE OF FUNDAMENTAL CIRCUMSTANCES OR CONDITIONS

It has been mentioned what kind of circumstances or conditions are so fundamental or essential to a distributorship agreement having no express duration that their change would lead to the termination. The rules mentioned therein are, as a rule, applicable to a distributorship agreement which contains an express duration clause. However, in the cases where the duration is expressly stated in the contract, a party alleging the termination shall bear heavier burden of proof to establish that such change of circumstance or condition is so serious as to amount to a justifiable reason for termination. Because the express duration clause will lead to the interpretation by the court that the parties have impliedly agreed that unless otherwise provided for in the contract, the contract could not be terminated for an agreed period of time or that the parties have fixed the duration at the risk or in expectation that circumstances or conditions might be changed for such period.

WORSENING OF DISTRIBUTOR'S FINANCIAL STANDING

Japanese case law provides that if a distributor's financial standing has become so serious that he can no longer perform his duties or obligations under the contract, a manufacturer is entitled to temporarily stop shipment of the goods until the distributor's financial condition has become sound. When such financial condition is too serious for the distributor to overcome, a manufacturer will be entitled to terminate the contract.

RENEWAL CLAUSE

It is a general practice to insert a renewal clause whereby the duration of the contract can be automatically renewed for a certain period, unless either party gives the other party notice of termination within a certain period before the expiration of the term of contract. In a recent ruling, the Sapporo High Court[3] denied a termination which had been effected by the manufacturer in compliance with the same type of renewal clause as mentioned above. The relevant facts can be summarized as follows:

(Facts)
    In 1961, Y appointed X an exclusive distributor to sell Y's agricultural machine in the territory of Hokkaido, the northern island in Japan, and in 1970 the contract period clause was amended as follows:

> 'This contract shall become effective from 1 October 1970 and continue until 30 September 1971. Unless any of the parties to the contract has given notice of termination at least three months before the end of the contract, this Contract will be automatically renewed under the same condition and thereafter.'

---

3. Sapporo High Court (Ra) 49/1987 *Hokkaido Ford Tracter KK* v. *Minoru Sangyo K.K.*

Y gave notice of termination to X in accordance with this clause and appointed a new distributor. X filed an application for injunction in order to prevent Y from distributing the products through a new distributor. The court granted the injunction order, denying the termination of the distributorship agreement by X.

In determinating whether a distributorship contract can be terminated, the following factors have been considered by the Japanese courts:

- Period of contract term. If a period of contract term is shorter than one year, such period may be deemed to be a period to review the terms and conditions.
- Period and costs for a distributor to establish a distributorship network.
- Contract term is sufficiently long to recover the investment by a distributor.
- Chance of distributors starting another business after termination.
- Damages suffered by distributor due to Termination.

Therefore, one must bear in mind that in some cases the contract cannot be terminated in the manner as expressly provided for in the contract.

Bankruptcy

Japanese Bankruptcy Law provides in Article 59 that:

(1) if the bankrupt and the other party have not yet completed performance of all the duties or obligations under a bilateral contract at the time of adjudicating bankruptcy, the administrator in bankruptcy may execute his option of rescinding the contract or performing obligations of the bankrupt and demanding the other party to perform his obligation;
(2) in the case mentioned in the preceding paragraph, the other party may give notice to the administrator in bankruptcy, designating a reasonable period of time and demanding that a definite answer be given within the said period as to whether he rescinds the contract or demands performance of obligations. If the administrator in bankruptcy fails to respond with a definite answer within the designated period, it shall be deemed that he has rescinded the contract.

This Article is applicable to a bilateral contract under which both parties to the contract shall perform duties or obligations. distributorship agreements and sales contracts concluded thereunder are 'bilateral contracts' within the meaning of Article 59.

Under the Bankruptcy Law, as mentioned above, the administrator in bankruptcy has the option to rescind the contract. On the other hand, the other party to the contract has no right to terminate the contract. Therefore,

51

it is advisable to provide in the termination clause and acceleration clause that, in the event that an application or petition for bankruptcy or commencement of composition or corporate reorganization is submitted, the contract shall be immediately terminated and all the payments under the contract shall become due and payable. Under Japanese Bankruptcy Law, such clause is permissible.

Anti-Monopoly Law Aspect

International distributorship agreements must be reported to the Fair Trade Commission within thirty days after conclusion. The Fair Trade Commission screens such agreements in accordance with its guideline of 22 November 1972, entitled 'Anti-monopoly Act Guidelines For Sole Import Distributorship, etc. Agreements'. The guideline states in paragraph 5 of Article 1 that it will constitute an unfair business practice to impose an unduly advantageous condition for the termination of the agreement. For example, the condition that a manufacturer can unilateraly terminate at any time even if a distributor is not in breach of contract will be considered as an unfair business practice under the Anti-monopoly Law and the Fair Trade Commission will demand such condition be deleted or modified.

Conclusion

Distributorship agreements normally continue for a fairly long period of time and the distributor may contribute to the establishment of a manufacturer's goodwill in Japan by spending a substantial amount of money for advertisement, sales promotion, after-sale service, etc. Distributors are, therefore, very much concerned to continue the distributorship relationship. Consequently, if a manufacturer rescinds or terminates the contract, the distributor will persistently struggle against it to protect his interests and, if the dispute is not resolved by way of settlement, such cases will inevitably end up in court. In some cases where a new distributor is involved in the dispute, the prolonged dispute will certainly lead to loss of business opportunity and be disadvantageous to both parties and, in particular, to the manufacturer. Therefore, in drafting a distributorship agreement, attention should be focused on making the termination clause as unamibigous as possible in order to avoid a later dispute. As a rule, the parties' freedom to contract is fully protected under Japanese law and one can freely negotiate and agree to contract terms and conditions. Therefore, it is strongly recommended that one draft a detailed termination clause.

However, one must always remember the guidelines of the Fair Trade Commission, and be sure the condition for the termination is not unduly disadvantageous.

Chapter 4
Technology Transfer, Cooperation and Joint Venture Agreements with Korea

by Duck Soon Chang

Central International Law Firm
Seoul, Korea

Introduction

There is little doubt that Korea, known as one of 'Asia's Four Tigers', is an important player in today's international economic arena. Strategically located in the Pacific rim region that is receiving world-wide attention, Korea is an emerging venue of successful cooperation between East and West. More and more foreign business entities, from the gigantic multinational enterprises to the small and medium-sized businesses, are developing economic relationships with Korean firms.

It is important to remember that it was only about three decades ago that Korea, long known as 'the Hermit Kingdom', embarked on its path of development. Gaining independence in 1945, Korea has grown from an under-developed country without international experience and the benefit of principal natural resources to a newly industralized country. It wasn't until the early 1960s that Korea was able to begin its economic development. In 1962, the Korean government launched its first Five-Year Economic Development Plan in order to pursue systematic economic development and to recover from the devastation of the Korean War. Following the success of the first plan, subsequent Five-Year Economic Development Plans have been successfully accomplished, with an average annual rate of economic development of nearly ten per cent.

Two critical components of this successful development of the Korean economy have been the capital and technology from advanced foreign countries, since Korea herself did not initially have the capital or technology necessary to carry out the economic progress. In an effort to make Korea's transition as orderly as possible, the government in 1966 passed the Foreign Capital Inducement Act ('FCIA') to promote and facilitate the influx of foreign capital and technology. The FCIA originally offered a variety of incentives and guarantees on the remittance of dividends and principal. In order to keep abreast with the rapidly changing economic conditions, the FCIA has been revised several times. These revisions have gradually liberalized the restrictions on foreign investment of capital and technology. In particular, since last year, the Korean government has been rapidly reducing or eliminating many of the former restrictions and regulations on foreign investment. This has been due to the considerable pressure from its principal trading partners, the US and several European countries. In conjunction with this rapid liberalization, the Korean government has also started withdrawing various incentives, such as tax benefits, which had been available to foreign investors.

There is no denying that Korea's rapid development to date should be substantially ascribed to the capital and technology introduced from foreign countries. The developing Korean economy will continue to depend on this infusion of foreign capital and technology in the foreseeable future. In exchange for these investments, Korea provides foreign enterprises with strong profit opportunities as well as a large and attractive consumer market composed of over 40 million people and hard-working and well-educated workers. Consequently, the opportunities in Korea for foreign business participation continue to abound.

As stated above, foreign investment of capital or transfer of technology into Korea is primarily governed by the FCIA. However, the FCIA provides only a basic framework of controls. Instead, various Ministers formulate regulations and guidelines to implement the FCIA. These regulations and guidelines are constantly being reviewed and revised. Consequently, it is very exciting and challenging to keep pace with rules and regulations governing foreign investment in Korea. The comments which will be made herein are based on the FCIA and their regulations and guidelines effective as of today.

The purpose of the FCIA, as described in Article 1 of the Act, is to effectively induce, regulate and protect foreign capital and technology conducive to the sound development of the Korean economy and the improvement of the international balance of payments. In the past, the Korean government has provided a variety of incentives to foreign investors to promote the influx of valuable foreign capital and technology. However, until quite recently, the Korean government was more concerned with protecting Korean nationals from their foreign partners who usually had superior bargaining power. The government also wanted to select the foreign capital and technologies which would be of help to Korea's economic progress. Recently, this governmental position has been changing. For example, the government has been loosening regulations on foreign investment into Korea, while, at the same time, removing a variety of incentives for foreign investors. What this means to foreign investors doing business in Korea is that foreign-invested enterprises will soon be competing on an equal footing with their Korean counterparts.

Joint Ventures

A foreigner may establish a new Korean company, either a wholly-owned subsidiary or a joint venture with a Korean party, or may acquire newly-issued shares of an existing Korean company. However, it is still prohibited for a non-resident foreigner to acquire previously-issued shares of an existing Korean company. Compared to the wholly-owned subsidiary, the main practical advantage of the joint venture is that the foreign investor can utilize the expertise of the local Korean partner to more easily participate in the Korean market while avoiding some of the pitfalls which acting alone might entail.

When a foreign party intends to establish a joint venture in Korea, he must obtain approval from the Minister of Finance ('MOF'). An exception to this general rule is known as the 'Automatic Approval System' whereby the Bank of Korea can independently approve specific types of joint ventures without referring to the MOF or any other Minister. To qualify for automatic approval, the joint venture must involve a foreign investment of less than US$1,000,000 in a non-manufacturing industry or US$3,000,000 in a manufacturing industry and this foreign investment must result in foreign ownership of less than 50 per cent of the total shares of the venture. Furthermore, the proposed joint venture may not request any of the tax benefits and the joint venture may not engage in a restricted or prohibited project. Although this 'Automatic Approval System' is effective in some cases, this report will describe situations where the automatic approval system is not available and thus where the regulations and procedures of the various Ministers raise issues for the foreign investor.

The MOF has established 'Guidelines for Foreign Investment' ('MOF Guidelines') under the FCIA. Under the MOF Guidelines, in principle, a minimum foreign investment of US$100,000, or its equivalent, is required.

Areas in Which Foreign Investment Is Allowed

In 1984, the Korean government enlarged the areas in which foreign investment would be allowed by switching from a 'positive system' to a 'negative system'. Under the present negative system, if the proposed business activity does not fall within a Restricted or Prohibited category, there will be no governmental restrictions on the establishment of the joint venture.

Of the total 999 industrial sectors listed in the Korean Standard Industrial Classification (Economic Planning Board Notification No. 71, amended on 26 January 1984), 788 industrial sectors accounting for 78.9 per cent of the total sectors are open to foreign investment. The remaining sectors are either Restricted or Prohibited.

At present, there are 51 industrial sectors in which foreign investment is prohibited. The Prohibited project list includes activities that involve the production of various agricultural products, such as tobacco; and the providing of services such as postal services, publishing newspapers, radio and television broadcasting.

Also, there are 160 sectors that are classified as 'Restricted'. The Restricted project list mainly includes sectors which are in the initial stages of development. The Korean government has decided, for public policy reasons, to protect these specific sectors from competition from sophisticated and developed foreign competitors. Generally, foreign investment in activities listed in these Restricted projects will be approved only in the following cases:

(1)   when the foreign invested enterprise exports 100 per cent of its products;
(2)   when the project is the construction and/or management of a 'resort complex' which meets the standards of the Tourism Industry Act; or
(3)   where the MOF establishes an exception for foreign investment in specified industry sectors. Currently, exceptions have been granted in eight sectors including the manufacture of blood preparation, manufacture of medicaments, general foreign trade, international trade brokerage, non-monetary institution, advertising agency, motion picture production, and motion picture rental services and distribution.

Apart from these Prohibited or Restricted projects, most business projects are open to foreign investment. There are no restrictions on the foreign shareholding ratio for a joint venture in industrial sectors in which foreign investment is allowed.

ESTABLISHMENT PROCEDURE

(1) Application for approval

In order to establish a joint venture in Korea, the foreigner must submit an application to the MOF, along with several supporting documents such as a copy of the Joint Venture Agreement and a description of the proposed investment plan.

In addition, if the applicant wants to receive a tax exemption benefit, he must, at the time of applying for the approval, submit an application for tax exemption, specifying the tax exemption period he wants.

Upon receiving an application, the MOF reviews and examines the following items:

  (i)   terms and conditions of the Joint Venture Agreement;
 (ii)   amount of foreign capital required;
(iii)   production and sales plans;
 (iv)   production process and technology required; and
  (v)   conditions of the plant site (except for manufacturing industries).

At this stage, the MOF usually refers the application to the relevant minister who regulates the specific industry in which the foreign investment is proposed. This minister then conducts an economic and feasibility study of the project and submits his opinion to the MOF.

The MOF also sends a copy of the Joint Venture Agreement to the Economic Planning Board ('EPB'). The EPB will examine whether or not the Agreement contains any unfair provisions which are prohibited by the Korean Monopoly Regulation and Fair Trade Act ('MRFTA'). According to the EPB Guideline (EPB Notice No. 87/14), the following are considered to be unfair provisions in a Joint Venture Agreement:

  (i)   any provision by which the joint venture is unreasonably obligated to purchase raw materials, parts, equipment and relevant products, from the foreign investor or a person designated by him;
 (ii)   any provision which prohibits the joint venture from selling or exporting its manufactured products in territories other than 'restricted territories' or any provision which obligates the joint venture to obtain the foreign investor's prior approval to sell or export there. Restricted territories are:
        (a)   territories in which the foreign investor has regularly been engaged in sales activities with respect to the products manufactured by the joint venture; and
        (b)   territories in which a third party has acquired the right to sell the products exclusively from the foreign investor;
(iii)   any provision by which the joint venture is obligated to export its manufactured products through the foreign investor or a person designated by him, unless the foreign investor or the person designated by him is obligated to purchase such products at prices and on terms appropriate in the international market;
 (iv)   any provision by which the foreign investor is entitled to select a certain number of directors so that the ratio of directors selected by him would, or could in the future, exceed the ratio of the shares held by him; and
  (v)   any provision by which a director selected by the foreign investor

57

in a fifty-fifty joint venture is entitled to make the final decision in the event votes by the Board of Directors are tied.

If the EPB determines that the Agreement contains any unfair provisions, the EPB notifies the MOF. The MOF will then request the applicant to delete or amend the unfair provisions before approval will be granted. The request by the MOF for the deletion or amendment of such provisions shall be made in writing stating reasons for the deletion or amendment. Such a request is generally complied with by entering into an amendment agreement between the parties.

The MOF has issued a Standard Joint Venture Agreement which can be referred to when a foreign party intends to establish a joint venture in the form of a stock company. If the Standard Agreement is used, this will expedite the examination procedures because it will not be necessary for the EPB to examine the Joint Venture Agreement.

After the proposed joint venture project is approved by the MOF, the foreigner will be permitted to remit dividends from the joint venture and proceeds received from the sale of shares of the joint venture. An approved joint venture may, in principle, engage in only the projects for which the MOF approval has been made.

(2) Report of foreign capital inducement

Once the project is approved, the foreign investor must complete the financing investment plan within two years from the date of the MOF approval. Although the foreign investor is not required to contribute the entire capitalization at one time, he must report to the MOF within one month from the date of each capital investment.

(3) Incorporation

A foreign investor may choose, as the legal form of the joint venture, any of the four different types of companies described in the Korean Commercial Code. However, in practice, the joint venture almost invariably takes the form of the *Chusik-Hoesa* (stock company).

Where the amount of partial investment made by a foreign investor and his Korean partner exceeds 50 million Korean Won (approximately US$66,000) for the establishment of a new joint venture in the form of a *Chusik-Hoesa*, the incorporation of the venture may be registered with the relevant local court even before the entire capitalization has been completed.

(4) Registration of the foreign invested enterprise

When a foreign investor completes the capitalization of the company, he must submit to the MOF an application for registration and subsequently receive a certificate of registration of a foreign invested enterprise. This registration is the prerequisite to qualifying for tax benefits.

Tax Benefits

Foreign invested enterprises are incorporated under the Korean Commercial Code. Thus, theoretically, they are subject to the same tax liabilities as any other Korean company.

However, as an important means of encouraging foreign investment in Korea, the FCIA has offered a broad range of tax benefits to foreign invested enterprises and the foreign investor when the investment is deemed to contribute to the development of the Korean economy. As these incentives have been so successful, the current trend is for amendments to the FCIA to restrict and eliminate the various tax benefits. The criteria for receiving tax benefits are found in the 'Standards on Income and other Tax Exemptions Granted to Foreign Investors' promulgated by the MOF (MOF Notice No. 87–10). According to the MOF Standards, the following types of projects are still eligible for tax benefits:

(1)   a project, the export ratio of which is greater than the basic ratio of 50 per cent plus the ratio of imported raw materials to gross sales;
(2)   a project which is accompanied by advanced technology which meets the following criteria:
    (a)   the induced technology must be necessary to the development of specific Korean high technology industries as specified by the MOF including testing, measuring and optical instruments, the defense industry, fine chemicals, and biogenetic engineering;
    (b)   the manufacturing process requiring the technology shall be performed in Korea; and
    (c)   the technology must have a positive economic and technological impact on the Korean economy;
(3)   a project located in a Free Export Zone (the Korean government has designated Free Export Zones in the cities of Masan and Iri);
(4)   a project in sectors reserved for the promotion of small and medium-sized enterprises by the relevant Act. (In this case, the foreign investor shall not be a multi-national enterprise and the foreign investment ratio shall be less than 50 per cent).

Tax benefits are not endowed automatically. To enjoy the tax benefits, the foreign investor must submit, along with the application for approval of the joint venture, an application for the tax benefits.

If the company is granted approval for receiving tax benefits, it may be eligible for various methods of tax exemptions or special depreciations on capital goods and equipment.

If the foreign investor chooses tax exemption, he may enjoy a five-year 'tax holiday' from corporate income tax on the dividends for any consecutive five-year period during the first ten years after the joint venture is registered with the MOF.

The joint venture may also qualify for a five-year reduction (in proportion to the ratio of foreign investment) in the corporate income tax and other taxes such as acquisition tax and property taxes.

As an alternative to a direct income tax exemption, a joint venture may choose to enjoy special depreciation on capital goods used in the foreign investment.

Regardless of whether the joint venture project qualifies for these various tax benefits, foreign expatriates employed by a joint venture will be exempted from Korean personal income tax for five years from the date of registration of the foreign invested enterprise with the MOF.

Technology Transfers into Korea

As stated above, foreign technology transfers into Korea are regulated principally by the FCIA. A Technology Transfer Agreement generally falls under the category of a Technology Inducement Agreement ('TIA') which is defined by the FCIA as 'an agreement whereby a Korean either obtains a license to use, or purchases, industrial property right or any other technology which belongs to a foreigner in exchange for the payment of royalties denominated in a foreign currency and where the term of the agreement is not less than one year'. Therefore, technology (including know-how) transfers or licensing agreements and patent assignment or licensing agreements which meet the above requirements fall within the definition of a TIA.

A Korean who enters into a TIA with a foreigner must submit several documents to the minister who has jurisdiction over the goods or services which comprise the subject technology of the TIA. For example, for healthcare products, the relevant minister is the Minister of Health and Social Affairs. The documents would include a copy of the Agreement and a description of the project plan that involves the introduced technology, etc. Once the minister approves the report, the remittance of royalties will not be subject to governmental interference.

If a Technology Transfer Agreement does not fall within the definition of a TIA as defined in the FCIA, the Korean licensee must obtain approval for each royalty remittance pursuant to the Foreign Exchange Control Regulations. In this case, the contents of the Agreement will not be reviewed by any governmental authorities.

It must be noted that prior to 30 June 1986, a Korean was not permitted to enter into a TIA whose main purpose was merely to allow the Korean the use of a foreigner's trademark. Consequently, it was impossible for a Korean to pay a foreign licensor royalties under a simple trademark license agreement. However, the Korean Government amended the FCIA, effective from 1 July 1986, so that the relevant minister can now approve a TIA based solely on a trademark, provided that the foreign licensor waived the tax exemption benefits.

REPORT AND ACCEPTANCE OF TIA

As stated above, every Korean who enters into a TIA with a foreigner must report the Agreement to the minister with jurisdiction over the subject technology of the Agreement.

Under the present reporting system, the relevant minister may reject the TIA or may request an amendment or adjustment to the TIA.

The main factors to be reviewed are as follows:

(1) value of the technology to the development of the Korean industry;
(2) conditions in the TIA (especially, the amount of royalties and the contract term); and
(3) whether the technology to be induced is:
    (i) contrary to the interests of national security or the maintenance of public order;
    (ii) likely to have a negative effect upon the sound development of the national economy; or
    (iii) in violation of the laws of Korea.

As a practical matter, the relevant minister is usually most concerned about the level of the technology, the duration of the license and the amount and method of calculating royalties. For example, if the technology already exists in ample supply in Korea or is not sufficiently sophisticated to have a beneficial impact on the development of local industries, it will likely not be deemed to be favorable.

Although there is no official policy, contract terms of up to ten years are sometimes granted for particularly valuable high technology, but five years is usually the maximum allowable duration for the licensing of less sophisticated technology.

There is also no published policy concerning the maximum amount of allowable royalties. However, as a rule, royalties in excess of five per cent of the net sales value are seldom accepted, except where valuable and sophisticated high technology is involved. In any event, it should be understood that consultation and negotiation with the relevant minister is an important part of the process and, if properly handled, can sometimes lead to special concessions.

The relevant minister must send a copy of the TIA to the EPB so that it can determine whether the Agreement includes any unfair provisions that violate the MRFTA. According to the EPB Guidelines (EPB Notice No. 87/14), the following are considered to be unfair provisions in a TIA:

(1) any provision by which the technology recipient is unreasonably obligated to purchase from the foreign investor, or a person designated by him raw materials, parts, equipment, and relevant products which are required by the technology recipient to manufacture the products (hereinafter referred to as 'Contract Products') with the use of the

technology supplied by the foreign supplier (hereinafter referred to as 'Contract Technology');

(2) any provision which prohibits the technology recipient from selling or exporting contract products in territories other than 'restricted territories' or which obligates the technology recipient to obtain the technology supplier's prior approval to sell or export there. Restricted territories are defined as:

  (a) territories in which the technology supplier has previously registered the contract technology;

  (b) territories in which the technology supplier has regularly been engaged in sales activities with respect to the contract products; and

  (c) territories in which a third party has acquired the right from the technology supplier to sell the contract products exclusively;

(3) any provision by which restrictions are imposed upon sales outlets, amount of sales, method of sales, and resale price of the contract products; however, this provision does not apply where the technology supplier allows the technology recipient to sell or export the contract products into a restricted territory as described in (2) above and subsequently the technology recipient does sell or export there;

(4) any provision by which the technology supplier does not grant to the technology recipient a right to use the contract technology exclusively, and restrains him from dealing in competitive or similar products, or using competitive or similar technology during the term of the contract;

(5) any provision which restricts the technology recipient from dealing in competitive or similar products, or using competitive or similar technology for a considerable period of time after either the expiration of the term of the contract or the early termination of the contract; however, this provision shall not apply if the early termination of the contract is attributable to the malfeasance of the technology recipient and the period of the restrictions is within the term of the original contract;

(6) any provision by which the technology recipient is prohibited or restrained from using the following technology continuously after the expiration of the contract or the early termination of the contract: technology other than that which the technology supplier has exclusive rights to such as industrial property rights, or technology the exclusive nature of which is extinguished after the time of contracting but before the time of expiration or termination; however, this provision shall not apply in the event that the early termination of the contract is attributable to the technology recipient;

(7) any provision by which the technology supplier is entitled to unilaterally determine the method for the calculation of royalties without specifying it in the agreement;

(8) any provision by which royalties are imposed upon products other

than the contract products which are manufactured or sold with the use of the contract technology during the term of the contract;

(9) any provision by which the technology supplier may supply the technology without reasonable cause long after the effective date of the contract or the date of advance payment by the technology recipient;

(10) any provision by which the technology supplier determines the scope of sales promotion expenses including advertising, and charges the technology recipient for the expenses;

(11) any provision by which the technology recipient is required to acquire a patent license concerning additional patented materials once he acquires a patent license concerning the patented materials; and

(12) any provision by which the technology supplier is entitled to unilaterally designate an arbitral organization or a court to resolve a dispute between the parties to the contract.

If the TIA includes any of these provisions, the EPB will notify the relevant minister, and then the relevant minister will request that the local technology recipient delete or amend the unfair provisions. However, as the wording in the Guidelines is somewhat vague, the ministers enjoy broad discretionary authority in their review of the TIA and exceptions are sometimes allowed. Therefore, when we initially file a TIA for review even if some of the provisions of a TIA appear to be in contravention of the Guidelines, we sometimes leave provisions as they are and then see whether the relevant minister objects to them. If the relevant minister does object and requests a supplement or amendment, it is easy to overcome the problem by simply amending the agreement.

If the relevant minister requests a supplement or an amendment to the TIA, the technology recipient must subsequently resubmit within sixty days from the date of receipt of the request, a report which evidences compliance with the request. This 60-day period may be extended one time with the approval of the relevant minister. The technology recipient usually complies with such a request by entering into an amendment agreement with the foreign technology supplier.

The TIA must come into effect within six months from the date of the final acceptance of the report. Otherwise, the acceptance of the report of the TIA will be deemed null and void. However, this period may be extended with the minister's approval.

TAX BENEFITS

The royalties remitted to the technology supplier who is a party to the TIA are exempt from income tax (in case of an individual) or corporate tax (in case of the juridical person) for five years from the date of acceptance of the report of the TIA. This tax benefit is provided automatically unlike the tax benefits which are granted to foreign invested enterprise only upon the request of foreign investors.

Unfortunately, it has recently been reported that the Korean government will abolish in the near future, this tax exempt status for royalties arising from a TIA. Consequently, the 'high-tech' industries will soon be the only areas where the government will continue to offer foreigners incentives to participate in Korea's development.

As mentioned above, a TIA whose main purpose is merely to allow the Korean licensee the use of a foreign licensor's trademark will be accepted by the ministers only if the foreign licensor has waived his rights to any tax exemption benefits. However, in practice, it is difficult to determine whether the main purpose of a TIA is to allow the Korean licensee the use of the foreign licensor's trademark. Therefore, the Korean government has established guidelines which provide that a TIA falling under any of the following categories is regarded as a TIA whose main purpose is merely to license the use of a foreigner's trademark, regardless of whether or not the agreement also includes transfer of a technology:

(1) a TIA which includes the use of a foreigner's trademark on certain consumer goods ('certain consumer goods' are textile goods, footwear goods, soap and other cleaning materials, household electronic products, bags, toys, furniture, musical instruments, sports equipment, stationery, cosmetics, non-pharmaceutical medicaments, processed foods and natural goods, alcoholic beverages, and other goods for daily life);

(2) a TIA whose extension of duration has been applied for solely for the purpose of continuing the use of a foreign trademark; or

(3) a TIA which includes a trademark license and the Korean licensee is not engaged in the manufacture of the products concerned.

Any TIA falling under any of the above three categories may be accepted by the relevant minister only if the foreign licensor has waived his rights to any tax exemption benefit at the time the Korean licensee submits the TIA to the relevant minister for acceptance.

Conclusion

As the Korean economy continues to mature, Korea will become an integrated and substantial part of the world economy. Consequently, the Korean government in order to guarantee fair competition between foreign investors and domestic businessmen, will further liberalize its regulations on foreign investment while reducing and ultimately eliminating the various incentives currently offered to foreign investors.

Chapter 5

Legal Aspects of Trade and Investment in Singapore and Malaysia

by Robert D.A. Pick

Baker & McKenzie
London, England

Introduction

It is common to link the countries of Singapore and Malaysia together when discussing not only investment but other aspects of South East Asia. Not just because they are physically adjacent. Malaysia also borders on Thailand, and Singapore is but a few miles from the coast of Indonesia. The reason is that the two countries have a common heritage and have only been independent of one another since 1965 and independent of the United Kingdom since, in the case of Malaysia (then 'Malaya'), 1957, and in the case of Singapore, 1963.

Ever since the Englishman, Captain Francis Light, obtained a cession over Penang from the Sultan of Kedah in 1786 on behalf of the British East India Company (this was the first territory in Malaysia to be acquired by the British, Singapore having been founded in 1819 by Stamford Raffles), English law has been part of the law of both Singapore and Malaysia in one way or another, alongside local customary law and Muslim law (which applies only to Muslims). The reception of English law took many forms. Sometimes legislation was enacted following closely on English models or those of other colonies, such as British India; and members of the bar and bench were almost all educated and trained in England, so naturally they applied English principles to local cases too. In fact, from time to time, the judges had to be reminded by the appellate courts to give more cognizance to local laws.

There is much argument in academic circles as to when, and the degree to which, English laws are applicable in both Malaysia and Singapore. Both countries contain legislation to do so. The Civil Law Act 1956 in Malaysia and the Civil Law (Amendment No. 2) Act of 1979 in Singapore both provide that the Common Law and rules of equity as administered in England will apply in their respective countries but subject to the limitation that local law, both case law and statute, will take precedence.[1] Further, English commercial law is specifically brought into the laws of Malaysia and Singapore but in the case of some States in Malaysia, it is the English law on the date of the coming into force of the Act (7 April 1956) and in others it is the English law as it changes subsequently. Hence, new legislation or case law in England can automatically change the law of Malaysia and Singapore, subject always to local statutes dealing with commercial subjects.

Whilst the question of the relationship between English and local law is a confused one, one can say for certain that as the two countries introduce more and more legislation to regulate commercial activities in their jurisdictions, so the influence of English law declines. In Singapore, the highest Court of Appeal is still the Privy Council sitting in London but the right of appeal to the Privy Council was abolished in Malaysia in 1980 for criminal and constitutional cases and in 1985 for other cases.[2]

Because of the way in which Malaysia grew from a number of States into a single country (the States of Sarawak and Sabah in East Malaysia are separated from the other States in West Malaysia by about 200 miles of water), there are still differences in the laws as applied to the Malaysian States – so much more so do the laws of Malaysia and Singapore differ, particularly in the area of foreign investment which is the main topic of this paper. The two countries are keen competitors in the all important area of attracting foreign investment, which makes the subject all the more interesting.

Trading with Singapore and Malaysia

Exports

Before dealing with investment as such in Singapore and Malaysia, mention should be made of that aspect of business which involves the sale of goods

---

1. Section 3 of the Malaysian Civil Law Act 1956 and Section 5 of the Singapore Civil Law (Amendment No. 2) Act 1979.
2. Sections 74 to 79 of the Malaysian Courts of Judicature Act 1964 dealing with appeals to the Judicial Committee of the Privy Council were repealed with effect from 1 January 1985.

without the degree of commitment which an investment necessarily involves, that is the sale to and in the country of goods. Both countries have, to a greater or lesser extent, a free-market economy and permit free enterprise to exist with the minimum of restrictions. There are therefore no formal anti-trust or anti-monopoly laws, and no laws covering market dominance such as exist in the European Community or the United States. In Malaysia, however, the Control of Supplies Act prohibits the purchase, sale or barter of certain products without the permission of the Controller of Supplies, but the prohibition is only applied in extreme circumstances to such public necessities as oil and certain foodstuffs. Just as in Singapore there are price controls[3] on a few essential goods, in Malaysia they exist on, for example, petroleum products, essential foodstuffs such as milk, rice, sugar and flour and on certain building materials but generally there is a free market for prices.[4]

So far as concerns import duties and barriers, both Malaysia and Singapore are members of ASEAN (the Association of South East Asian Nations) along with Brunei, Indonesia, Thailand, and the Philippines, but it would be a mistake to think that ASEAN is a common market to any extent approximating that of the European Community. An agreement on preferential trading arrangements was signed by the then ASEAN members in February 1977 and was certainly a step forward in the direction of freedom of trade since it provided, *inter alia*, for the gradual reduction of tariffs and the liberalization of non-tariff barriers (by the end of 1986, some 18,000 items had been accorded tariff cuts under the preferential trading arrangements,[5] but in spite of this progress, ASEAN cannot be considered as a single market in which to operate).

Import duties are imposed to a greater or lesser extent in both countries not only for the purpose of raising revenue, such as the duties on liquor, tobacco and petroleum products, but also to protect local industries. Generally speaking, however, most goods enter into Singapore free of duty whereas in Malaysia there is a variety of duties on a wide range of imports ranging from zero to 100 per cent of the value. Both countries have established successful free trade zones ('FTZs') and these are particularly important to Malaysia, in view of the stricter tariff system which applies there. Companies which export at least 80 per cent of their production and rely on imported raw materials and components are able to benefit from goverment concessions on tariff rates. FTZs are situated mainly on Peninsular Malaysia's West Coast but due to labor shortages and the need to develop the economy of the East Coast, similar benefits are being granted to the new so called 'licensed manufacturing warehouses' (LMWs).[6]

---

3. Section 4 of the Price Control Act (1985 Rev. Ed.) allows the Price Controller to fix maximum prices or charges.
4. *See* the Price Control Act 1946 and the regulations thereunder.
5. The system operates by giving a margin of preference, ranging from ten per cent to 50 per cent or more, on the full rate of duty.
6. *See* Section 65A of the Customs Act 1967.

Non-tariff barriers are certainly more in evidence in Malaysia than in Singapore where fairly normal labelling requirements exist for imported food, drugs and liquor. In Malaysia, there is a requirement for the use of Bahasa Malaysia, the language of the majority of the indigenous population, on the labelling of certain products for domestic use, though foreign languages may be used too. The labelling guidelines are generally quite comprehensive.

There should also be mentioned the fact that the Malaysian government will favor Malaysian firms entering into joint ventures with foreign firms when awarding public works and service contracts of up to M$50,000 in value. Preference margins are also given to Malaysian firms in the case of tenders of less than M$25,000. This means that a contract will be awarded to a Malaysian firm even if its price exceeds that of a foreign firm by no more than five per cent. If there is no Malaysian firm bidding, a joint venture with a Malaysian firm will take priority over a foreign firm. Apart from these guidelines, it is often advisable for local know-how to be brought in by foreign firms when tendering or selling into Malaysia.

All firms bidding for government contracts must have at least 30 per cent Bumiputra equity, so that foreign companies may have to bid through local agents or distributors which have this percentage of Bumiputra ownership.

DISTRIBUTORS AND AGENTS

Rather than selling direct into Malaysia or Singapore, a foreign company may consider appointing a local agent or distributor. This is a very common practice. Generally, there is no problem from the legal point of view in establishing this relationship but care must be taken for the relationship to be properly set up and documented. In some countries in South East Asia, such as Indonesia, the termination of a distribution or agency agreement can cause unusual problems but in Singapore there is no particular protection for a distributor or agent whose appointment is terminated in accordance with its terms. In Malaysia a principal agent agreement must be terminated with sufficient cause.[7] In one reported case, a sole distributor was held to be an agent and sufficient cause was required for termination.[8]

One of the reasons for a foreign company appointing a local agent or distributor is to avoid the deemed establishment by it of a local presence. It is, therefore, important to ensure that the agent does not cause the foreign company to be liable to local taxes which may be higher than taxes in the home base and therefore not wholly available for credit against home base taxes.

As to whether a foreign company will be liable to local tax depends on

---

7. *See* Section 158 of the Contracts Act 1950.
8. *See Chan Chow Kian* v. *International Trading Co.* (1969), 2 MLJ* 223.

local tax laws, but the impact of double taxation may be alleviated by double taxation treaties.[9] Both Singapore and Malaysia have entered into double tax treaties with the UK, but not with the US, and with most European countries.[10] The double tax treaties differ in detail but they use the basic concept that local tax is only payable by the foreign enterprise where it is 'carrying on business through a permanent establishment' which means:

(a) if it has a fixed place of business in which the business of the enterprise is wholly or partly carried on, e.g. branch, place of management, office, factory, etc.; or

(b) where the business is carried on through an agent who has, and habitually exercises, an authority to conclude contracts on behalf of the foreign enterprise.[11]

It is not always easy to draw the lines between a dependent and independent agent but the OECD[12] model provides that for an agent to be independent he must be independent both legally and economically and, when he is acting on behalf of the foreign enterprise, he is acting in the ordinary course of his business.

Naturally, the appointment of an agent in the strict sense of the word, where the agent does not purchase goods himself, but merely receives commission on sales introduced by him, is likely to cause more problems from this point of view than the appointment of a distributor who purchases goods as a principal.

If the foreign enterprise does attract local tax, this is normally on the basis of the 'Attribution Rule', tax is assessed on the portion of the profits of the foreign enterprise attributable to the permanent establishment. This is the case, for example, in the double taxation treaties between the UK and both Singapore and Malaysia.

LICENSING

Licensing can be looked on as a half-way house between direct selling into a country and the establishment of an investment, such as a manufacturing facility, in the foreign country. Hitherto, licensing in Singapore and Malaysia has not been a common practice, partly because of the lack of adequate intellectual property protection for licensors and in Singapore, for example, because of the country's small domestic market and the compara-

---

9. *See* Section 49 of the Income Tax Act (1985 Rev. Ed.) on double taxation arrangements.
10. In the case of Singapore, these include Belgium, France, West Germany, Italy, The Netherlands, Switzerland, Finland, Norway, Denmark and Sweden.
11. As an example, *see* The Income Tax (Singapore United Kingdom) (Avoidance of Double Taxation Agreement) Order, 1966, Article 2(1)(1).
12. OECD Model Agreement, 1977 Edition, Article 5 paragraphs 2 and 6.

tive ease with which foreign investment can be made. However, the situation may change as intellectual property protection laws are tightened and if, in Malaysia, for example, foreign companies are required to divest themselves of their equity in direct investments.

Certainly there are advantages as well as disadvantages to the licensing route. One advantage is that it is easier to extricate oneself from a license agreement than an equity investment; a second is that the income paid to the licensor by a licensee by way of royalty or license fee is usually more tax effective than payment by dividend from a subsidiary. The main danger is that licensing involves a transfer of know how to a third party whom the licensor may not be able to control as much as he would wish.

In Singapore, it is not usually necessary to obtain government approval to the terms of licensing or technical assistance agreements but in Malaysia applications to enter into such agreements for manufacturing projects, where applicable,[13] have to be submitted to the Ministry of Trade and Industry and to the Malaysian Central Bank to ensure that no unreasonable demands are placed on the local party. The Ministry would want to ensure, for example:

(a) that the agreement does not impose unfair or unjustified restrictions on the Malaysian party;
(b) that the agreement is not prejudicial to the national interest; and
(c) that the payment of fees is commensurate with the level of technology to be transferred.

The technology to be supplied must incorporate the latest developments known to the licensor, and the licensee should have access to improvements to the technology.

Whilst payment for a license can be made either by way of a lump sum payment, running royalties or a mixture of both, lump sum payments are discouraged and should generally relate only to the actual expenses incurred by the licensor for preliminary services provided to the licensee.

Where royalties are imposed, the approved rate is between one and five per cent of net sales depending on the degree of sophistication of the technology being transferred.

The duration of the license agreement should be adequate for the full absorption of the technology. Normally a five-year initial period is approved and any renewal is subject to prior approval of the Ministry.

The licensee should be free to sell licensed products throughout Malaysia and in all other countries except where the licensor manufactures directly or

---

13. The Industrial Coordination Act 1975 spells out the instances when a license will be needed for manufacturing. Applications for a manufacturing license have to be submitted to the Malaysian Industrial Development Authority ('MIDA') which is under the Ministry of Trade and Industry. Usually conditions reflecting the Malaysian New Economic Policy will be stipulated on the license.

he has given exclusive rights to other licensees or where he is not legally empowered to allow sales based on his technology.

The governing law should be Malaysian, and arbitration proceedings must be conducted in Malaysia.

Payment of royalties and technical fees by Singapore or Malaysian companies are generally subject to witholding tax which in the case of Singapore is at the rate of 33 per cent[14] and in the case of Malaysia at a special rate of 15 per cent.[15] These rates may be wholly or partially reduced if the payment is made to a licensor in a country with which Malaysia or Singapore has a double tax treaty.

Whilst the withholding tax rates are therefore higher in Singapore, the Minister of Finance does have power under the Economic Expansion Incentives (Relief from Income Tax) Act 1967 (as amended)[16] to reduce withholding tax on royalties and technical assistance fees and to exempt them from tax completely.[17] It is understood that this exemption is rarely granted and more commonly applicants are given a reduction in the rate. However, no such reduction will be granted if the reduction is offset by a corresponding increase in tax on the licensor in his country of residence[18]; in other words, the Singapore government will not grant this reduction if the beneficiary is the foreign government rather than the foreign licensor. Thus, no reduction is possible in the 33 per cent rate imposed on royalties payable to US companies since the US government will tax the royalties or fees in full.

INTELLECTUAL PROPERTY

Undoubtedly one of the main problems in doing business in South East Asia, particularly by way of direct selling or licensing, has been the likelihood of intellectual property rights, whether patent, trademark, copyright or just know how, being infringed or exploited. The situation, however, is improving, as a result of considerable pressure having been exerted over the years by foreign governments.

As recently as October 1986, the only way to obtain patent protection in Malaysia was to first register a patent in the United Kingdom. Now, however, Malaysia has implemented the Patents Act 1983 establishing a Patents Board. It is therefore now possible to apply for a patent directly in Malaysia and such a registration will be effective for the whole of the country. The new law is similar to the patent law in other countries, with

---

14. *See* Section 45A of the Income Tax Act (1985 Rev. Ed.).
15. *See* Section 6 and Schedule I of the Income Tax Act 1967.
16. Amendment Act 22 of 1987, with effect from 18 September 1987.
17. *See* Section 64 of the Act.
18. *See* Section 63 of the Act.

protection being granted for fifteen years with a provision for renewal, the patent owner having the exclusive right to exploit the patented invention and to assign and license the patented invention. The law also gives protection for five years to 'utility innovations', a utility innovation being any implement, tool, product or process which is of practical utility by reason of its form, configuration, construction or composition which is new to Malaysia.

Malaysia has not yet acceded to the Paris Convention for the Protection of Intellectual Property but is understood to be seriously considering doing so.

Nor is Singapore a member of the Paris Convention. Patent protection in Singapore is granted by the registering of a UK patent which must then be filed with the Singapore Registrar of Patents within three years thereafter, although the Registrar has a discretion to accept for registration a patent lodged outside the three-year period.[19] Since 22 September 1982, patents granted under the European Patent Convention designating the UK as one of the countries in which protection is granted have been accepted by the Registrar for registration in Singapore.

So far as trade marks are concerned, it is worth making a general comment on the value of a registered trade mark as against an unregistered mark. Whereas registration of a trade mark will entitle a trade mark owner to succeed in a suit against an infringer merely by proving the registration and the infringement, many well known brand names, logos or get ups, although not registered as trade marks, can nevertheless be protected since they identify particular products as being manufactured and sold by a particular company. The company in effect acquires a form of goodwill. The action against an infringer of an unregistered mark is called in Malaysia and Singapore, as in the UK, a 'passing off' action and is more likely to give rise to difficulties than bringing an action on a registered trade mark. The reason for this is that the owner has to prove that the infringer represented his goods for sale in such a manner as to mislead the public into thinking that they were the owner's goods or that the infringer's business was in some way related to the owner's.[20] In common law jurisdictions such as Singapore and Malaysia, it is necessary to show that the owner already had a local reputation for the product in that country and not just an international reputation. This can cause problems for an international company. A registered trade mark, on the other hand, will give protection before any goodwill or reputation has been built up. It is therefore extremely important to obtain trade mark protection in countries where products are being or are likely to be sold, and Singapore and Malaysia are no exceptions.

Both Singapore and Malaysia have their own system of registration of

---

19. *See* Section 3 of the Registration of United Kingdom Patents Act (1985 Rev. Ed.).
20. *See* the Privy Council decision (Singapore) in *White Hudson & Co.* v. *Asian Organisation Ltd* (1965) 1 MLJ* 186; *Clairol Incorporated* v. *Too Vit Company* (1980) 2 MLJ* 112; *Lee Kar Choo* v. *Lee Lian Choo* (1967) 1 AC** 602.

trade marks. Protection lasts for seven years and is subject to successive fourteen-year renewal periods.[21]

Both Singapore and Malaysia introduced new copyright legislation in 1987.[22] One of the main features of both Acts is that computer programmes are specifically referred to as being copyrightable[23] thus removing one of the major uncertainties of the old law. Copyright protection is obtained without registration and lasts for 50 years after the year of death of the author.[24] The situation is still not entirely satisfactory, however, since original works will only be protected if they were first published in Singapore or Malaysia respectively or the author was a citizen or resident in Singapore or Malaysia[25] at the time when the work was first published. However, the harshness of this rule has been softened in Singapore. Portection under the 1987 Act has been extended to works first published in the US or the UK and to works authored by citizens or residents of the US or UK. Copyright owners of foreign countries other than the US or the UK will also have protection under the Acts if the work is published in Singapore within 30 days of first publication elsewhere. The position is the same in Malaysia except for the additional protection afforded in Singapore to US and UK copyright owners. The Acts introduce much greater powers for the authorities to enforce infringement of copyright and stiffer penalties for infringers. Unfortunately, however, despite pressure from interested parties, neither Singapore nor Malaysia has become signatories to any of the international conventions and therefore most foreign copyright owners will continue to lack the protection which they can expect in many other countries.

Finally, a word about know-how and trade secrets. In common law jurisdictions such as Singapore and Malaysia (just as in civil law jurisdictions), know-how and trade secrets can be protected by contract (that is by an express reference in the license or other agreement that certain confidential information will not be disclosed) so it should be possible to bring an action for failure to retain this confidentiality. Under English law, and in Singapore and Malaysia too, it may also in certain circumstances be possible to protect confidentiality even where there is no contractual relationship between the parties. However, since this is not the case in certain other countries in South East Asia such as the Philippines and Thailand, it is advisable to avoid disclosing confidential information unless it is done so on the basis of a contractual agreement that the information will be kept confidential.

---

21. *See* Sections 32 and 34 of the Singapore Trade Marks Act (1985 Rev. Ed.) and Section 32 and 41 of the Malaysian Trade Marks Act 1976.
22. The Singapore Copyright Act 1987 came into effect on 10 April 1987. The Malaysian Copyright Act 1987 came into effect on 1 December 1987.
23. *See* Section 7(1) of the Singapore Copyright Act which states that 'literary work' includes 'a computer program or compilation of computer programs'.
24. *See* Section 23(2) of the Singapore Copyright Act.
25. For a contrary view, *see Lee Yee Seng & Ors* v. *Golden Star Video* (1921), 2 MLJ* 43, 44, which held that a work first published in Malaysia will be granted protection by the Copyright Act notwithstanding that the author is neither a citizen nor resident of Malaysia.

Investment

INTRODUCTION

Both Singapore and Malaysia recognize the benefits to be gained by their economies through inward foreign investment and foreign investment is therefore encouraged by means of various tax incentives and concessions. As competition for foreign investment has increased throughout the developing countries in Asia, so have both Singapore and Malaysia increased the number of incentives on offer and adopted great flexibility in their attitude towards foreign investment applications. Part of this renewed enthusiasm has been due to the need for these countries to pull themselves out of the serious economic recession which hit them both in 1985 and 1986 although Singapore in particular has recovered swiftly to record an 8.8 per cent growth in GDP for 1987. The figure for Malaysia in 1987 was 2 per cent.

The main bodies through which foreign investment is channelled are, in Malaysia, the Malaysian Industrial Development Authority ('MIDA') and, in Singapore, the Economic Development Board ('EDB').[26] If clear evidence is needed of the encouragement of foreign investment, one has only to see that MIDA has established overseas offices in three cities in the US, four in Europe, and five in Asia.[27] The EDB has an even wider international profile with some overseas offices in North America, Europe and Asia.

Whilst foreign investors are encouraged in both countries, the degree to which their activities are restricted as compared with local investors differs, although the contrast is becoming less pronounced.

SINGAPORE

Singapore has the most open economy of all the ASEAN countries and whereas equity participation by Singaporeans in businesses established by foreign investors is certainly encouraged, it is not a general requirement. except in the case of shipping and retail companies. In view of this, joint ventures in Singapore are not very common although the company law, which is essentially similar to UK company law, is perfectly well able to cope with this structure.

---

26. The EDB was established pursuant to the provisions of the Economic Development Board Act (1985 Rev. Edn.).
27. For a description of policies, incentives and procedures adopted by MIDA *see* MIDA (1988) 'Malaysia Investment in Manufacturing Sector' (3rd Edition), which can be obtained from MIDA, Wisma Damansara, Kuala Lumpur or local MIDA offices.

MALAYSIA

Restrictions on foreign investors in Malaysia are imposed by the New Economic Policy ('NEP'), a policy whose application has been considerably relaxed in the past two years or so. The NEP comprises a set of guidelines laid down by the Malaysian government in 1970 and provides the basis for the regulation of foreign investment and ownership of assets by foreigners in Malaysia. In accordance with the policies of the NEP, the Industrial Coordination Act was passed in 1975 with the primary purpose of achieving the objectives of the NEP, in particular regulating the manufacturing sector by requiring substantially all manufacturing companies in Malaysia having shareholders' funds of M$2.5 million and above or engaging 75 or more full time employees to be licensed.

The NEP is somewhat different from localization policies in other Asian countries and elsewhere since its purpose is not to control the amount of foreign ownership of the economy but rather to redistribute wealth amongst different racial groups in the country thereby achieving a better economic and social balance. The reason for this is that the population of Malaysia consists of about 55 per cent Bumiputras (or indigenous people), 35 per cent Chinese and about ten per cent Indian and others. There is nothing particularly remarkable about this except that the 55 per cent Malays (who are Bumiputras) owned, at the time the NEP was first promulgated, only about 4.5 per cent of the corporate sector. It has now risen to about twenty per cent. The long term objective was therefore set that by 31 December 1990 ownership in the corporate sector should consist of 70 per cent Malaysian, and only 30 per cent foreign, the Malaysian content including 30 per cent Bumiputra and 40 per cent other Malaysian, and it is these percentages that are applied to equity ownership. A popular misconception has always been that these proportions apply to every individual company. This is not the case because the targets are global ones so that within, for example, a particular industry, one foreign company might be permitted in excess of 50 per cent ownership and another less than 30 per cent.

There is no doubt that over the years the NEP has achieved a substantial increase in Malay participation in the economy but it has also tended to discourage foreign investment because of the, often wrongly perceived, difficulties put in the way of foreigners. In view of this, and because of the government's concern about the lack of growth in the private sector, steps have been taken to stimulate further foreign investment by relaxing the rules. This relaxation began in July 1985 with new guidelines linking the level of equity of foreign partners in a joint venture with the export level of the project. If the project was 100 per cent export orientated, 100 per cent foreign ownership would be permitted and so on. Even if the export content was below 50 per cent but above twenty per cent, 51 per cent foreign equity would still be permitted.

In October 1986, the Malaysian Prime Minister, Dr. Mahathir Mohamad, announced a further relaxation of the guidelines by extending the ability of foreign companies to retain 100 per cent equity ownership. These new guidelines need to be set out in some detail.

New investments

(a)   Foreign investors may hold up to 100 per cent of the equity if the company exports 80 per cent or more of its production, irrespective of whether its products compete with products presently being manufactured locally for the domestic market.

(b)   Foreign investors whose applications are submitted between 1 October 1986 and 31 December 1990 are also permitted to hold up to 100 per cent of the equity provided they meet the following conditions:

    (i)   the company exports 50 per cent or more of its production or it employs 350 full-time Malaysian workers and the employment of Malaysians at all levels approximately reflects the racial composition of the country; and

    (ii)   the company's products do not compete with products presently being manufactured locally for the domestic market.

(c)   Local equity participation for other export orientated projects is permitted as follows:

    (i)   for projects exporting between 51 per cent and 79 per cent of their production, up to 51 per cent foreign equity ownership will be allowed. Additional foreign equity ownership up to 79 per cent may be allowed depending on factors such as the level of technology, spin off effects, size of the investment, location, value added and the utilization of local raw materials and components;

    (ii)   for projects exporting between 20 per cent and 50 per cent of their production, foreign equity ownership of between 31 per cent and 51 per cent will be allowed, depending upon similar factors as mentioned above;

    (iii)   for projects exporting less than 20 per cent, foreign equity ownership will be allowed up to a maximum of 30 per cent;

    (iv)   for projects producing products that are of high technology or are priority products for the domestic market, foreign equity ownership of up to 51 per cent will be permitted.

(d)   Detailed rules have been laid down as to the level of distribution of the Malaysian equity in respect of new investments, with priority being given to bumiputras as against other Malaysians.

The new guidelines are retrospective to some extent since companies which have been licensed between 1 April 1986 and 30 September 1986 and which have not yet made any investment in respect of the implementation of the projects are also eligible for the same equity guidelines which are set out above.

Further, although a company which has been licensed before 1 October 1986 must comply with the equity conditions as stated in its license, the foreign partner is permitted to own up to 100 per cent of the expanded equity as a result of an expansion in capacity or diversification provided, once again, that the new guidelines are fulfilled and provided, of course, that it is permitted to do so under any agreement with the other shareholders.

The new guidelines contain an important assurance in respect of equity ownership in that a company which has been approved under the new equity guidelines will not be required to restructure its equity at any time, even after 1990, provided that the company continues to comply with the original conditions of approval and retains the original features of the project. In this context it should be noted that Malaysia has concluded Investment Guarantee Agreements with fourteen conuntries, including the US, the UK and other European countries. Whether the government will exert pressure in other ways to increase local participation remains to be seen.

Tax

A word needs to be said about the general basis of corporate taxation in Singapore and Malaysia so that a better understanding can be achieved of the various tax incentives which have been introduced in both countries to encourage foreign investment. The scope of tax is territorial, which generally speaking means that a company's income is subject to tax in Singapore or Malaysia if it accrues in or is derived from Singapore or Malaysia (as the case may be), or is received in Singapore or Malaysia from outside. For a non resident company, its income is taxable only to the extent that it accrues in or is derived from Singapore or Malaysia for example, as a result of the receipt of royalties. The residence of a company depends not only on the place where it is incorporated but also on the place from where it is controlled and managed. The corporate tax rate in Singapore is 33 per cent, and in Malaysia 40 per cent plus development tax of five per cent (*see* below). An additional excess profits tax of three per cent on companies whose taxable income exceeded M$2m was abolished in the Malaysian Budget in October 1987.

There are no capital gains taxes in Singapore, and in Malaysia there are capital gains taxes only on gains made from the sale of land or buildings under the Real Property Gains Tax.[28] The rates of tax depend on the length of time which the assets have been held and now range from twenty per cent if disposal is made in the first or second year after acquisition, down to five per cent if made in the fifth year for companies and to zero per cent for individuals if made in the sixth year onwards after acquisition. There is also a share transfer tax on the sale value in excess of M$1m on the disposal of the shares of a land based company, the tax being levied at the rate of two

---

28. *See* the Real Property Gains Tax Act 1976.

per cent.[29] A 'land based company' is one that owns land in Malaysia as its main or one of its main assets; if a company which does not own land itself has an interest in a land based company it may itself be treated as a land based company. There is an exemption from share transfer tax for inter company transfers made within a group for the purpose of increasing operating efficiency or in compliance with government policy on capital participation. The 1988 Budget introduces a withdrawal of such exemption in certain instances.

Development tax, as mentioned above, at the rate of five per cent is also charged on any income derived by a resident or a non resident from a 'development source', namely, 'a source consisting of a business or the letting of property situated in Malaysia'.[30] In effect, therefore, all income derived from a business will be subject to development tax. The principal income of a company which falls outside the scope of the development tax is dividends or interest (except where they contsitute business income, for example, for banks).

There is no dividend withholding tax in Singapore or Malaysia. A company is allowed to deduct tax on dividends paid to its shareholders at the rate, in Singapore of 33 per cent and in Malaysia of 40 per cent.[31] If a resident company pays the dividend without the deduction of tax, the dividend is then deemed to be of a gross amount and the difference between the gross amount and the net amount paid is deemed to have been deducted as tax. The tax deducted or deemed to have been deducted is not a final tax, but is set off against the income tax of the company payable to the Inland Revenue. If the tax deducted or deemed to have been deducted exceeds the tax payable by the company on its chargeable income, the difference is payable by the company as an additional tax. If the tax payable by the company on its chargeable income exceeds the tax deducted or deemed deducted, the difference is carried forward and set off against tax deducted or deemed deducted from dividends in the following year.

Problems arise where a Singapore or Malaysian resident company derives non Singapore or non Malaysian source income which is not remitted to Singapore or Malaysia. The income is not, at that stage, subject to tax. However, when the company declares a dividend, it deducts from the dividend tax which would be payable to the tax authorities. Therefore, even if the company does not in fact have any tax liability, because its profits do not have a Singapore or Malaysian source, nor are they actually received in Singapore or Malaysia, the company may still effectively pay tax on such profits if a dividend is declared out of them. This obviously discourages the use of a Singapore or Malaysian resident company as a regional holding

---

29. *See* the Share Transfer (Land Based Company) Transfer Tax Act 1984.
30. *See* the Supplementary Income Tax Act 1967.
31. *See* Section 44 of the Singapore Income Tax Act (1985 Rev. Edn.) and Section 108 of the Malaysian Income Tax Act 1967.

company. Recent amendments to the relevant section of the Income Tax Act have not addressed this problem.

Mention should be made here of a far reaching change to the Singapore Income Tax Act brought about in January 1988 for the purpose of stamping out blatant tax avoidance schemes. The Revenue have previously had the right, under Section 33, to disregard transactions which were artificial or fictitious, thereby reducing the amount of tax payable. Under the new Section 33, however, the Revenue can make adjustments to any transaction or arrangement unless it is for *bona fide* commercial reasons and had not, as one of its main purposes, the reduction of tax.

This means in effect that even if the transaction has a commercial purpose, it may be caught if one of its main purposes is the reduction of tax. Clearly the level of tax payable on a transaction is often going to affect the manner in which the transaction is structured. However, as a result of representations made to the Revenue, it has given an assurance that ordinary commercial transactions will not be caught and it will be prepared to give advance rulings where possible. It will be interesting to see how this new legislation is used.

Singapore Tax Incentives

As mentioned above, one of the main areas in which developing countries compete for foreign investment is the granting of tax incentives.

One of the leaders in this development is Singapore where a large number of incentives are available under the Economic Expansion Incentives (Relief from Income Tax) Act and other legislation, including the Income Tax Act itself. Most of the incentives are administered by the EDB referred to earlier.

The list of incentives includes pioneer status, and incentives relating to expansion, investment allowances, operational headquarters, post pioneer operations, venture capital, warehousing and servicing, countertrade, international consultancy services, approved foreign loans and approved royalties. Set out below are brief details of some of the major incentives.

'Pioneer status' is one of the original incentives given by the Singapore government and remains its flagship. Under the Act, the Minister of Finance has the discretion to declare an industry which has not been carried out on a scale adequate for the development of Singapore to be a pioneer industry and a manufactured product to be a pioneer product if he considers it expedient 'in the public interest to do so'.[32] He will declare an industry to be a pioneer industry if the company is engaged in a particularly specialized or innovative area of manufacture. Recently, pioneer status has been extended to the services sector and is available to companies which can demonstrate

---

32. *See* Section 4(1) of the Economic Expansion Incentives (Relief from Income Tax) Act.

that they will be making a substantial investment involving new technology transfer and expertise.[33]

The consequence of obtaining pioneer status is that a company will be exempt from tax on its profits arising from that pioneer activity for a period of between five and ten years,[34] depending on the level of the capital investment involved or the scale of the technology transfer. Whereas previously a minimum investment of S$1m was generally required for pioneer status, this rule has been waived and there is now no requirement as to the amount of capital expenditure to be incurred. The tax exemption starts when the pioneer product is produced in marketable quantities. Shareholders receiving dividends out of profits during the tax holiday do not generally pay tax on those dividends. One disadvantage of pioneer status is that losses incurred during the pioneer period cannot be set off against subsequent profits arising after the pioneer period has expired. As a concession, the Revenue will permit some of these losses to be carried forward but it is generally inadvisable for a company which is not confident of making profits during the pioneer period to apply for pioneer status, nor is pioneer status suitable for projects which have a long gestation period.

There was a tendency for companies whose pioneer status had expired to remove their operations from Singapore in order to obtain continuing tax free status in other locations which were offering similar incentives. However, pioneer companies can now also take advantage of the Export Incentive Scheme which allows companies benefitting from this Scheme to enjoy corporate tax exemptions on 90 per cent of their export income over a specific base calculated by reference to the current export performance of the industry (in the case of a new company) or its own performance (in the case of an existing company). Further, a company which enjoyed pioneer status or export incentive status and incurs additional investment is able to obtain a reduction in corporate tax rates of not less than ten per cent, for up to a further five years, on the expiry of its pioneer or export incentive status.

As a result of the extension of qualifying activities for pioneer status, countertraders are now specifically encouraged to apply and if successful they will be exempted from tax for a period of five years. A separate company must be formed to engage in countertrading activities only. The company must show that it has established international trading links and employs an agreed number of specialist countertraders, and at least one leg of each countertrade transaction, whether it is financial or physical movement of goods, must be routed through Singapore. The five year tax holiday may be extended upon a favourable review by the Trade Development Board.

Another incentive is the Expansion Incentive which can be given to manufacturing and service companies. In order to qualify for this incentive,

---

33. *See* Section 17 of the Act.
34. *See* Section 18 of the Act.

manufacturing companies must incur or intend to incur new capital expenditure of not less than S$10m in new productive equipment and machinery.[35] The benefit consists of a tax free period of up to five years[36] on all its 'incremental income' which means the income directly attributable to the new capital expenditure over and above the income it was earning prior to the expansion. It is understood that this incentive has not proved to be very successful, probably due to the large amount of capital expenditure which is required for qualification.

One of the most important incentives is the Investment Allowance Scheme. Where the Minister 'considers it expedient having regard to the economic, technical and other merits of a project',[37] he may qualify a company for an investment allowance of up to 50 per cent of the fixed capital expenditure incurred within a specific period not exceeding five years[38] on productive equipment such as machinery and computers. The allowance is credited against chargeable income and is carried over until it has been used up.[39] Originally, the benefit was given to companies carrying out manufacturing projects but it is now available for approved research and development, service and construction activities. Investment allowances can be an attractive alternative to pioneer relief for those projects which involve large capital expenditure and/or long gestation periods during which time there is little profit which can be exempted from tax.

The final incentive to be mentioned here is a fairly new one, the incentive for operational headquarters ('OHQ'). An OHQ is defined as an entity incorporated or registered in Singapore for the purposes of providing management services to subsidiaries and/or associated companies (or their branches) in other countries. An OHQ is expected to hold equity in regional subsidiaries or associated companies and to provide supporting services, such as administration, management, technical support, R&D, fund management, to them. Companies that have a corporate policy to own subsidiaries through a single parent company can still qualify but the regional companies are expected to be related to the parent company.

Each application will be considered on its merits and in evaluating applications the EDB will take into account factors such as the level of paid up capital of the proposed OHQ, whether there will be a significant presence of management personnel and professionals of quality and capability to provide the supporting services, and whether there will be substantial work done in Singapore which makes a significant contribution to the operations of the OHQ's subsidiaries. This means that letterbox companies set up solely for tax purposes will not be considered and subsidiaries and associate

---

35. *See* Section 21 of the Act.
36. *See* Section 22 of the Act.
37. *See* Section 67(2) of the Act.
38. *See* Section 68 of the Act.
39. *See* Section 71 of the Act.

companies which form the network of the OHQ must be involved in real commercial activities.

The benefits under the Scheme include the following:

(a) income arising from the provision of services by the OHQ in Singapore to overseas subsidiaries and associated companies will be taxed at a concessionary rate of ten per cent and where the services are provided by the OHQ at cost, the 10 per cent concessionary rate will apply to the usual imputed profit margin of five per cent;

(b) dividends paid by overseas subsidiaries will be exempt from tax in Singapore and no further tax will be levied when dividend income is distributed through Singapore to its overseas parent company;

(c) other income such as royalties payable to the OHQ for research development work may also be exempt from tax on a case by case basis.

The incentive period will be for up to ten years in the first instance with the possibility of renewal periods.

In conclusion, there are a wide range of incentives available but it is clear that the nature of them is changing as Singapore changes its emphasis towards encouragement of the services sector[40] whilst not neglecting major innovative and capital intensive projects which will help to develop Singapore's economy further. As the Finance Minister, Dr. Hu, said in a recent Budget statement, 'We recognize that incentives are still useful and necessary at this stage of our economic development. At the same time, I should emphasize that it is our intention to eventually move towards a broader based, low tax regime'.

Malaysian Tax Incentives

In Malaysia, as in Singapore, there are a host of incentives given to investors, and no distinction is made between local and foreign investors. Unlike Singapore, however, Malaysia does not seek to encourage investment in service industries except the hotel and tourism industries. The incentives are based on the three mainstays of the economy, namely manufacturing, agriculture and tourism.

Malaysia offers pioneer status too. Pioneer status will now be granted irrespective of the size of the capital investment but the investment must be in an area which the government has declared eligible for that status. These areas are periodically reviewed and the list published by MIDA. Pioneer status gives tax relief for five years with the possibility of an extension for a further five years, after which the company is still able to apply for other incentives under the Act.[41]

---

40. *See Straits Times*, 5 March 1988, 'Service Sector Gets Lion's Share of Perks'.
41. *See* the Promotion of Investments Act 1986.

Another major incentive is the Investment Tax Allowance under which a company may be given an allowance of up to 100 per cent in respect of qualifying capital expenditure incurred within five years from the date of approval of the project.

The so-called 'Tax Abatement Programme' allows firms to reduce their taxable income by certain percentages. Thus, a five per cent abatement is given for a minimum of five years to manufacturing companies located in designated 'promoted industrial areas'. A five per cent abatement is given to small scale manufacturing companies for five years, small scale being defined as those with shareholders' funds of less than M$500,000. These companies, and indeed other companies, may claim an additional five per cent abatement if they have complied with the NEP on equity participation or employment. There are also accelerated depreciation and environmental allowances on plant, machinery and factory buildings in respect of qualifying capital expenditure incurred, in the case of the environmental allowance, prior to 31 December 1990.

There are also incentives for exports such as the abatement for adjusted income which is granted to resident manufacturing companies exporting, directly or through agents, products which are manufactured in Malaysia. An abatement is given equivalent to 50 per cent of the proportion which export sales bears to total sales, plus five per cent of the value of most indigenous Malaysian materials which are incorporated into the exported products. There is also an export allowance of five per cent based on the FOB value of export sales of trading companies which export products manufactured in Malaysia.

In addition to these specific incentives, there are a variety of others designed to encourage, for example, reinsurance business, shipping, the agricultural sector, exports, research and development and the hotel and tourist industries as well as additional incentives for investors in Malaysia, whether they have pioneer status or not, in the form of loans from government sponsored lending institutions.

Exchange Control

One area of vital importance to foreign investors is exchange control and here, both Singapore and Malaysia should cause no problems.

Singapore abolished exchange control in 1978 so that no exchange control approvals are required for any investment in Singapore, for the remittance of dividends or profits or for the repatriation of capital.

Exchange controls still exist in Malaysia but they are not generally restrictive. In general, businesses are able to deal freely in most currencies and investors may bring into Malaysia unrestricted capital. Foreign exchange is also freely available for resident companies wishing to purchase imported goods and services. There are restrictions on taking money out of Malaysia but at present these are of an administrative nature only. No permission is needed for payments abroad of less than M$10,000 and for payments of over

M$10,000 the approval of an authorized bank is required. This is usually given as a matter of course provided that proper supporting documentation is submitted.

Borrowing by residents from non resident lenders of amounts in excess of M$1 million requires approval. However, in order to enable the Central Bank to monitor large loans from overseas, information about the borrowing must be notified to the Exchange Control Department where the borrowing exceeds M$200,000.

Non-resident controlled Malaysian companies require permission to borrow more than M$10 million from all sources in Malaysia.

Enforcement of Judgments and Awards

As was mentioned at the beginning of this paper, the legal systems in Singapore and Malaysia are based on that of England and therefore court procedures are not dissimilar. The courts of both countries will accept jurisdiction and foreign governing laws in similar manner to England, that is if there is a substantial connection with the subject matter of the dispute, or if there is express consent of the parties. Singapore and Malaysia will automatically enforce foreign judgements made in jurisdictions with which they have reciprocal agreements, consisting of the UK and certain other Commonwealth jurisdictions. As I have mentioned, there are certain agreements in Malaysia, such as some government contracts and technology transfer agreements, which are required to be subject to Malaysian law or arbitration.

So far as arbitration is concerned, it is possible for arbitrations to be held in both countries and equally for arbitration clauses to provide for arbitration elsewhere. Malaysia has established a regional centre for arbitration in Kuala Lumpur and is keen for the services of this Centre to be used. It has adopted a set of rules which are basically the same as the UNCITRAL Rules. There are obvious disadvantages in conducting arbitration in Malaysia but one of the advantages will be easier enforcement of an award against the Malaysian party. Although Malaysia may not be a party to the 1958 New York Convention on the Recognition and Enforcement of Foreign Arbitral Awards, it has recently given effect to this Convention and a Convention Award will be enforceable subject to the provisions of the Act.[42]

Singapore has recently taken an important step forward with the passing of the Arbitration (Foreign Awards) Act of 1986 which came into force on 19 November 1986. Under the Act, Singapore acceded to the New York Convention which will have the effect both of encouraging Singapore as a

---

42. *See* the Convention on the Recognition and Enforcement of Foreign Arbitral Awards Act 1985 which came into effect on 3 February 1986.

venue for international arbitration and encouraging parties in contractual relationships with Singapore companies to choose arbitration as a means of resolving disputes. There are apparently no proposals for Malaysia to accede to the New York Convention.

Establishment of a Presence in Singapore and Malaysia

In Singapore, the establishment of a corporate entity is a very simple procedure and is governed by the Companies Act which is not dissimilar to the English Companies Act. The procedures are the same whether the investor is foreign or local based. A local incorporated company can be established once the proposed name[43] is approved by the Registrar of Companies. There is no minimum capitalization requirement as such but for practical purposes the minumum authorized capital is S$25,000, with only two shares of S$1 each being required to be issued. No par value and bearer shares are permitted. Once the name is approved, the process of incorporation can generally be completed in under two weeks. As has been said earlier, a Singapore company must have at least two directors, at least one of whom must be resident in Singapore[44] and for this purpose an expatriate in Singapore on an employment pass is acceptable. All directors must be natural persons.

The Singapore Companies Act lays down various continuing filing and reporting requirements which must be observed by a Singapore company. The most important of these is the requirement to prepare audited accounts annually, comprising a profit and loss account, balance sheet and directors' report.[45] Copies of the accounts must be filed with the Registrar of Companies and are open to public inspection. This filing requirement does not apply to an 'exempt private company' but a company which has corportate shareholders does not qualify for this exemption.[46]

The Companies Act also contains a number of other restrictions, for example, on loans to directors,[47] which are designed to ensure that the privileges of limited liability are not abused. The Act is administered firmly by the Registry of Companies which can be expected to take action against any contraventions of the Act which come to its attention.

A foreign company can also establish a place of business or carry on business in Singapore without the local incorporation.[48] It must, however,

---

43. Before a company may be registered with the Registry of Companies, a name must be reserved for it under Section 27(1) of the Companies Act (1985 Rev Ed).
44. *See* Section 145 of the Act.
45. *See* Section 201 of the Act.
46. *See* the Eighth Schedule to the Act. Under Section 4, an exempt private company is a private company where none of its shares are held by corporations and which has no more than twenty members.
47. *See* Section 162 of the Act.
48. *See* Division 2 of Part XI of the Act.

register with the Registry of Companies at least seven days before commencing operations in Singapore. A branch established in this way is subject to similar filing and reporting requirements as applied to companies incorporated in Singapore. In particular, audited branch accounts must be prepared and filed annually together with a head office balance sheet. The performance of certain restricted types of activity in Singapore by a foreign company will not give rise to the need to register a branch. Activities which fall into this category include the soliciting of orders which are accepted and become binding contracts only outside Singapore, the maintenance of a bank account and the investment of funds.

Another common form of entity in Singapore is a representative office which will be administered by the Trade Development Board ('TDB'). Its status is not acknowledged by any statute but is governed by a number of reasonably well defined administrative guidelines. Numerous foreign companies have established representative offices in Singapore. Application to establish a representative office is made to the TDB and should be accompanied by a copy of the foreign company's audited accounts for the past three years and preferably also by a brochure describing the company's activities and its products. Whereas previously TDB approval for representative offices was given without time limit, it has recently appeared that this practice has changed and approval is being granted for one year only. Renewal of the approval will then have to be sought. It appears that the TDB is reviewing its policy on registration of representative offices.

The activities of a representative office are strictly limited to 'promotion and liaison'. It may carry out marketing, advertising and market research but must not become involved in negotiating contracts, the order/acceptance process, invoicing, collection of payments or after sale service. Moreover, the functions of a representative office must be carried out only on behalf of its head office and other branches of the same company. A representative office should not act on behalf of other companies in the same group.

The Malaysian Companies Act has provisions both for local incorporation and the registration of branches of overseas companies, as in Singapore. However, it is now virtually impossible for a foreign company to carry on business in Malaysia through a branch except for a short term project, such as might arise in the construction industry.

So far as local incorporation is concerned, the subject of foreign equity requirements has already been dealt with at length. Formalities for incorporation of a company in Malaysia are similar to those in Singapore but it should be noted that the Malaysian companies Act requires a local company to have at least two directors, both of whom must have their principal or only place of residence in Malaysia. They need not be Malaysian citizens.[49]

Where the company is involved in manufacturing and requires a license

---

49. *See* Section 122 of the Companies Act 1965.

under the Industrial Coordination Act, the Minister of Trade and Industry may lay down requirements as to Malaysian representation on the Board.

Finally, it should be mentioned that Malaysia adopted a Code on Takeovers and Mergers effective from 1 April 1987 which, unlike the self regulating Takeover Code in London, is statutory and has the full force of law.[50] A mandatory offer is required to be made to other shareholders when 33 per cent of voting control of a company is acquired (in London the threshold is 30 per cent and in Singapore 25 per cent). Before the mandatory offer is made, approval must be obtained from the Foreign Investment Committee[51] or the Capital Issues Committee[52] as appropriate and the Takeover Panel. The unusual feature of the Code is that it applies not only where the company subject to a takeover is a public company (whether listed or not) but also to private companies which have shareholders funds exceeding $5 million and the purchase consideration involved is not less than M$10 million.[53]

---

50. *See* Section 179(3) of the Companies Act 1965 and the Malaysian Code on Takeovers and Mergers.
51. Where an offer comes within the 'Guidelines for the Regulation of Acquisition of Assets, Mergers and Takeovers' ('the Guidelines') it should be a condition of the offer that it should lapse in the event of the Foreign Investment Committee ('FIC') not giving its approval. The Guidelines are prescribed by the FIC and the FIC is in the Prime Minister's Department.
52. Where an offer comes within the jurisdiction of the Capital Issues Committee under Section 6(2) of the Securities Industries Act 1983, it should be a condition of the offer that it should lapse in the event of the Capital Issues Committee not giving its approval.
53. *See* Practice Note No. 3 by the Panel on Takeovers and Mergers.
*   *The Malayan Law Journal*
**   *The Law Reports, Appeal Cases*

The author gratefully acknowledges the valuable assistance in the preparation of these footnotes of Wong Kien Keong, Ph.D., B.A., Solicitor of the Supreme Court of England and Wales and Advocate and Solicitor of the High Court of Malaya, Associate of Baker & McKenzie, Singapore.

Chapter 6
Legal Considerations for Investment in Taiwan

by Jui-Ming Huang

Baker & McKenzie
Taipei, Taiwan

Introduction

With an area of 36,000 square kilometers and a current population of approximately nineteen-million, Taiwan, the Republic of China (ROC), is one of the most-densely populated areas in the world. In the past 40 years, Taiwan has sustained rapid economic growth. The per capita GNP has consistently increased to attain a level of US$3,751 in 1986 and estimated US$4,991 in 1987, one of the highest in Asia. Taiwan belongs to East Asia's newly industrializing countries (or NIC) which are always regarded as paragons of development.

Foreign trade is the backbone of Taiwan's economy and the prime mover of its economic growth. By 1986, the total foreign trade had grown to US$63.8-billion with US$24.1-billion in imports and US$39.7-billion in exports. The development of industry and allowing access to investment from overseas have always been the policy of the government. As a result, Taiwan has changed from an agriculturally based to an industrially based economy. Since the 1960s, the industrial sector has changed significantly from labor intensive to the capital and technology intensive industries. Agricultural and processed agricultural products declined from 91.9 per cent of total exports in 1950s to only 6.2 per cent in 1980s while industrial products grew from 8.1 per cent of total exports to 93.8 per cent during the same period. Comsumer goods, on the other hand, dropped from 19.9 per cent of total imports in 1952 to 8.5 per cent in 1985 while capital goods rose from 14.2 per cent to 23.8 per cent of total imports. Taiwan has also accumulated one of the world's largest foreign reserves. According to the statistics complied by the Central Bank of China, net foreign exchange assets rose to US$76-billion in March 1988, second only to West Germany.

A steady increase of investment from overseas parallels the steady growth of Taiwan's economy. Many enterprises with foreign capital are on the top of the 'List of Manufacturers and Traders of the Republic of China with Good Export Record' published each year by the Ministry of Economic Affairs. The annual amount of new investments from foreign nationals has increased from US$108.7-million in 1974 to US$660.7-million in 1985. Taiwan has been rated as one of the good investment countries in the Asian Pacific Region. Qualities such as human resources, good infra-structure, free foreign banking facilities and political leadership were considered in making this assessment.

The ROC government has planned to change its industrial structure by raising the proportion of technology intensive industries to 35 per cent of the manufacturing sector by 1989.

Fourteen key projects have been announced to be implemented or completed between fiscal year 1986 and 1991:

(1) third phase expansion of China Steel Corporation;
(2) important power projects:
    (a) Fourth Nuclear Power Plant;
    (b) Mington Pumped Storage Project;
    (c) Taichung Thermal Power Plant;
(3) oil and natural gas projects;
(4) expansion of highways:
    (a) second freeway in Northern Taiwan;
    (b) the North-South highway along the West coast-line;
    (c) No. 3 provincial North-South highway;
(5) expansion of the railway System;
(6) modernization of telecommunication;
(7) the underground railroad project in downtown Taiwan;
(8) initial phase of the rapid mass transit system for metropolitan Taipei;
(9) flood control and drainage;
(10) exploitation of water resources;
(11) ecological protection and domestic tourism;
(12) urban garbage disposal;
(13) medical care programs;
(14) grass-roots development projects.

In the quest for such targets, investments from overseas have always been sought. They are considered essential for their fulfillment.

While Taiwan's overseas markets include some 150 countries and territories, the United States remains the leading export market representing more than 40 per cent of total exports. Japan has been the leading source of imports, controlling around 30 per cent of the total import market. Over the past ten years (1974–1985), Europeans have completed 115 foreign investment projects in the ROC, which is relatively small in comparison with the 505 projects from the US and 900 projects from Japan. Recently, efforts have been made to diversify away from the US and Japanese markets. Europe, for this traditional high-level technology and vast market potential, is regarded by the Taiwan government as an ideal area for mutual development. The year 1986 was announced by the Taiwan government as a 'Europe Action Year'. These efforts bring the result that the total amount of trade between Taiwan and Europe in 1986 has increased by 46.8 per cent in comparison with the amount in 1985. This indicates that there is a promising future for the business development between Taiwan and European countries.

Form of Business Organizations

There are various forms of business activities in which a foreign company may consider operating in Taiwan, depending on the nature and range of its business involvement. Following are brief descriptions of the various forms most frequently adopted.

APPOINTING AN AGENT/DISTRIBUTOR

A foreign company may appoint a company in the ROC as its agent or distributor to conduct business on its behalf. A local company or a recognized branch office of a foreign company is entitled to act as agent or distributor of a foreign company.

REPRESENTATIVE OFFICE

The representative office of a foreign company in the ROC can legally bind it but is not permitted to conduct business activities. Such an office is ideal for a company which conducts only purchasing activities in the ROC. There are no capital contribution requirements. The office is not liable for any tax on reimbursements of cost received from its head office. Registration of the office requires only a resident representative, either a domiciled national or a resident alien. All matters in relation to the purchasing, such as locating suppliers, inspecting merchandise, and arranging shipping schedules can be handled by this office.

LIAISON OFFICE

A liaison office is also non-taxable, but it may not be registered with government authorities. All business and legal relationships of such an 'office' must be conducted in the name of the individual acting as liaison person.

BRANCH OFFICE (WITHOUT FOREIGN INVESTMENT APPROVAL)

A branch office of a foreign company in the ROC can conduct full-range business activities. There is a modest capital contribution requirement in establishing a branch office. The branch manager can be either a domiciled national or a resident alien.

AN ORDINARY LOCAL COMPANY

If a foreign national or overseas Chinese fails to qualify for investment under the Statute for Investment by Foreign Nationals or the Statute for Investment by Overseas Chinese, he may still organize an ordinary local company under the ROC. Company Law jointly with local nationals and may hold a majority share in it. The company will be treated equally as a 'normal' local company.

FOREIGN INVESTMENT APPROVED COMPANY (FIA COMPANY)

Foreign nationals making investments under the Statute for Investment by Foreign Nationals are generally called Foreign Investment Approved Companies (FIA Companies). The ROC government offers many incentives to the FIA Company status which will be discussed below.

FIA Companies can be established in the form of a branch office or a subsidiary company of a foreign company to engage in manufacturing industries, while certain service business now also qualify for FIA but may only be organized in subsidiary form. Normally, the form of company limited by shares is used by the foreign investor in establishing a subsidiary company, because of its eligibility for tax benefits under the Statute for Encouragement of Investment. Foreign investors are permitted to hold 100 per cent of the shares in the FIA subsidiary companies.

Legal Framework for Foreign Investment

FOREIGN INVESTMENT GENERALLY

A FIA Company will be eligible for certain incentives and benefits set forth in statutes aimed at encouraging foreign investment. The most relevant of these statutes are the Statute for Investment by Foreign Nationals ('SIFN') which sets forth guidelines regulating the various aspects of investment made by foreign nationals in the ROC and the Statute for Encouragement of Investment ('SEI') which encourages investment by providing certain tax benefits and other advantages to qualifying enterprises and industries.

Non-FIA enterprises may also do business in Taiwan but will not be able to enjoy the special benefits. Under the current restrictions on inward remittance of foreign exchange, a foreign investor seeking to invest in an existing non-FIA enterprise, or to establish a new non-FIA enterprise, with funds from outside Taiwan will encounter significant difficulties. It may thus be necessary for non-FIA foreign investment to be made with New Taiwan dollar funds available locally in Taiwan.

To obtain foreign investment approval, a foreign investor must submit an application which consists of the investment plan and other relevant documents, to the Investment Commission ('IC') of the Ministry of Economic Affairs ('MOEA'). The IC then approves or disapproves the FIA investment plan, with the former in a few rare cases accompanied by certain conditions and restrictions.

BENEFITS OF FIA COMPANY

The investment incentives granted to FIA companies are stipulated in SIFN and SEI. The major benefits of FIA status are:

Repatriation of capital and earnings

Under the Republic of China's ('ROC') previous foreign exchange control system, foreign investors could not repatriate equity investment, the principal of any intercompany loan 'investment' or the profits or interest derived therefrom, unless the original investment received approval under SIFN.

Effective 15 July 1987, the Executive Yuan suspended four key articles of the Foreign Exchange Control Act and issued or amended a series of regulations in connection with this suspension. Under the Rules Governing Applications for Exchange Settlement of Private Outward Remittances ('Outward Remittance Rules'), any ROC individual or entity may remit abroad up to US$5-million annually, without the need for supporting documentation being presented to the Central Bank of China for approval. This dollar limitation does not apply to business expenditures such as payments for imported goods or expenses of 'invisible trade', with the latter including commissions, royalties and other compensation for technology transfer, construction payment expenses and expenses of foreign subsidiaries.

In sum, if the invested enterprise is not expected to remit more than US$5-million in any year (from 15 July of one year to 14 July of the next) in the form of profits, interest, loan repayment or reduction of capital, the foreign investor could under the current rules not rely on the repatriation privileges under SIFN in order to remit such funds abroad. If such projection may not be made with certainty, or in the event of an amendment to the Outward Remittance Rules which reduces the amount of foreign exchange which may be remitted freely, the foreign exchange privileges of the SIFN are still important.

Under SIFN, the following rules must be observed in order to repatriate FIA-status investment.

(a) Equity investment
100 per cent of the equity investment is repatriable only one year after the commencement of operations of the foreign invested enterprise. A foreign investor may apply for repatriation of equity investment under the following circumstances:

(i)   the invested enterprise reduces its capital and returns the same to its foreign investors;
(ii) the invested enterprise is dissolved and liquidated; or
(iii) the foreign investor transfers all or part of its shares for local currency payment.

Additionally, except for gains resulting from the sale of land owned by the invested enterprise, capital gains are now repatriable.

(b) Profit derived from equity investment
The profit must first be distributed to shareholders as dividends since a FIA invested enterprise, unless it is an approved venture capital enterprise organized as a partnership, may only be organized as a corporation.

Although SIFN does not limit the amount of dividends which can be remitted, under the ROC Company Law a corporation may not declare a dividend before offsetting losses in prior years, payment of income tax, payment of the employee bonus required by its Articles of Incorporation, as well as the establishment of a legal reserve and possibly a special reserve.

The Company Law also requires that a ROC company stipulate in its Articles a certain percentage of profits which will be paid to employees as bonus. The actual percentage is determined at the discretion of the promoters.

If an IC investment approval requires a certain export percentage of total sales and the invested enterprise fails to meet that export ratio in a particular year, then any profits earned that year cannot be remitted out of Taiwan. At present, the ROC government faces a trade surplus with most countries and is enjoying huge foreign exchange reserves; thus the IC usually no longer requires an export ratio as a term of its approval.

If a FIA company is presently required to export a certain percentage of its output, under an approval letter issued prior to change in IC policy, it may apply to the IC for the removal of such an export ratio.

(c) Application for repatriation

Application for repatriation of any of the above items must be filed within six months after the investor becomes entitled to do so, otherwise the right of repatriation will be extinguished. An extension of the repatriation period can be obtained, usually for up to an additional 12 months.

Waiver of domicile requirement

The Company Law sets domicile requirements for responsible persons of companies incorporated in Taiwan. At least one half of the seven promoters of a company limited by shares must be domiciled in Taiwan, though there is no minimum requirement for the percentage of stock held by these promoters. The chairman and vice-chairman of the board, one half of the managing directors and at least one supervisor must be domiciled in Taiwan. A FIA company need not observe these requirements because of an express waiver in the SIFN. It may be a wholly foreign-owned company with all officers domiciled outside of Taiwan with only managers resident on Taiwan.

No requisition/expropriation

A FIA company that is at least 45 per cent foreign owned will not be subject to requisition or a period of 20 years after commencement of business, so long as the foreign investors continue to hold 45 per cent or more of the total capital.

Waiver of issuing shares to the public

A corporation which has a minimum total capital of NT$200,000,000 must issue shares to the public in accordance with the Company Law. If 45 per cent or more of the stock of a FIA company is foreign-owned, this requirement is waived.

Waiver of employee subscription of new shares

Under the ROC Company Law a corporation is required to offer to its employees ten per cent to fifteen per cent of any new shares issued unless the shares represent capitalization of retained earnings or capital surplus. The employees' right of subscription is waived for FIA companies that are at least 45 per cent foreign-owned.

Reduced witholding tax rate on dividends

The withholding tax rate on dividends is 35 per cent though investors in an FIA company enjoy a reduced rate of only twenty per cent.

Special appeals to the Executive Yuan

Upon obtaining special approval from the Executive Yuan, a FIA company would no longer be subject to the domicile requirements contained in the Mining Law, Land Law, Maritime Law and Civil Aviation Law.

REQUIREMENTS FOR FIA STATUS

A foreign investment will be approved only if it will benefit the economy of Taiwan, a standard which is both arbitrary and flexible, allowing the Investment Commission significant discretion in reviewing each application. The IC's discretion is, however, limited by policy guidelines regarding foreign investment established by the MOEA and in some cases the Executive Yuan. Usually the IC examines the following issues:

(a) the need in either the local or export market for the proposed product;
(b) the technology which may be introduced into Taiwan in conjunction with the investment;
(c) the amount of investment to be brought into Taiwan.

Under SIFN, only an investment project in one of the following categories will be approved:

(a) productive or manufacturing enterprises which are needed domestically;
(b) service industries which are needed domestically;
(c) industrial, mining, communications enterprises;
(d) scientific and technical research and development enterprises; or
(e) other enterprises conducive to the economic/social development of the ROC.

Currently, manufacturing industries, particularly those employing advanced technology, and certain selected service and other industries routinely receive approval. Industries such as the automobile or motorcycle, shoe, textile and certain other industries with quotas are subject to strict scrutiny and conditions for foreign investment.

To date, the Investment Commission has not formulated special written guidelines for approval or rejection of investment applications. Various government agencies are now preparing proposals for a 'negative list' of industries which may not be approved under SIFN. Once the list is finalized, all investments not included in this list will be approved.

Service industries

The IC reviews service industry investment applications on a case-by-case basis. It has not established definite guidelines for approval in this area but foreign investment have been approved in the following service industries:

(a)   management consulting;
(b)   securities investment services;
(c)   leasing;
(d)   construction;
(e)   advertising;
(f)   inspection services;
(g)   cleaning.

Trading activities

Government policy towards trading activities engaged in by foreign-invested companies was relaxed considerably in the summer of 1987, thus IC foreign investment approval is no longer limited to trading activities of FIA manufacturing enterprises and large-scale trading companies. Under the new policy, the prior restriction that trading activities may be established only after the commencement of manufacturing operations has also been eliminated.

Leasing

A foreign investor may obtain approval under SIFN for investment in a finance leasing company with local partners if some stringent requirements are met.

Venture capital

Venture capital companies are a recent development in Taiwan. Under the Regulations Governing Venture Capital Investment Enterprises ('Regulations') promulgated by the Ministry of Finance ('MOF') in 1983 and recently amended in April 1986, foreign investors can now receive FIA under SIFN for this kind of investment. These Regulations require that: (a) the FIA company have a minimum fully-paid capital of NT$200 million and (b) the capital must be contributed in one lump sum. The former requirement that a venture capital company organize as a company limited by shares has been amended to permit a venture capital enterprise to be organized as a partnership. The Rules contain restrictions on the scope of permitted business activities, types of investments, borrowing, and limits on the maximum investment allowed in a particular project. Prior to or concurrent with the submission of an application for foreign investment approval, a special application must be made to the MOF for permission to establish a venture capital enterprise.

HUANG

FORMS OF INVESTMENT

Loan v. equity

The foreign investment may be made in the form of equity or loan with a permissible equity/ loan ration of 1:3 in the case of FIA companies. A 1:4 ration is permitted by the IC in exceptional cases.

The advantage of a loan rather than equity investment is that a loan can be repatriated more easily than capital, without affecting the registered capital of an invested company. Also, loan repayments from profits are not subject to the withholding tax applicable to payment of dividends. One other advantage of a loan investment is that the investor is also a creditor of its invested enterprise, which gives the investor priority over other shareholders against the assets of the invested enterprise.

Further, the interest on a loan is a deductible expense of the invested enterprise. However, if the invested enterprise enjoys a tax holiday, the interest expenses would not result in any savings in corporate tax. Finally, interest payments may be repatriated before a fiscal year end while dividends may be repatriated only when declared out of earnings at the end of a fiscal period.

The disadvantage of a loan rather than equity investment is that interest is subject to twenty per cent withholding tax. Dividends are also subject to the same withholding rate, but if the invested enterprise incurs losses, it is not allowed to declare a dividend. Losses may be carried forward for only three years. Two other disadvantages relate to the fact that certain calculations are made on the basis of equity investment, which does not include loan investments by shareholders. For example, the maximum amount of retained earnings is calculated based on a percentage of equity investment. The maximum amount of capitalization of technical know-how or patent rights is also limited to a percentage of equity investment.

The Composition of investment

The foreign investment may be composed of the following:

(a) *Cash in the form of foreign exchange, which is remitted or brought in:* the cash investment may be reserved and deposited in its original form, but is usually limited to US$ and HK$. If the funds are remitted by telegraphic transfer, the message should state that such funds represent investment approved by the IC with reference to the number of the IC meeting when approval was obtained, and the amount of foreign currency to be retained, if any. If the cash is to be brought in by an individual, the cash must be registered with the customs office at the port of entry. For loan investments, only cash is permissible but it may be remitted out again for procurement of machinery, equipment and materials.

(b) *Imports, against self-provided foreign exchange, of domestically needed*

98

machinery, equipment, raw materials for own use, or commodities for sale which are permissible imports to raise funds for working capital or planterection: an equity investment in the form of machinery, equipment, materials and commodities will be recognized only when the goods have been imported and examined by the IC. This procedure may in turn delay the incorporation of the invested enterprise. Investors, therefore, generally invest cash first in order to incorporate the enterprise as soon as possible, and then remit the cash abroad to acquire the needed machinery, equipment and materials.

(c) *Technical Know-How or Patent Rights:* technical know-how may only represent up to fifteen per cent of total paid-up capital; technical know-how in the form of patent rights may account for up to twenty per cent. Other than in the case of patented know-how, a matching cash investment equal to the value of technical know-how invested must also be made.

The shares issued corresponding to the know-how contribution may not be transferred until two years after the completion of investment. Shares issued corresponding to patent rights may not be transferred during the valid period of the patent rights. Patent rights are limited to those registered in Taiwan. Moreover, patent rights and technical know-how may not be reinvested in any other enterprise in Taiwan.

Evidence substantiating the declared worth of technical know-how or patent rights must be provided to the IC. Although no tax is imposed on the investment of know-how or patent rights, the full amount of the proceeds from the sale of such shares will be considered capital gain for tax purposes.

(d) *Those portions of principal, net profit, interest or any other income from investment which have been approved for exchange settlement:* as the capital increases, such increase can be formally capitalized after related taxes have been deducted and paid. Where a productive enterprise re-invests its undistributed earnings for purposes such as to add or renovate machinery and equipment or transportation facilities, to re-pay loans borrowed for the addition or renovation of machinery and equipment, or to re-invest in industrial mining, the newly issued registered stocks of its shareholders will not be included in the shareholders' consolidated income or profit-seeking enterprise income of the current year for taxation. If such stocks are thereafter transferred due to sale, donation, or distribution of estate, the total amount of the price or of the current value of such stocks at the time of transfer will be deemed as income of the year in which the transfer is made and be reported for income tax purposes.

INCENTIVES FOR COMPANIES IN EXPORT PROCESSING ZONES (EPZ)

Export Processing Zones are a combination of a free trade area and an industrial park, designed to promote export-oriented industries by providing favourable climate for industrial investment. FIA investors engaged in export-oriented manufacturing operations may wish to consider establishing their business in the Export Procession Zones. The advantages provided to the export enterprises located in the zones are:

Tax incentives

- **Exemption from customs duties**
  No customs duties are levied on importation of raw materials, parts, components, machinery and semifinished products for own use.

- **Tax holiday**
  A five-year tax holiday on products which are in conformity with the 'Categories and Criteria of Productive Enterprises Eligible for Encouragement', even if the enterprise is not an FIA company.

Simplified procedures

The EPZ Administration is authorized to handle all matters relevant to the management of the zones, such as investment application processing and approval, import and export licensing, foreign exchange settlement, company registration, construction licensing, etc.

Convenient facilities

Adequate public facilities as well as power and water supply are available within the zones. There are now three export processing zones, all are conveniently located near transportation centers.

The Kaohsiung EPZ is situated in Kaohsiung Harbor, which is the largest international seaport in Taiwan. The Nantze EPZ is situated in Kaohsiung city, about twenty kilometers north of the Kaohsiung EPZ, and the Taichung EPZ is located about nine kilometers north of the city of Taichung, less than 30 kilometers away from seaport and airport.

Financing support

For purchasing standard factory building, bank loans of up to 70 per cent of the purchase price are available with ten-year installment repayment provisions. Loans are also available for the construction of self-designed factory buildings.

INCENTIVES FOR COMPANIES IN THE SCIENCE-BASED INDUSTRIAL PARK ('THE PARK')

To promote the development of advanced technology industries, stimulate research and innovation in industrial technology and import high-technology industries and highly-trained scientists, a science-based industrial park was established in 1980 in Hsinchu, about 80 kilometers southwest of Taipei.

The tax incentives and facilities offered to investors are similar to those offered to Export Processing Zones.

Legal Framework for Transfer of Technology

The rules and regulations governing the transfer of technology into the ROC vary greatly depending on the nature of the technology involved and the manner in which it is transferred. The principal groupings of technology for these purposes are: (i) unpatented technical know-how; (ii) patents; (iii) technical assistance and services; (iv) trademarks; and (v) copyrights.

PATENTS/UNPATENTED TECHNICAL KNOW-HOW

The applicable law governing the transfer of technology in the form of patents or unpatented technical know-how depends on whether the transfer will be made as a license of the technology or as a contribution to the capital of an ROC company: (i) the Statute for Investment by Foreign Nationals ('SIFN') and the Statute for Investment by Overseas Chinese ('SIOC'), as supplemented by the Regulations Governing the Use of Patent Rights and Technical Know-how As Equity Investment ('Technology Investment Regulations'), govern investments in the form of patent rights and technical know-how; and (ii) the Statute for Technical Cooperation ('STC') governs the license from abroad of patent rights and 'technical skills'.

Capital investment in the form of technology

A foreign investor may make a capital contribution in the form of patent rights provided that the patent rights have been granted pursuant to the ROC Patent Law for a new invention, utility model or design. Likewise, a foreign investor may contribute technical know-how. In either case, if approved as outlined below, the foreign investor will be able to repatriate his investment if he ever sells his equity in the ROC company.

Licensing of technology

'Technical cooperation' as used in the STC refers to technical cooperation between foreign nationals and the government, nationals or legal entities of the ROC in which the former agrees to furnish the latter with technical skill or patent rights not as a capital investment but for a royalty. The patent rights which may be licensed pursuant to the STC are those granted under the ROC Patent Law for new inventions, utility models and designs. The STC does not contain a specific definition for 'technical skills'.

The Investment Commission of MOEA will approve license of 'technical skills' or patent rights only if the license complies with one of the following purposes:

(i) Production or manufacturing of new products;
(ii) Increase of the volume of production, improvement of product quality or reduction of production cost; or
(iii) Improvement of skill of administration, management, design or operation and other improvements.

The royalty rates approved by the Investment Commission usually range from three to five per cent of the licensee's 'net sales'. In special cases involving technology valuable to the national security interests of the ROC, the approved rate may be as high as seven to nine per cent.

For these purposes, the Investment Commission defines 'net sales' as:

'The gross sales of the licensed products, less taxes, freight and miscellaneous costs, packing fees, insurance, advertising, sales commissions and discounts, as well as less the CIF value of, the customs duties on, and the freight and miscellaneous expenses of any raw materials or parts imported by the licensee for use in the manufacturing of the products.'

The Investment Commission will usually permit the license agreement to exclude from the definition of 'net sales' the value of raw materials imported from anyone other than the licensor, thus effectively increasing the base for calculation of the royalties. The royalties may be either a one-time, lump sum royalty or a continuing royalty; and the royalty may be paid only after notice to the Investment Commission that the implementation of the project involving the licensed technology has commenced, which commencement must occur within six months of the Investment Commission approval. The ROC does not prohibit the payment to a foreign licensor of royalties not approved by the Investment Commission, however, as mentioned earlier, only approved royalties may be deducted by the licensee for ROC tax purposes.

TECHNICAL ASSISTANCE AND SERVICES

The definition of 'technical skills' for purposes of the STC does not encompass, *inter alia*, technical assistance and services. Technical service fees for engineering services relating to the design and construction of a plant in the ROC are nevertheless now eligible for repatriation, under the relaxed foreign exchange controls, without the need for the supplier to obtain the prior approval of the Central Bank of China ('CBC'). However, at the time the licensor wishes to repatriate such royalties or fees, an application for the remittance of foreign exchange must still be submitted to CBC which routinely approves such applications so long as the licensee has not utilized its US$5 million annual limit.

TRADEMARK LICENSES

Under ROC Trademark Law ('TML'), the owner of a trademark has exclusive right of use of the mark and may not license another person to make use of the mark except by way of assignment of the trademark or by obtaining approval of the National Bureau of Standards ('NBS') regarding the fulfillment of certain conditions. These conditions include:

(a)   the goods bearing the proposed mark will be made by the trademark user under the control and supervision of the trademark owner in such a way as to maintain the quality of these goods; and
(b)   the proposed license meets certain needs arising from the economic development of the ROC, as evidenced by guidelines issued by the MOEA.

On 15 June 1980, the MOEA promulgated 'Guidelines for Screening Trademark License Applications Filed by Foreign Companies' ('Guidelines Regarding Trademark Licenses'). The Guidelines indicate that license agreements will be approved under any of the following circumstances:

(i)   if a foreign company has been granted approval under the SIFN to establish an invested company in the ROC and the investment of that foreign company represents twenty per cent or more of the total capital of the invested enterprise and if the products to bear the trademark are products of the invested company;
(ii)   if a technical cooperation has been approved under the STC, a foreign company may obtain approval of a trademark license to the domestic licensee for use on the licensed products of the technical cooperation, so long as the duration of license is no longer than that of the approved license agreement; or
(iii)   if products to bear the trademark owned by a foreign company are quality products sold in international markets, so long as the licensor can supervise and control the production of the domestic company so as to maintain quality equal to that of products by the foreign company itself.

The parent company or subsidiary of a foreign company meeting the conditions of the immediately preceding subparagraph (i) above may also receive approval to license the invested enterprise to use trademarks owned by it (even though it is not the direct investor on products of the invested enterprise).

103

ROC law is silent regarding the approval and/or registration of a copyright license. In practise, however, copyrights are licensed or the copyrighted work is leased to a user. In either case, in order for the foreign copyright holder to be able to repatriate the proceeds obtained in the ROC from either the license or lease, the licensor or lessor must obtain prior approval from the Central Bank of China.

Tax Minimization Strategies

CORPORATE TAX STRUCTURE

Local business entities, including branches of foreign corporations, are subject to a maximum corporate income tax rate of 25 per cent on their net income. Foreign corporations are generally taxable only on their ROC-sourced income at flat withholding rates applicable to the particular types of income. If a foreign corporation has a certain type of fixed place of business or a business agent in Taiwan, it may, however, expose itself to income tax liability in Taiwan (including filing of returns) for ROC sourced income.

Withholding tax

Dividends are generally subject to a 35 per cent withholding tax rate, unless the investment is an FIA investment in which case the tax rate is reduced to twenty per cent. This twenty per cent withholding rate is also applicable to payments to foreign individuals or companies in the form of interest, royalties, service fees (other than certain approved technical services) and other forms of income. The 35 per cent rate is applicable to capital gains income from the sale of shares of the invested enterprise. Exemptions from these taxes will be discussed below.

Tax status of different corporate entities

The distinction between a liaison and a representative office lies in their method and basis of registration. The latter is registered with the MOEA pursuant to Article 386 of the ROC Company Law, while the former is an entity which reports its presence only to local tax authorities. So long as both types of entities remain within the guidelines of Article 10 of the Enforcement Rules to the ROC Income Tax Law, neither is required to file tax returns and neither is subject to income tax liability in Taiwan. Article 10 provides that a liaison person sent to Taiwan to gather market information, quote prices and establish contacts and who does not execute contracts nor make deliveries nor accept orders on behalf of his employer will not be considered a 'business agent' for purposes of the Income Tax Law. Branch offices of foreign corporations, other than those specializing only in purchasing activities for their head offices, are taxed on the same basis as subsidiaries. Purchasing branches with restricted activities and no source of income, receiving only reimbursements of expenses from their head offices, are not regarded as taxable entities. Subsidiaries of foreign corporations, whether or not one hundred percent foreign-invested, are treated for local tax purposes the same as ROC companies.

One major distinction between a branch office and a subsidiary, from the viewpoint of the foreign investor, is that after-tax profits remitted from non-FIA branches are not subject to any ROC income tax in contrast to dividends which are subject to the withholding tax rates earlier described. In addition, to further weigh the scale in favor of branches, branches do not encounter the maximum retained earnings limitations applicable to ROC companies which force the declaration of dividends if no capital increase from re-investing retained earnings is desired.

An FIA manufacturing branch is subject to a twenty per cent 'profits transfer tax' which is meant to place such transfers on profit on par with dividends paid by a subsidiary. The rationale is, of course, that beginning in 1987 an FIA branch is eligible for all the tax incentives applicable to a subsidiary, unlike non-FIA branches which would not qualify for any tax incentives.

AVAILABILITY OF TAX INCENTIVES

Tax incentives in the ROC are available to enterprises in certain industries or engaged in specific activities which conform to the requirements of various laws and regulations, regardless of the investors' nationalities. In addition, there are also certain incentives available by geographic location of the invested enterprises, such as enterprises which qualify for establishment in the Export Processing Zone or Hsinchu Science-Based Industrial Park.

A summary of the major types of tax incentives available in the case of equity investments in the ROC is presented below:

- tax holidays from income taxation;
- twenty per cent maximum corporate income tax rate;
- investment tax credits;
- higher ceiling for permitted retained earnings;
- installment payment or exemption from customs duties on imported machinery and equipment;
- exemption from capital gains tax;
- export incentives (zero per cent value-added tax, refund, deferred payment or exemption from duties in connection with imported raw materials or components, exemption from commodity tax);
- reduced real property taxes for industrial land and factory buildings.

In addition, there are also certain exemptions from income tax in the case of royalties paid for licensing of various intellectual property rights or certain technical services fees, as described below:

- licenses of patents registered in the ROC, with the licensing approved by both the Investment Commission ('IC') and the National Bureau of Standards ('NBS');
- licenses of trademarks registered in the ROC, with the licensing approved by the NBS;
- licenses of know-how approved by the IC where the licensee is in an industry designated as 'strategic';
- technical services fees paid in connection with plant design and construction by certain encouraged enterprises.

Finally, certain other technical services qualify for a 3.75 per cent reduced withholding rate from the standard twenty per cent though prior approval of the Ministry of Finance is required in order to confirm that the services for which the reduced rate is being sought are indeed 'technical'.

TAX STRUCTURING TO MINIMIZE CORPORATE TAX LIABILITY

Form of local entity

With the lifting of exchange controls, foreign investors wishing to engage in activities not qualifying for tax incentives, i.e. not manufacturing or technical services, but which may be conducted through a branch may now take advantage of the tax advantages of the branch form described above. Note that venture capital investment and finance leasing activities may not be conducted through a branch, though a multitude of other activities such as trading, managing of chain stores and provision of various services may be operated in branch form. To enjoy the branch tax advantages, the foreign investor would be required to forego the benefits of the SIFN. Most benefits of the SIFN are simply not necessary in the case of a branch as a result of the difference in corporate form. The primary benefit which absence may in the future still be crucial is the lack of repatriation privileges with respect to capital and profits. As a result, this route should be selected only if the projected profits, as well as return of working capital upon liquidation or any other special foreign exchange remittances required, would not exceed US$5 million per year. This US$5 million guideline is, of course, based upon the current foreign exchange regulations. It is important that the operations of the branch be sufficiently flexible to allow shifts in the flow of income or assets in the case of a change in these regulations.

Categorization of payments

To take advantage of the exemptions or reduced rates available for certain intellectual property rights royalties and technical services, a licensor or provider of technical services should separate by category and by amount the compensation for those tax-exempt items such as offshore services fees, special technical services fees and royalties for approved patent or trademark licenses. The second category of fees to be distinguished would be those services which would qualify as 'technical services' for the reduced 3.75 per cent rate. Only the remaining royalties or fees would be taxed at the twenty per cent standard withholding rate.

Basic Labor Law Structure

The Labor Standards Law took effect on 1 August 1984. Presently, only the following industries are required to conform with the Law:

- agriculture, forestry, fishing and animal husbandry;
- mining and quarrying;
- manufacturing;
- construction;
- water, electricity and gas supply;
- transportation, warehousing and communications;
- mass media; and
- other lines of business as may be designated by the central competent authority.

Some basic contents of the Law are summarized below:

Work hours

Regular work house may not exceed eight hours a day and forty-eight hours a week. If overtime is necessary due to specific reason, the employer, with consent from the labor union or the workers, may extend the regular work hours. However, the extended work hours may not exceed 46 hours a month for male workers and 32 hours for female workers.

Retirement

Workers may apply for voluntary retirement if they meet one of the following conditions: (a) have worked for fifteen years or more and are 55 years of age or older; or (b) have worked for 25 years or more. Retirement is compulsory when an employee has reached the age of 60, has developed a mental impairment, or is otherwise totally disabled.

Retirement payments

The unit of measure for retirement payment calculations is the employee's last monthly wage prior to retirement. Retiring employees are eligible for retirement payment equal to two units times the number of years of continuous employment with the same enterprise for the first fifteen years of employment, with one unit increments for each year past fifteen years to a maximum of 45 units of total retirement benefits.

Pension funds

Employers must make monthly contributions to a workers' pension fund, which amounts are deposited into a special account. The deposits constituting the fund may not be assigned, seized or attached, offset or used as security. The contribution rates may be set at fifteen per cent of the salary payments, upon approval by the appropriate authorities.

Termination

Employers may terminate a labor contract by advance notice in the following situations:

(1) the business ceases to operate or has been transferred;
(2) the business suffers an operating loss or contraction;
(3) business suspension for more than one month is necessitated by force majeure;
(4) a change in business nature requires a reduction in the number of workers and the particular worker(s) cannot be assigned to another suitable position; or
(5) a particular worker is clearly not able to perform satisfactorily the duties required of the position held.

Severance payments

Employees who are laid off are entitled to a severance payment equal to one month's average monthly wage for each year of continuous employment with that enterprise.

LABOR INSURANCE

According to the Regulation of Labor Insurance, any business employing five or more workers must enter into labor insurance contracts with the Labor Insurance Bureau for every employee between the age of fourteen and 60. The insurance premium is six to eight per cent of the insured salary. The insurance provides maternity benefits, hospitalization expenses for normal or occupational benefits in the event of disability, death benefits for the insured and his family members and retirement payments.

STRIKES

Compulsory mediation is first required in settling labor disputes. Although there is a recognized right to strike after mediation fails to settle a labor dispute, in fact no strike occured under the martial law. The martial law was lifted in 1987, at this time strikes are legally permissible under certain conditions.

Protection for Foreign Investments

PROTECTION AGAINST EXPROPRIATION

The ROC is a member of the Convention on the Settlement of Investment Disputes between States and Nationals of other States of 18 March 1965. The convention provides protection against expropriation or requisition of foreign investments in Taiwan. In addition, Article 16 of the Statute for Investment by Foreign Nationals provides a twenty-year guarantee against government expropriation or requisition if the foreign investment comprises 45 per cent or more of the total registered capital.

PROTECTION OF REPATRIATION

The following privileges are provided in the Statute for Investment by Foreign Nationals to protect the repatriation of the invested capital:

-   foreign investors in FIA companies may have 100 per cent ownership of the enterprises they invest in;
-   foreign investors may, one year after the commencement of the business operations, apply for repatriation of up to 100 per cent of the invested capital;
-   capital gains (excluding gains accrued from the disposal or reappraisal of land) qualify as FIA status invested capital, and therefore can be converted into foreign exchange and remitted abroad;
-   FIA companies with foreign investment comprising at least 45 per cent of the total registered capital are exempted from the requirement of Article 267 of the Company Law that ten to fifteen per cent of any new shares issued by a company be allocated for employee purchases.

TRADEMARK LAW

The ROC is not a party to any international convention for the protection of trademarks. It is advisable for a foreign trademark owner to register its mark in Taiwan in its own name as early as possible. The legal life for registration is ten years from the date of the approval of the application and may be extended each time for another ten years. A trademark not registered in Taiwan is protected under the Trademark Law only when the trademark is considered to be 'well known'. Any infringement of an ROC registered trademark may be punished with imprisonment of up to fifteen years, which imprisonment may not be converted into a fine. The criminal

The maximum punishment is four years imprisonment for infringement of patent rights, five years imprisonment for infringement of trademarks, and two years imprisonment for copyright piracy.

Civil proceedings

The infringed party may initiate civil proceedings to enjoin infringement and to claim damages.

(a) Injunction

In an injunction, the infringing party can be enjoined from manufacturing, processing, selling, delivering, importing, exporting, displaying for sale or any other activity connected with the infringing product. A deposit in an amount equal to thirty per cent to fifty per cent of the amount of the claim is usually required to institute the injunction.

(b) Damage compensation

A civil suit may be brought, to recover the damages suffered from the infringement and to compensate for any profit realized by the infringing party. Evidence proving the damage would be required.

Administrative measures

If a company is found guilty of infringing another person's intellectual property, the Board of Foreign Trade may suspend or cancel its export license.

Chapter 7
Current Regulations on Foreign Investment in Indonesia

by Amin Azeharie

Gani Djemat & Partners
Jakarta, Indonesia

Introduction

Indonesia strongly believes in international cooperation, because it fully realizes that in today's World, no country can ever develop properly solely on its own, and that no country can be an island unto itself!

Cross-fertilization is needed to ensure healthy growth and political as well as economic cooperation among states is a crucial aspect of the world today and will be even more important in the future, if mankind is to achieve the peace and prosperity that are the dream of every nation.

I come from a developing country which is situated far away from Europe, in a region which is often referred to by Europeans as the 'Far East'. In the past it took indeed about one year or more for a ship sailing from Amsterdam, Spain, or Portugal, to reach the Spice Islands which is present day Indonesia. However, in our age of modern and fast communication, it is now only a matter of hours by jet plane. Thus, the Far East is not far anymore and Indonesia, to be exact, is one of the member countries of South East Asian Nations (ASEAN).

Although the name Indonesia may not be unfamiliar to many of you, yet I presume that it is sometimes still difficult for many people to know properly

113

the present economic situation and the economic potentialities of the country, as well as the prevailing investment climate, which are so important to would-be investors.

I therefore believe that before embarking on the discussions of the substance of the topic, namely the Current Regulations on Foreign Investment in Indonesia, it will be useful to give a brief explanation on the abovementioned factors, which after all are so closely connected with the regulations themselves.

The Economic Environment

The Republic of Indonesia is strategically situated in South East Asia, between the vast continents of Asia and Australia and between two large oceans, the Pacific and the Indian Ocean. Through all its history it has been the crossroad of many seafaring and or trading nations and numerous ships have sailed through the narrow straits or sealanes separating its islands, or through the Strait of Malacca separating the Indonesian island of Sumatera from the Malaysian peninsular.

Stretching 3,200 miles from East to West and spanning the equator for more than 1,000 miles North to South, Indonesia is the world's largest Archipelago, comprising more than 13,000 inhabited islands. It is a nation of vast natural resources, immense cultural and geographic diversity, and with a population of presently more than 165-million people, it has demonstrated its potential and ability for sustained economic growth.

Indonesia's economy is diverse. It has a broad agrarian base and growing industrial and manufacturing sectors. Economic gains have been fostered by an increasingly comprehensive and advanced infrastructure and a regulatory environment that encourages entrepreneurship.

Private investment, both foreign and domestic has been made integral to this development process, and the role of the investor is expanding as the economy develops further.

The economy of the country is primarily based on smallholder agriculture, export oriented estate agriculture, mineral and oil exploitation.

Manufacturing is at present also becoming increasingly important to the economy. Much of Indonesia's labor force, which is expected to increase by some 9.3-million during the present Fourth Five-Year National Development Plan (Repelita IV, Fiscal Year 1984–1989), is employed in smallholder agriculture, mainly producing food crops for domestic consumption as well as rubber, coffee, pepper, and tobacco for export.

Export agriculture, developed since the (Dutch) colonial period, produces primarily rubber, palm oil, coffee, tea, sugar, tobacco and other export products. Although fisheries are until now relatively not much developed, they have in recent years become an important source of foreign exchange earnings. Especially in the shrimp cultivation for export the country has made much progress.

Crude oil is the country's major export item, but Indonesia's mineral wealth includes also substantial coal, tin, copper, nickel, gold, silver, bauxite, iron sands and manganese reserves.

The importance of wood products and copper as export products has also increased, while in the manufacturing sector the production of textiles, pharmaceuticals, fertilizer, and cement has expanded rapidly.

THE NEW ECONOMIC POLICY

Since its independence in 1945, Indonesia's economic growth has been remarkable. Equally impressive has been the country's social and political stability, which has been so important and conducive to the development of its economy.

With the change of Government in 1966, when the New Order Government under President Soeharto took over from the administration of President Soekarno, a new economic policy was adopted. The major objectives of this policy were to slow down the rate of inflation, rehabilitate the economic infrastructure, increase exports and provide adequate food and clothing for the population.

The Government pursued a stabilization policy in which expenditures were limited to levels that could be financed from its own revenues and receipts from international financing assistance. At the same time, inflationary financing of budgetary deficits was stopped and growth in the money supply moderated.

Since 1979, the Indonesian Government has sought to implement development policies that would raise the living standards and the well being of the Indonesian people. It has also worked to achieve a more equitable distribution of the fruits of development and to lay the necessary strong foundations for further continued development of the country. The goals of the country's development plans relate to what is called the 'Development Trilogy', centering on a more equitable distribution of development and its gains, leading to improved welfare for all Indonesians, an emphasis on hight rates of economic growth, as well as sound and dynamic national stability.

Equitable distribution of the benefits of development is to be reflected in every aspect of the development and will include:

- access to basic human needs, especially food, clothing, and shelter;
- access to educational and health services;
- a reasonable income;
- employment opportunities;
- access to business opportunities;
- access to participation in development, particularly for the younger generation and the women;
- development efforts throughout the various regions of the country;
- opportunities to obtain justice.

The five-year plans

The blueprint for the country's rapid economic turnaround has been a series of five-year plans (*Repelita*), the first of which began in fiscal year 1969/70, and which are designed to accelerate the country's economic development. The first plan which ended in 1973/74, stressed the development of industries that support the agricultural sector.

The second plan (Fiscal Year 1974/75 – Fiscal Year 1978/79) concentrated on the development of industries producing processed raw materials.

The third five-year plan (Fiscal Year 1979/80 – Fiscal Year 1983/84) emphasized the development of industries producing manufactured goods. Increased attention was also given to those problems that were not fully solved during the second plan period, such as raising economic growth rates in certain geographic areas, bolstering economically weak groups, developing cooperatives, increasing growth of food and staple production, expanding population transmigration, as well as improving public housing and social welfare, including the further expansion of educational opportunities throughout the nation.

The fourth five-year development plan (*Repelita* IV) for the period of Fiscal Year 1984/84 – Fiscal Year 1988/89, emphasizes the continued development of the agricultural sector and the industries – especially labor-intensive ones – that improve the national balance of payments by raising exports and meeting domestic needs as well as on industries that add value to domestic resources.

The Government anticipates the active participation of the private sector in national development during this plan period and projects that a substantial number of jobs will have to be created during the Fourth Plan in order to meet the needs of new job seekers.

The projected annual growth rates for each sector of the economy during this fourth plan are as follows:

Agriculture	–	3	per cent
Mining	–	2.4	per cent
Industry	–	9.5	per cent
Construction	–	5	per cent
Transport & Communications	–	5.2	per cent
Other	–	5	per cent

Agriculture's contribution to the country's gross domestic product is expected to fall from 29.3 per cent level recorded in 1983 to 26.5 per cent by 1989. This shift is in line with the Government's strategy of developing a more balanced economy.

The Government projects an economic growth rate averaging five per cent annually over the next five years. This rate is regarded as realistic given a relatively weak recovery in the world economic system.

During Repelita I, Indonesia's economy grew at an average annual rate of 8.5 per cent. This growth rate declined slightly to an average annual rate of

7.2 per cent in Repelita II and dropped again to an annual rate of 5.7 per cent in Repelita III. The reduced economic growth during Repelita III was primarily due to low rates of growth of somewhat more than two per cent in 1982 and about 4 per cent in 1983.

Indonesia's development that began seriously in the 1960s, advanced dramatically in the 1970s, and continues until today. One of the clearest indicators of this progress is the inflation rate. A high rate of inflation persisted since the country's independence in 1945 until the late 1960s and resumed in the early 1970s. In 1974, the inflation rate was still 47.4 per cent, however, thanks to the stabilization policy taken by the New Order Government this rate was reduced to 16 per cent in 1981, 8.7 per cent in 1982, and 1.3 per cent in 1985.

INFLUENCE OF WORLD RECESSION

Indonesia's international trade has maintained a healthy level of growth, despite the dampening influence of the world economic recession and the drop in the nation's most important export commodity, oil. The country's 1984 exports were valued at $ 21.9-billion, up 3.4 per cent over those of 1983. Petroleum and gas exports, including exports of liquified natural gas (LNG), dropped from $16.14-billion in 1983 to $16.02-billion in 1984.

In 1984, Indonesia's non-oil exports were valued at $5.87-billion, and during the first nine months of 1985 the estimated value of non-oil exports was $4.84-billion.

The decrease in the value of oil exports was caused by falling world oil prices and Indonesia's adherence to production quotas set by the Organization of Petroleum Exporting Countries (OPEC). Petroleum and petroleum products have consistently been the largest foreign-exchange earners for Indonesia since 1969, with timber ranking second, followed by rubber and coffee. The Government has long been concerned with this heavy dependence on a few foreign-exchange earners and, as a result, has intensified diversification programs and boosted the exports of such non-oil and gas commodities as palm oil, coffee, pepper, rubber, tobacco, tin as well as textiles, electronic components, and other manufactured goods. Japan and the United States have been by far the principal destinations of products exported by Indonesia and are also the biggest importers of Indonesian petroleum.

Presently, Indonesia has also become the world's largest supplier of plywood, and the United States, several European countries, the Middle East and Hongkong are the primary destinations.

The Government has been engaged in a longterm program to expand and diversify its export markets. In the past few years, export to the European Economic Community and to Asian countries other than Japan, has increased significantly.

The Middle East and Eastern European Countries have also been targeted for export expansion, and the development in these areas has been considerable. With rapid growth in the manufacturing sector in Indonesia, the composition of imported goods has changed considerably. Raw materials and capital goods now account for most imports.

THE ASSOCIATION OF SOUTHEAST ASIAN NATIONS (ASEAN)

ASEAN was established on 8 August 1967, by the Foreign Ministers of the member countries (Indonesia, Malaysia, the Philippines, Singapore, and Thailand). In January 1984, the newly independent State of Brunei was also admitted to the organization. Headquartered in Jakarta, Indonesia, the group's main purpose is to strengthen multilateral cooperation among the member nations in such areas as economic, social, cultural, technical, scientific and administrative fields.

The basic framework for economic cooperation within Asean is provided by preferential tariff arrangements (PTAs). Specific instruments identified under the PTAs are extension of tariff preference, purchase financing support at preferential interest rate, longterm quantity contracts, preference in procurement by governments, and liberalization of non-tariff trade restriction on a preferential basis. The PTAs have also received approval from the General Agreement on Tariffs and Trade (GATT).

Over 18,400 items have been listed under ASEAN PTAs, and across-the-board tariff cuts of between twenty per cent and 25 per cent have been established for items with an import value of up to $10-million.

Intra-ASEAN industrial cooperation takes various forms, including the production of basic industrial products, joint-venture schemes, and complementary industrial development in specific sectors.

ASEAN industrial projects, which are supported by all ASEAN countries, seek to establish ASEAN-sponsored facilities in each of the member nations. Indonesia is the site of an ASEAN-sponsored facility for the production of urea fertilizer. This project, which began operation in October 1983, will supply urea fertilizer throughout the ASEAN region. Each of the ASEAN member countries will participate in at least one of the ASEAN industrial projects. For example, another urea factory has just been completed in Malaysia, a hepatitis-B vaccine project is nearing completion in Singapore, and projects for other ASEAN member nations are in the planning stages.

Intra-ASEAN cooperation in the private sector is encouraged through the ASEAN chambers of commerce and industry. The chambers have been important factors in encouraging standardization in various fields among the ASEAN nations, increased entrepreneurial cooperation, and intra-regional flows of trade and investment.

ASEAN member countries have also undertaken programs to combat the introduction and spread of plantpests in the region, an emergency rice reserve maintenance program, a collaboration program on post harvest technology, a forest-tree-seed center, a coal study project, and an emergency petroleum-sharing program.

An advanced communication system is one of the key elements needed to ensure that this regional cooperation continues to develop. Significant efforts have been made in this regard, including the development of submarine cable transmission systems between Indonesia and Singapore and, more recently, between Penang in Malaysia and Medan in the provice of North Sumatra, Indonesia.

The Investment Climate

In 1966, Indonesia began consolidating and restructuring the country's economy and its political life after so many years of neglect and mismanagement. As stated above, the Indonesian national development effort began in earnest in 1969 with the launching of the first Five Year Development Plan (Repelita I). Since then a great deal of progress has been made. The following statistics will give an illustration:

The per capita gross domestic product of the country in 1966 was equivalent to only US$80. In 1981, by comparison, it has already reached 570, a seven-fold increase, so that Indonesia is no longer classified by the World Bank or the United States as a 'low income' country.

The economic growth of the country has indeed been rapid and steady. From 1960 to 1966, the economy grew at an average annual rate of only 1.67 per cent. By comparison, in 1980 the economic growth rate was 9.6 per cent and in 1981, despite the world economic downturn, it continued to grow at the high level of 7.6 per cent. In contrast we observe that even in some advanced industrial countries growth was only around two per cent, with in certain cases advanced countries even experiencing a decline.

CONTROLLING INFLATION

Over the years, substantial progress has also been made in controlling inflation. The inflation rate in 1966 was 625 per cent, while in 1981 it had decreased a great deal and was only a modest six per cent. In 1982, it was 9.69 per cent despite the slackening oil demand and continued worldwide recession. Finally, notwithstanding the rise in the price of petroleum products for domestic fuel consumption in January 1983, the inflation rate for the country's budget year 1982/1983 (1 April to 31 March) was only 8.4 per cent, and the rate of inflation for the following year was also kept under control at a one digit figure, the rate for 1985 being only 4.4 per cent. These figures have been achieved during a period of extraordinary difficult world economic conditions, characterized by recession and very serious inflationary tendencies. This success demonstrated the ability of the Indonesian economy to still develop even in the face of adverse world economic conditions.

COMBINED DEVELOPMENT DRIVE

It is in fact the fruit of a systematic effort carried on with great patience over many years. The Indonesian New Order Government has consistently maintained a balanced budget policy. Besides it has also consistently applied policies designed to maintain economic stability in the country without restraining economic growth and without diminishing efforts to improve the social welfare of its people by means of programs designed to promote a more equitable distribution of income.

During these difficult periods, steps have been taken to keep the Government expenditures within the State's budgetary capabilities. In the meantime, completed development projects have succeeded in increasing productive capacity in a number of sectors, and this in turn has had the effect of increasing the economic growth.

The Indonesian private sector is also continuing its investments, even in the midst of the world recession. It is this continuing combined governmental and private development drive that makes the Indonesian investment climate quite attractive in spite of the current world situation.

Indonesia has indeed much to offer to the foreign investors. The biggest among the ASEAN NATIONS, in size it is also bigger than any country in Europe (except Soviet Russia), stretching 5,000 kilometers from East to West, or more than the distance from London to Moscow, and almost 1,800 kilometers from North to South. It is a country with more than 165-million people, the fifth biggest nation in the world.

COMPARATIVE ADVANTAGES

As stated previously, Indonesia's geographical location, lying on the crossroads of two continents (Asia and Australia) and of two oceans (the Indian and the Pacific oceans) gives it an important strategic position. It commands sealanes, making it open to the world and easily accessible to other markets nearby. Indonesia is part of the Pacific basin area that economic analysts predict will be one of the most dynamic economic growth centers of the 21st Century.

The 'comparative advantages' that Indonesia can offer the enterprising businessman, foreign or domestic, are great and of a variety and combination that are rare in the world, especially in the developing world. Indonesia has a variety of natural resources such as minerals and agricultural and marine products that are ready for extraction, cultivation, processing and export. It is one of the biggest oil producers in Asia, next to China and Iran, and is the biggest exporter of liquid natural gas or LNG in the world. It is also the world's second largest producer of rubber, palm-oil and tin, the fourth largest exporter of coffee, and the fifth largest of tea. Besides, it is one of the largest producers of tropical timber and the largest exporter of plywood.

The country's 165-million people provide a ready source of low-cost yet hard-working and, as many existing investors can attest, easily trainable and intelligent labor. At the same time, the big population represents also a large potential market for many products. This market can function as a cushion for exports to other markets in the region, or elsewhere in the world.

A COUNTRY GEARED TO DEVELOPMENT

The Government realizes that the country lacks sufficient indigenous capital and technology to develop the national economy entirely on its own. That is why the Government welcomes foreign investment. To maintain the pace of development at a desirable level and speed the country needs a steady flow of foreign investment into Indonesia. In order to ensure that Indonesia remains both attractive and competitive with other countries also seeking foreign investments, the Government is fully committed to an ongoing process of continuous improvement of Indonesia's investment climate through progressive reforms of the regulations.

The Indonesian Government is aware that vast natural resources, a large population, liberal investment legislation and incentives by themselves may not be sufficient to make a country attractive to investors. It is the totality of the comparative advantages together that counts. A certain country may offer a one hundred percent tax haven, but that does not necessarily make it an attractive place to set up a business. Other factors such as the availability of raw materials, labor, access to markets, etc., must also be considered. Indonesia believes that it offers advantages in most of these areas.

Another fundamental factor for consideration by a would-be investor in selecting the country in which to place his money is stability, in particular political and economic stability. Generally speaking Indonesia is politically one of the most stable countries in the world.

Although the country has of course certain problems, there is, however, little strife in Indonesia, whether political, labor, racial, or sectarian. Compared with the situation in many other developing or developed countries, the big cities as well as the country side are safe in Indonesia.

Furthermore, the present day Indonesian economy is well organized, prudently managed and planned and geared for growth and development. Over the last twenty years the national efforts have been concentrated on development and on maximizing the economic well-being of the people and, in particular, the quality of life in general. As stated above the country has enjoyed between 1969 and 1983 a high economic growth rate averaging 7.2 per cent per annum. At the same time the Government has also been able to keep the rate of inflation under control at a one digit figure, the one for 1985 for example being merely 4.4 per cent.

SOUND MANAGEMENT OF THE ECONOMY

Indonesia, like many other countries in the world, is facing today an economic down-turn of big dimensions. In short course the country has been hit by the vagaries of the international commodity and money markets, over which it has no control. About 65 per cent of Indonesia's export earnings were derived from oil, but in a matter of a few months only the world market price of oil plunged from US$29 per barrel to less than half of that amount. Unfortunately, the prices of most of the country's other export

121

commodities have also dropped, including those of tin, tea, palm-oil, rubber and several others.

As a result, the growth rate fell to 5.2 per cent in 1984 and to around two per cent in 1985, and there was even the possibility that the growth rate would be zero in 1986.

Yet, in the face of this adversity the Government of Indonesia has shown its ability to maintain economic stability and to fulfil its international commitments, including debt servicing and repayment. It has gained praise from its creditors and international financial institutions such as the IMF and the World Bank for the sound management of its economy.

The Inter-Governmental Group on Indonesia (IGGI) convened in Amsterdam in the second half of 1986 concluded that despite all the difficulties that the country is now facing, Indonesia is still on the right track. The IGGI therefore agreed to extend development aid and loans to the country totalling over US $2.5-billion. This and the fact that the assistance was more than what was sought by Indonesia, provide a further testimony to and reinforcement of the trust of the International community in the present-day economy of the country.

INVESTMENT IS WELCOME

Indonesia has shown over the years that it is prepared to take appropriate actions, sometimes very painful ones, to ensure the stability and viability of its economy. In 1982, for instance, when the first signs of recession hit the country, the Government immediately cancelled or rephased its development projects up to the amount of US$20-billion.

These measures demonstrated clearly Indonesia's willingness to sacrifice economic growth in order to maintain stability, and the Government's determination to be very careful not to incur debts that would be beyond its capability to repay in the future.

These steps were followed by a series of drastic and fundamentally more important reforms, including the revamping and modernization of the country's tax laws and liberalization of its banking system. In 1985, another radical measure was taken to reform Indonesia's customs and port procedures, so that the flow of goods into and out of Indonesia as well as within the country itself was made more smooth and faster, and cost of doing business in the country itself was made more smooth and faster, and costs of doing business in the country were cut down a great deal.

Further strong measures were taken in May 1986, this time with the purpose of promoting Indonesia's exports and opening up more investment opportunities. Investment requirements that were regarded as restrictive to foreign investment were relaxed, so that as far as investment procedures are concerned Indonesia is now at least as attractive as most other developing countries. A foreign investor, for instance, may now establish a joint-venture company with only minimal local participation (that is, five per cent under certain circumstances), while permits for employment of expatriate experts by joint-ventures are now more liberally granted. Besides, investments by medium and small enterprises have also been made easier.

Indonesia thus welcomes and appreciates any investment – whether large or small – in the country, because its need is not only capital, but also know-how, technology and access to export markets.

The Investment Regulations

LAW NO. 1 OF 1967

The Indonesian Government from the very beginning realized that for the overall development of the country substantial investment is needed to sustain the level of growth which is necessary to improve the standard of living of the people and in the longer run to give Indonesia enough momentum and strength for a self-propelled growth by the end of this decade. Parts of the investments will be generated out of Government expenditures, but an increasingly substantial part is expected to emanate from the private sector, from foreign as well as domestic investors. The Indonesian Government is well aware that notwithstanding the overall favorable investment climate investments do not necessarily happen without inducement and that investors need certain assurances, before entering into ventures.

It was with this understanding that a law was passed in 1967 governing foreign investment, followed in 1968 by another law on domestic investment. These two laws provide the legal framework in which investors operate in Indonesia. Under the two laws a range of incentives are offered to the investors, foremost among them are exemption from duties and postponement of value added tax on imported capital goods for investment projects. Against his wishes but succumbing to the demand of reality, President Soekarno, Indonesia's first President enacted on 10 January 1967, Foreign Capital Investment Law No. 1/1967. Over two months later, Soekarno, however, officially stepped down as the President of the Republic of Indonesia and General Soeharto who was appointed as Acting President on 11 March 1967, took the responsibility of implementing the new Foreign Capital Investment Law. The Government of Indonesia realized that although foreign private investment by itself can never make a country a viable economy, its role in a recovery period could be crucial. The response of the International community to Indonesia's Foreign Investment Law and invitation to invest in the country was quite impressive and the new order government saw the possibility to initiate at long last an effective economic development program for the country.

The Foreign Capital Investment Law No. 1/1967, as amended by Law No. 11/1970, offers to foreign investors various attractive regulatory assurances if they are doing business in the country. The intention of this policy is to give the foreign investor a better profit margin when they are investing in Indonesia than in any other country.

Among the tax incentives are:

(a) exemption from corporation taxes for priority projects;
(b) exemption from dividend tax for the same period of time as the above tax exemption, provided that no tax is levied by the investor's country of origin where he is subject to tax liability;
(c) exemption from capital stamp duties;
(d) an Investment allowance which is to be deducted annually from pretax profits but is limited only to the first four years of investment;
(e) a carry forward of losses;
(f) accelerated depreciation of fixed assets;
(g) additional tax privileges for investment ventures considered by the Government to be exceptionally important for the economic development of the country;
(h) exemption from import duties for fixed assets; and
(i) exemption from property tax.

Although the 1967 Investment Law refers only to direct investment, the Government in fact from the very beginning encouraged the establishment of joint ventures between the foreign investor and Indonesian partners. After 22 January 1974, a Resolution of the Cabinet made it mandatory for foreign investors operating in Indonesia to have local partners. Other important incentives in the FCI Law of 1967 are:

(a) right to appoint management;
(b) foreign investors are assured that they may determine the management personnel of their ventures in Indonesia. They are allowed to bring and employ foreign managerial and expert personnel in positions which cannot yet be filled by Indonesian nationals;
(c) right of foreign exchange transfer.

The foreign capital enterprise is guaranteed that the money it earns in Indonesia may be transferred to its home country according to the prevailing rate of exchange. This stipulation became later somewhat superfluous, because the Government decided on 17 April 1970, that from that date onward all foreign exchange transactions can be concluded freely. Thus except for the formal transfer which must be channelled through special accounts at the Central Bank, all other foreign exchange transactions can easily be conducted by foreign investors without any restraint whatsoever from the Government. The formal foreign exchange transfer may include: net operating profits, allowance of depreciation of capital assets, proceeds from the sale of shares by the foreign investors to Indonesian nationals, expenses of foreign personnel in their home countries, expenses for Indonesian trainees abroad, principal and interest on foreign loans and compensation in the case of nationalization of capital assets. Indonesia's policy regarding the transfer rights of the foreign investor is clearly very liberal.

The foreign investors are also guaranteed that the Government will not undertake nationalization or revocation of their ownership rights, or take steps to restrict their rights of control and or management of their enterprises, except when it shall be declared by law that interest of the State requires such a step.

In case one of the measures referred to above still takes place, the Government has the obligation to provide compensation, the amount, type and method of payment of which shall have been agreed upon by both parties, in accordance with valid principles of International law. In case no agreement can be reached between the two parties, arbitration shall take place which shall be binding on both parties.

DOMESTIC INVESTMENT LAW OF 1968 (LAW NO. 6/1968)

Closely related to the Foreign Investment Law of 1967 is the Domestic Investment Law of 1968 (Law No. 6/1968), which was originally meant *inter alia* to attract capital of Indonesian origin, but owned by foreigners domiciled in the country. However, above-mentioned Government Regulation No. 16, of 17 April 1970, which totally liberated foreign exchange transactions, made Law No. 6/1968 rather meaningless as far as the origin of capital is concerned.

THE INVESTMENT COORDINATING BOARD (BKPM)

To facilitate investment in Indonesia, the Government has established the Investment Coordination Board (BKPM) and has given it authority (Presidential Decrees No. 33/1981 and No. 54 of 1977) to provide a one-stop service for potential investors. This Government Agency is not only responsible for planning and administration of investments, but it is also there to help investors find suitable projects in which to invest, to ease their way into the country, to help investors overcome any problem that might develop during the implementation of their projects, etc. Since the end of 1977, the BKPM has been a truly one-stop investment agency. In order to obtain all the approvals, licenses, and permits required to establish or expand production facilities in the country and to receive fiscal facilities, grants and other incentives, the investor need deal solely with BKPM (except for oil and mining projects). Moreover, the processing of applications is undertaken completely by BKPM. The Board administers the foreign and domestic investment acts and is the central point of investment authority under Presidential Decrees No. 35 of 1985 (concerning the status, duties and functions of BKPM) and No. 54 of 1977 (concerning the principal rules regarding capital investment procedures). These Decrees have streamlined processing procedures and provide a single point of advice and guidance for prospective investors.

The BKPM has, *inter alia,* the following major obligations:
(a) coordinating and planning sectoral and regional investments and synchronizing these plans with a master plan;

(b)   formulating investment policies;
(c)   preparing and publishing investment priority lists;
(d)   encouraging the spread of investment activities in accordance with development policies;
(e)   supervising the implementation of approved investments;
(f)   developing and processing priority projects;
(g)   encouraging and fostering the completion of investment projects;
(h)   establishing effective promotional communications with investors in particular and the business community in general;
(i)   evaluating and screening investment applications;
(j)   Submitting evaluated foreign investment applications to the President for his approval;
(k)   approving domestic investment applications;
(l)   issuing required permits and licenses;
(m)   providing general investment services.

OIL, MINING AND FORESTRY

The Board also oversees investment in oil-related industry, mining and forestry.

Foreign Participation in the *oil and gas industry,* specifically for exploration and production, is accomplished through a production sharing contract with Pertamina, the state-owned oil company. Under this kind of an arrangement, a contractor is required to finance all exploration, development and production costs relating to oil and gas resources within a specified area, while Pertamina is responsible for the management of operation.

The contractor is entitled to recover all operating costs, including capital investments, out of crude oil production. The balance of oil production is then divided between the Government and the contractor, in a ratio of approximately 85:15 in favour of the Government.

The duration of production-sharing contracts is 30 years, but they expire after an unsuccessful six to ten-year exploration period. Cost recovery is not limited and followed generally accepted accounting practice at an accelerated rate.

Foreign participation in the petroleum processing and petrochemicals sector may be accomplished through joint-venture arrangements.

Terms of production-sharing contracts for natural gas are similar to the arrangements for oil. The contractor is entitled to recover all operating costs, including capital investments, out of the natural gas produced.

Foreign investment in mining must be done under either production-sharing contracts or work contracts with the Government. For mining investment purposes, minerals are divided into three categories:

(1)   strategic minerals: oil, coal, nickel, tin, uranium and other radioactive minerals, cobalt, asphalt and others;

126

(2) vital minerals: gold, silver, lead, zinc, copper, bauxite, manganese, iron and others;
(3) other minerals: primarily industrial minerals, such as limestone, clay, sulphur, gypsum, etc.

In principle, only the state can mine strategic minerals, but arrangements have been made to extend this right to private companies, both domestic and foreign. The principle underlying the system of production-sharing contracts or work contracts is that the foreign party conducts all stages of the operation, including general prospecting, exploration, refining and processing, transport and marketing of the mineral products, as a contractor to the Government or state enterprise. The foreign party, as the operating company, must be incorporated in Indonesia, unless special exemption is granted. It has control and management of all its activities under the agreement and has full responsibility for all risks of operations. The various stages of work stipulated in general in the contract comprise:

(a) general prospecting for a period of up to 12 months;
(b) exploration: 36 months;
(c) evaluation: 12 months;
(d) construction: 36 months;
(e) operation: 360 months.

The foreign company must endeavor to use Indonesian services, raw materials produced from Indonesian sources, and products manufactured in Indonesia. It should also provide a genuine opportunity for Indonesian capital participation as soon as production of the project commences. The company is subject to the payment of land rent in respect to the contract areas, royalties in respect to the company's production of minerals mined, corporation tax in respect to annual profits, sales tax of general application in Indonesia and tax upon transfer of ownership of motor vehicles and ships.

Exemption is provided from import and other custom duties in relation to the importation of machinery, equipment, tools, and ancillary supplies needed for the operation of the project. Any item imported by the company for the operation of the project and no longer needed, may be re-exported free from all export and other custom duties, or may be sold in Indonesia after compliance with customs and import laws and regulations.

Profits may be transferred, provided taxes and other official obligations have been met. Provision is also made for accelerated depreciation of fixed capital assets.

Investment opportunities have been made available by the Government to foreign investors through international tenders. In addition to specific nickel and tin deposits, tenders have been requested for general mineral exploration in 53 separate blocks of potential mineral-bearing land in various locations throughout Indonesia.

Incentives provided for mining activities are based on Government Regulation No. 21 of 1976 and Presidential Decree No. 49 of 1981, as modified by laws No. 7 and 8 of 1983.

The new simplified Government's policy with regard to foreign investment on the forestry sector is contained in Ministerial Decree of 12 April 1984. The foreign investor must submit an application to the Ministry of Forestry for a forestry agreement. Investors may now operate in various types of timber processing industries, securing timber supplies through contractual arrangements.

The foreign company operates under a contract-of-work agreement which requires them to share a certain percentage of the profits with the Indonesian Government. Incentives are provided *inter alia* in the form of loss-carry-forwards, accelerated depreciation, and duty-free import of project goods. The majority position, both in terms of management and equity, is held by the Indonesian partner from the formation of the joint venture company. Joint ventures in forestry may be established for the following operations:

(a) all stages of wood processing, from saw-milling to pulp and paper manufacturing;
(b) forest-related industries, such as the production/or assembly of light equipment and accessories for logging or wood processing, sea transportation and related services, and the establishment of new forest resources.

Such schemes can be combined with general land development proposals, embracing ranching, food crops, orchards, or plantations of rubber trees, oil palms, etc. The overall objective of the Government is to ensure that all log production is processed domestically. The Government realizes, however, that processing and support industries require adequate facilities and has therefore authorizes regional administrators to establish industrial complexes as a matter of urgency.

The Board has its main office in Jakarta and maintains regional offices in the capital cities of the 27 Provinces of the Republic of Indonesia to coordinate local investments. These offices, each under the direction of the provincial governor, monitor and evaluate capital investments at the provincial level.

SIMPLIFICATION

In order to create a more favorable investment climate and further assist investors, BKPM substantially simplified investment procedures in April 1985. Under the new regulations, the number of applications, procedures and restrictions has been significantly reduced and the time needed to process applications has been shortened.

A few examples of the changes are as follows:

(a) under certain conditions, a prospective investor may not have to obtain first a provisional approval (SPS) but may be able to apply immediately for the final approval (SPP President). In such cases, the investor will receive the SPP President within six weeks of application, compared with three of more months otherwise;

(b) a feasibility study for a priority project is no longer required to obtain an SPS;

(c) evidence that the venture's paid-in capital satisfies debt-equity ratio requirements is no longer required in order to obtain an SPP President;

(d) the cumbersome six-page project-modification application has been replaced with a one-page document.

Potential investors are advised to contact BKPM staff to determine if any new regulations or procedures might apply to the area of investment under consideration. One of the objectives of the simplification efforts is that the BKPM will be perceived more as an agency assisting investors and less as an Office which regulates investments. The BKPM is at present indeed better equipped than ever before to assist investors in facilitating investment in Indonesia, beginning with the dissemination of information on business prospects and continuing through to assistance on problem solving. The essence of the simplification measure is to make the issuance of permits and facilities as simple and automatic a procedure as possible.

For certain matters, authority was delegated to regional BKPM offices, such as the application for extension of an expatriate work permit, which save time and money for investors.

The BKPM in 1985 has also addressed the problem of stay and work-permits, including the extension of work-permits, for expatriate experts. At present, as long as their services are required by a company for the successful operation of its enterprise, the BKPM will issue the permits. Previously, several fees were levied on the employment of expatriates, including a US$400 per man per month levy on the extended employment of an expatriate beyond their originally scheduled expiry date. Now the Government has done away with any levy on the use of expatriate personnel. Foreign experts, whose skills are still needed, may continue working in Indonesia without any fee whatsoever levied upon them. However, when they are no longer needed and their tasks can be transferred to Indonesians, then it is expected that they be replaced by Indonesian workers.

INVESTMENT PRIORITY LIST (DSP)

The Foreign Capital Investment Law of 1967 determines *inter alia* that certain enterprises are reserved for joint ventures only and that certain business fields are totally closed to foreign investors. As of 15 February 1977, the Capital Investment Coordinating Board lay down a legal base for the List of Priority Scale, which is meant to guide the foreign investors, as well as to facilitate them in deciding which project is to be undertaken.

The Investment Priority List or *Daftar Skala Prioritas* (DSP) as it is called in the Indonesian Language is to support the Indonesian National Development plan, which is carried out on the basis of the Broad Outlines of State Policy (*Garis Besar Haluan Negara* or GBHN). The GBHN indicates the goals and targets that are to be achieved by the Indonesian people in realizing the aspiration of their national struggle, the methods to be used, and the stages of this development process.

The present long-term development program has been set at 25 to 30 years and will be implemented by stages of five years period through successive Five Years Development Plans (*Repelita*). The target of this long-term development program is to lay the foundation for take-off, i.e. to fuel growth and development through Indonesia's own resources. This target is to be accomplished in the coming *Repelita* VI.

With respect to capital investment, the GBHN provides that the role of domestic capital investment must be continually fostered and enhanced. Foreign capital investment is possible in certain sectors that produce goods that are urgently needed by the country, that can expand exports, that require large investments of capital and relatively high technology and that will neither endanger national economic and or security interest, nor hinder the development of national companies. Foreign capital investment is implemented in the form of joint ventures and is accompanied by the requirements to create significant job opportunities, to enable the transfer of skills and technology to the Indonesian people within the shortest possible time and to preserve the nature and quality of the environment. Foreign investment is also aimed at strengthening national economic growth by promoting the fulfillment of national development goals.

Based on the foregoing considerations, investment plans have been prepared to direct capital investment to those fields which will contribute to the achievement of development targets. These plans have been set forth in the Investment Priority List (DSP), which indicates the various possibilities for capital investment in Indonesia.

The DSP essentially reflects an integrated investment plan, with the basic aim of supporting development projects through efforts to increase income, employment and business opportunities, as well as to encourage development evenly throughout the provinces by making the best possible use of available natural resources.

The DSP indicates also fields of investments open to foreign investments (PMA Investments) and to Domestic Investments (PMDN investments), fields open only to small-scale entrepreneurs and to Domestic Investments which are not eligible for investment facilities under the laws on foreign and Domestic Investment, as well as fields declared closed to further investments. The DSP remains in effect for three years and is reviewed each year for adjustment to current conditions.

The 1986 DSP reflects adjustments to the DSP 1985 to account for changes in national economic conditions as influenced by the world economic situation. It also sets forth several new policies in the field of investments, both from domestic as well as foreign sources, to increase exports of processed goods, to protect domestic production and therefore to protect and assist also the growth of existing investments.

Fields of investments that are declared open, are open for new projects, as well as for the expansion of existing projects unless otherwise decided. The expansion of existing projects can be considered if construction or production has reached an appropriate stage of realization and the investor has fulfilled its obligations to report on the development of the enterprise conform the regulations in force.

Expansion means an increase in capital investment that expands the business capability of a company through the utilization of advanced technology, through an addition in type or in capacity of production or through an increase in the added value and or local content of licensed production with additional primary production equipment.

Diversification means the diversification of the business of a company through changes in type and capacity of licensed production without an increase in productive capacity and primary production equipment.

Additions to or reductions in the fields of investment in the DSP will be issued after agreement has been reached with the Minister responsible for the particular field of investment concerned. A potential investor who is interested in fields of investments that are not listed in the DSP may request clarification from the BKPM. The decision in respect of each particular request will be issued after taking into consideration the opinion of the Technical Department or Agency concerned.

'MAY 6TH PACKAGE'

On 6 May 1986, the Government of Indonesia issued several new regulations (Decrees), expressly intended to generate economic growth within targeted sectors of the national economy. These sectors offer the greatest potential for the longterm positive development of the national well-being. The 'May 6th Package' contains two basic components each with its underlying objectives: first, to stimulate Indonesia's non-oil and gas exports. The aim is to make other Indonesian products more competitive in the world market, and second, to stimulate investment, domestic as well as foreign.

The 'May 6th Package' provides a significant coordinated program of improvements and incentives for foreign investors. It is almost on a par with the far-reaching reform-measures initiated by Presidential Instruction No. 4 of 1985 on customs and import procedures, including port operations, designed to facilitate the smooth flow of goods in and out of and within Indonesia.

Regarding foreign investment, the 'May 6th Package' contains, *inter alia*, the following stipulations:

– the 'May 6th Package' reaffirms that the permit for a PMA (foreign capital investment joint-venture company) to operate in Indonesia is valid for 30 years as stated in the Foreign Capital Investment Law No. 1 of 1967. However, each PMA company that increases its capital or raises its investment by way of (1) diversification, or (2) an increase in its production capacity, or (3) an increase in its value-added or the local content of

131

its products in accordance with the applicable schedule set by the Government, may be granted an additional permit for up to thirty years, after the additional investment has been approved by the Government;
– foreign investment is permitted only in the form of a joint venture between a foreign company and an Indonesian national company or an Indonesian national. The Indonesian equity share ownership in the joint venture must be at least twenty percent at the outset.

However, PMA companies which:

(1) are high risk ventures;
(2) require large capital and high technology;
(3) are located in remote areas; or
(4) are producing entirely for export,

may be established with an initial five-percent Indonesian equity ownership, to be increased to twenty percent within five years after commercial production begins.

One very basic element in the Indonesian investment policy is that at the latest ten years after start of commercial production a majority (at least 51 per cent) of the equity shares of the PMA must already be Indonesian owned.

Investors thus should be prepared for total divestment by the end of the thirty years period, except of course if there is additional investment that allows for an extension. For the sake of the investor's investment the divestiture should be effected gradually so as not to disrupt the company's operation. The ten-year period is regarded, however, for certain ventures, particularly those that require large capital investment, as being too short. This sometimes gives rise to difficulties, because even if the foreign partner is willing to divest his shareholding, he may not always readily find buyers, certainly in many cases not his current joint venture partner.

The foreign partner in this case should give his Indonesian partner the first option to increase his equity share to acquire a majority in the enterprise (51 per cent or more). The same rule applies for any additional shares required to finance expansion. In case the Indonesian partner is not able or not willing to buy, the foreign partner may either: find other Indonesian buyers; or transfer his shares to Indonesian Banks or to a non-bank financial institution, or 'go public' and trade the shares on the stock market. If he is still not successful despite all these endeavors, then the foreign partner will be allowed to meet his obligation to divest his majority shareholding in stages (for up to five years). This means that in practice the divestiture period may be extended up to fifteen years.

A PMA company that meets certain requirements will be treated as a domestic investment company (national company). Those requirements are:

(1) if the Indonesian State and or Indonesian private nationals own at least seventy-five percent of the company's shares;
(2) if the company has gone public and at least fifty-one percent of its equity shares have been offered and sold on the stock exchange; or

(3) if the company has gone public and the shares owned by the Indonesian State and or Indonesian private nationals and the shares that have been offered on the stock exchange amount to at least fifty-one per cent. In this case, the shares that have been sold on the stock exchange must amount to at least twenty per cent.

This treatment as a national company will in no way change the PMA status of the company concerned. It however, provides three main benefits:

(1) it permits the PMA company to engage in domestic marketing and distribution of its products, whereas previously it was required to sell its products through an Indonesian distributing agent;
(2) it allows the PMA company to borrow from state banks; and
(3) it allows the PMA company to operate in business sectors that are otherwise closed to it but open to PMDN companies.

The 'May 6th Package' now allows the foreign investor to reinvest his profits as well as proceeds from other resources in new ventures or use them to buy shares in already existing companies. Before the 'May 6th Package', foreign investors had only two options: either reinvest their profits in their own companies, e.g. for expansion purposes, or repatriate the money.

Enterprises in which part or all of the equity shares are owned by a PMA enterprise will have the status of a PMA company.

The investment value of a foreign investment company (PMA) must be at least $1-million, with the exception of consultancy and engineering service enterprises and certain other business sectors to be determined by the departments concerned or by BKPM. The $1-million refers to the total investment and not to what the foreign investor has to bring in. Certain enterprises as mentioned above, may be now set up with even less than $1-million.

All business sectors declared either open or closed in the DSP, may be open to foreign and domestic investments if the production is intended 'entirely' for export. The term 'entirely for export' means that at least eighty-five percent of the production is sold for export, while the remaining fifteen percent or less, may be sold in the domestic market.

It is hoped that this new stipulation will promote investments that are geared for international markets, but still need a cushion in the local markets to boost the exports.

With the enactment of Law No. 7 of 1983 on Income Tax and Services and Sales Tax on Luxury Goods, Law No. 12 of 1985 on Land and Building Tax, and Law No. 13 of 1985 on Stamp Duties, fiscal facilities that can be extended to PMA/PMDN investors are as follows:

(1) exemption or reduction of import duties on imported equipment, machinery and spare parts;
(2) exemption or reduction of import duties on imported raw materials and

ancillary goods required for the production for a maximum period of two years;

(3) deferment of payment for up to five years of the value-added tax (PPN) on imported capital goods required for the production of goods or services, e.g. hotel business; and

(4) exemption from transfer of ownership duties with respect to the initial registration of ships in Indonesia.

The new Indonesian tax system replacing, *inter alia,* the old Company Tax Ordinance of 1925 inherited from the Dutch Administration is a modern one, straightforward and simple. It is also generous with a graduated scale for personal and corporate income tax with a top tax marginal rate of only 35 per cent, compared with a previous maximum tax of 45 per cent on corporate tax income and 50 per cent on personal income.

The Negative List

Goods produced in sufficient quantities in Indonesia (and of comparable quality to similar products produced overseas) as described in the List of Capital Goods not eligible for receiving Import Duty Facilities (the so-called 'Negative List'), will not receive any import duty facilities when imported. However, enterprises that produce entirely for export, may import those goods duty free. All other goods outside the negative list may still be imported duty free, both by foreign as well as domestic investment companies.

Investors, if they choose, may still import goods that are mentioned in the Negative List, but they will not get duty exemption and have to pay the normal payable duty.

Import duty facilities

Both foreign and domestic investment companies that buy capital goods made in Indonesia, will be granted import duty facilities for the imported raw materials and components required in making those capital goods. The enterprises producing those capital goods may obtain a rebate on duties already paid, through a draw-back system.

Land and location of investment projects

The right of Land Exploitation (HGU) is granted to the Indonesian partner in a joint venture. In accordance with Presidential Decree No. 23 of 1980, the Indonesian partner in a PMA company may, in turn, provide the PMA company the use of the HGU.

The Regional office of the BKPM is responsible for all matters concerning the location, provision of land, land grant, building permit, and permit under the Nuisance Law with respect to any investment project. The Minister for Internal Affairs determines applicable rules.

In order to obtain certain investment facilities, investors who intend to export part or all of their products may choose to locate their company in a 'bonded zone'. The rules concerning bonded zones are set forth in a Government Regulation on bonded zones. The rules and regulations concerning the import, export and transfer of goods into and from the industrial processing zone of 'Batam Island' follow the provisions of Presidential Decree No. 22 of 1978.

The following measures are adopted in order to protect and promote the efforts of economically weak group enterprises, small business sectors and cooperatives, as well as to induce companies to 'go public' and giving special investment opportunities to PMA companies.

New competing capital investments are restricted in traditional fields of economic activity that are operated by and reserved for economically weak entrepreneurs.

In certain business sectors, participation by economically weak entrepreneurs as business partners will be required in joint ventures, irrespective of whether these entrepreneurs are associated with a cooperative or not. Certain business sectors will be reserved for small entrepreneurs or cooperatives only.

Business sectors open only to small entrepreneurs and capital investments that are non-PMA/PMDN, may receive PMDN investment facilities, if operated by a small entrepreneur or a cooperative. A national company may invest in those sectors and be granted investment facilities extended to a PMDN, if it takes a cooperative as its business partner. In this case, the cooperative must hold at least twenty percent of the equity shares at the time the business venture is established.

Business sectors open only to domestic (PMDN) and non-foreign/domestic (non-PMA/PMDN) investment, may be opened to foreign (PMA) investment if the foreign enterprise takes a cooperative as its business partner. The cooperative must hold at least twenty percent of the equity shareholding at the time the foreign (PMA) joint venture is established.

For business sectors closed to further foreign investment, the permit for an expansion of an existing foreign joint venture operation may be considered so long as those sectors are open to domestic (PMDN) and non-foreign/PMDN investment. In this case twenty per cent of the equity shares with respect to the expansion must be sold to the public on the stock exchange, or a cooperative shall own at least twenty per cent of the equity shares with respect to the expansion at the time the application for expansion is submitted.

For business sectors closed to domestic investment (PMDN), the expansion of a domestic investment venture may be considered as long as the sectors concerned are declared open to non-foreign/domestic (non-PMA/PMDN) investment. In this case, twenty percent of the equity shares of the enterprise must be sold to the public on the stock exchange, or a cooperative shall own at least twenty percent of the equity shares with respect to the expansion at the time the application for expansion is submitted.

The 'May 6th Package' also provides an important relaxation in the rules relating to agro-business, particularly with regard to oil-palm estates and shrimp cultivation.

For oil-palm estates, the People's Nucleus Estate (PIR) Pattern has been established, with the investor serving as the nucleus and the individual farmer as the smallholder (*plasma*).

Similarly, investment in shrimp cultivation is based on a TIR Pattern (Smallholders Nucleus Ponds pattern). Under the old PIR system, the ratio between the acreage of the nucleus estate (operated by the investor) and the smallholders (*plasma*) estate, in principle, was to have been 20:80. Although the cost of the smallholders (*plasma*) estate will later be assumed by Banks and the former become debtors to the Banks, the nucleus and plasma ratio has often caused problems for lending Banks. Under the new policy, for the first 10 years of commercial operation the ratio may initially be 40:60 and the conversion of the plasma to 20:80 may be effected at the end of the ten-year period.

With regard to the TIR system for shrimp cultivation, the ratio is altogether changed from 20:80 to 40:60 (permanently) and even 60:40 for newly developed areas outside Java. Oil-palm estates and shrimp cultivation are among the most attractive fields of investment that the country is offering.

The 'May 6th Package' finally also reconfirmed that capital investment enterprises may employ foreign experts needed to ensure the successful operation of the enterprises, provided they set up an education and or training program for Indonesian nationals, and transfer both expertise and technology with the objective that in stages, at the time determined, Indonesians will assume the work performed by expatriates.

OTHER INCENTIVES, FACILITIES

Another important step in the progressive reform of Foreign Capital Investment Regulations is the Decision of the Chairman of the BKPM No. 17/SK/1986 dated 25 October 1986, regarding 'Foreign Shares Participation in Business Companies already in Operation'.

Owners of foreign capital, whether they have already a share or not in a PMA company in Indonesia, may invest their capital in an already existing PMDN company or in another national limited liability company. The investments may be realized by the purchase of the shares of national companies already in operation, both in the form of paid-up capital and subscribed capital, or in the form of new emissions.

The participation of foreign capital in 'national companies' must meet the following requirements:

(1) the field of business of the national company concerned is, according to the DSP (Investment Priority List) valid at the time of filing the application for investment, still open to foreign capital investment;
(2) increase of capital in the national company concerned is really needed

in order to improve the condition of the company, or to open the possibility of exporting all, or part of its products, which must be proven by the report of a public accountant or by the suggestion of the bank that supplies the credit.

The amount of the national shares shall be as follows:

(1) if the increase in capital is purely intended to improve the condition of the company, or to meet the company's need for capital and the command of technology, the national share in the company may not be reduced to less than 75 per cent;
(2) If the company exports parts of its products, the national share in the company may not be reduced to less than 51 per cent;
(3) If the company exports all of its products, the national share in the company may not become less than twenty per cent and shall be gradually increased again to 51 per cent in accordance with the valid regulation.

The national company mentioned above will henceforth operate as a joint venture, subject to the stipulations of Law No. 1 of 1967 on Foreign Capital Investment.

The participation of multilateral finance institutions in which the Indonesian Government has shares, such as the International Finance Corporation, the Asian Development Bank, etc., in national companies, both newly-established as well as those already existing, is considered as national participation.

A joint venture between a multilateral finance institution and a national capital owner may be approved as a company subject to Law No. 6 of 1968 regarding Domestic Capital Investment.

Foreign shareholding in a PMA company which is in need of increase of share capital for improving the condition of the company in order to export all or part of its products, or to boost its export, may be increased to maximum 95 per cent, in case the present national shareholder is unable to increase its shareholding, according to the existing ratio of shares.

The change in the foreign shareholding in a PMA company as mentioned above will be only possible after proof has been submitted in the form of a report of a public accountant or a suggestion from the credit-supplying bank, that an increase in the share capital is really needed for abovementioned purpose.

The national shareholding shall be restored to the original ratio within the period of five years; if the previous national shareholding is less than 51 per cent, the increase must become at least 51 per cent within the period of ten years after the increase in share capital has been approved by the BKPM.

Since 25 October 1986, the Government has been providing to joint venture companies producing for export, *rupiah* credit from state-owned banks, with a low concessional interest rate, enjoyed previously by domestic investors only. Furthermore, foreign banks can also participate in this scheme without any restrictions. The export oriented PMA Joint Venture Company can now obtain 85 per cent of its production cost as credit from the bank.

In order to further improve the business and investment climate of Indonesia, the Government decided early in 1986 that businessmen from 29 countries are henceforth allowed to come to Indonesia for a business visit of up to two months at a time, without having to obtain an entry visa. Previously this facility was only granted to tourists of those countries. Another Government decision subsequently states that, commencing 30 October 1986, multiple business visas for businessmen to Indonesia will be valid for twelve months, which is a great improvement compared with the four months validity period previously.

The '24th December 1987 Package'

On 24 December 1987, the Indonesian Government issued in continuation of its deregulation policy started in 1985, a series of 48 new regulations aimed at further boosting non-oil and non-gas exports as well as developing the tourist industry of the country.

This '24 December Package', comprising primarily simplifications of the procedures for obtaining licenses and exemption from certain charges, taxes, duties etc. provides *inter alia* the following facilities and advantages:

(a) any Indonesian company which is in possession of an official recognition in the field of trade or industry may from now on also act as an exporter of most Indonesian commodities. A special recognition as exporter is no longer needed;

(b) foreign Capital Investment Companies in the field of production are now allowed to export themselves their own products, or those from other processing companies in Indonesia. For this purpose, the foreign company must establish a joint venture company (a PT) with an Indonesian partner;

(c) exporters-producers which export most (i.e. at least 65 per cent) of their products, in meeting their needs for goods, basic material etc. for their production process, are allowed:

   (i)   to use domestically produced goods, basic material, etc. at prices whose ceilings are equal to import prices in the international market; or

   (ii) to import the goods, basic materials, etc. without being subject to trade arrangements (i.e. exempted from import duty, surcharges, etc.);

(d) to non PMA/PMDN companies which export their products, are given exemption from import duties and VAT, for the machines and equipments that they need for their production. Exemption from the VAT is given before their products are exported;

(e) foreign Capital Investment companies which export the largest portion of their products are free to employ expatriates that they need for this purpose;

(f) foreign companies or groups of foreign companies abroad are allowed to establish their regional representative office in one of the major cities of Indonesia, to take care of their interests in Indonesia as well as in several other countries;

(g) the import of used containers needed for the export trade is exempted from custom procedure, but the import of new containers is subject to the general provisions in the import sector. The containers may be transferred from one place to another within the Indonesian custom area according to need. Container terminals will be established in several cities in the interior of the country in order to expedite handling of the necessary documents and better facilitate the flow of export goods to the ports concerned.

The import of samples for use in the manufacture of products designed for export or for the domestic market is exempted from import duty, surcharges, VAT and sales tax for luxury goods.

The import of goods, materials and construction equipments for the realization of Government projects funded with foreign aid and or loans, which are not mentioned in the sale/purchase contracts of the projects concerned, may be exempted from import duties, surcharges, VAT and sales tax on luxury goods.

Imported goods and materials with their import duties and surcharges already paid, which subsequently are sent into a bonded area for export, may have their import duties and surcharges restituted.

Export goods of Indonesian origin that are reimported into Indonesian custom areas, will be treated as import goods but can be granted trade facilities, exemption from import duty and surcharges, as well as a suspension of VAT and sales tax on luxury goods. These facilities may be granted to the exporter producers or to the exporters that have exported those goods.

To foreign capital investment companies:

(a) of which at least 51 per cent of their shares are owned by the State and or national private persons or companies; or

(b) of which 45 per cent of their shares are owned by the State and or national private circles, provided that at least twenty per cent of the total stocks is sold through the stock market as national stocks,

shall be given equal treatment as a PMDN Company.

Foreign Capital Investment Companies (PMA companies):

(a) shall be established in the form of joint venture with national capital participation of at least twenty per cent of the value of shares at the time of establishment and which must increase to 51 per cent within fifteen years starting from the commencement of commercial production;

(b) which are located in bonded zones and export 100 per cent of their products, can, however, be established with national capital participation of five per cent or more, without the obligation to increase the national shares.

Above-mentioned provisions are also valid in case of any addition of share capital due to investment increase.

Foreign Capital Investment Companies (PMA companies):

(a) the investment value of which is at least US$10,000,000; or

(b) which are located in the provinces of Jambi, Bengkulu, Central Kalimantan, Central Sulawesi, South-East Sulawesi, West Nusatenggara, East Timor, Maluku, Irian Jaya and certain regencies in other provinces to be further stipulated; or

(c) the products of which are for the greater part exported, i.e. at least 65 per cent of the production is sold to the export market,

can be established with national shares of at least five per cent of the shares value, which must be increased to at least twenty per cent of the shares value within ten years starting from the commencement of commercial production.

Steel needed for construction works which before may only be imported through certain registered importers, e.g. PT Krakatau Steel, can now be imported by any other importer.

Producers in the jewelry industry are allowed to import the needed raw materials such as gold, platinum, silver and precious stones, free from any custom duty. They may also directly export their products themselves.

Procedures and or requirements for the establishment of hotels, restaurants, travel bureaus, tourist objects etc. are now simplified and made easy. There are only two kinds of permits in this respect (compared with 33 in the past) namely a temporary license and a permanent one. The tourist industry in the Investment Priority list (DSP) has been declared open to any company.

Chapter 8
Legal Aspects of Trade and Investment in Thailand

by Srisanit Anek

Anek & Associates
Bangkok, Thailand

Introduction

Thailand is an attractive country in which to do business because of its wealth of resources, steadily growing economy, excellent infrastructure and communication, and the intelligence, flexibility and tolerance of the Thai people. In addition, as a developing country, Thailand has recognized the importance of foreign investment for the purpose of the country's social and economic development, since foreign investment is, *inter alia*, the source of foreign capital and advanced technology and as such has employed various ways and means, both legal and non-legal, in order to promote investment in the country. At the present time, there is a large amount of foreign investment flowing into the country.

This paper will be confined to the laws and legal requirements in relation to investment in Thailand.

However, it will firstly give some information about the country. Secondly, it will focus on the laws and legal requirements in relation to investment, particularly foreign investment. It is worth noting that those matters treated in this paper are what is prescribed and required by the laws. However, in practice, these laws and requirements are not strictly implemented, some of them may be relieved and relaxed.

141

General Information on Thailand

Thailand lies in the central of South-East Asia, with a population of almost 60-million, nearly ten per cent of these living in and around Bangkok, its capital. Bangkok is the industrial and economic center of the country. It dominates the administrative, financial, industrial and commercial activities of the country.

Thailand is a constitutional monarchy. Under the written Constitution, His Majesty the King is the Head of State. Sovereignty is derived from the people of Thailand and is exercised by the King in the three ways: legislative power through the National Assembly, executive power through the Council of Ministers and judicial power through the Courts in compliance with the provisions of the Constitution. The Constitution recognizes the King as Head of State, Head of Armed Forces, Upholder of the Buddhist Religion, and Upholder of all Religions.

At the national level, executive power is administered and legislated by the Cabinet, in which all the Ministries are represented, and is headed by the Prime Minister. The Council of Ministers and the Prime Minister are appointed by the King, subject to the countersignature of the President of the National Assembly.

The National Assembly is the bicameral legislative organ of Thailand, consisting of the Senate and the House of Representatives. The Senate is appointed by the King, and the House of Representatives is popularly elected. Thailand has a civil law system. Most laws have a form of brief, simple statements of general principle and therefore leaving considerable scope for interpretation and flexibility. The basic legislation of Thailand is in a codified form such as the Civil and Commercial Code, the Land Code, the Revenue Code and the Penal Code.

The courts in Thailand follow the traditional pattern of courts: court of first instance, court of appeals, and the supreme court. Judges are appointed and removed by the King according to the recommendation of the Judicial Commission established under the law on judicial service. There are no juries in Thailand, and decisions of the Supreme Court are highly authoritative but do not establish binding principles of law.

Way of Doing Business in Thailand

There are some cases where the businesses of foreigners in Thailand have failed because of a lack of awareness of the socio-cultural values. Thai people have their own socio-cultural values different from those of other countries due to their historical foundation and religions. The values of the Thai people in respect of doing business which foreign businessmen should be aware are loyalty and trust. Hierarchy and seniority are also important. Senior officials or businessmen expect to be treated with respect and may not be accessible to their junior.

The Thai businessman usually has a short business horizon and does not want to get involved in a complicated manufacturing process. Therefore, manufacturing in Thailand tends to be the processing of raw materials and the simple fabrication of industrial materials into consumer products. And, in the case where it requires a complicated process, the manufacturer would generally prefer to buy technology rather than to develop it. However, this position has been changing, and the number of real manufacturers and investors with horizon beyond three to five years is growing in number and importance. In addition, the awareness of the necessities of the adoption of new technologies requiring higher investments and a more skilled professional workforce is also growing.

Legal Aspects of Trade and Investment in Thailand

FORMS OF BUSINESS ORGANIZATION

Business in Thailand may be conducted in many forms, i.e. sole proprietorship, partnership, limited company, joint venture, branch of foreign company and representative office of foreign company.

Sole proprietorships

An individual solely carrying out a business is deemed to be a sole proprietor. There are no specific laws governing business in a form of sole proprietor. However, the provisions of the Civil and Commercial Code relating to obligations and specific contracts wil basically govern the sole proprietorship business.

The sole proprietor retains a full and exclusive control over the business operation and also retains all profits and bears all the losses of the business. The establishment of a sole proprietorship requires no legal formalities, since it is an unincorporated business.

A sole proprietorship is owned by only one individual and all properties of the proprietor, both personal and business, are subject to attachment or other legal action which may be brought in respect of the business. In addition, the proprietor may be more financially restricted in the course of his business venture than other forms of business organization in terms of attracting capital from outside source. Therefore, this form of business organization is not attractive to investors.

Partnerships

Under the Thai law, a partnership is defined as a contract whereby two or more persons agree to unite to form a common undertaking with a purpose of sharing profits which may be derived therefrom. There are three different types of partnerships which are recognized by the Civil and Commercial Code relating to Partnerships and Companies which is the law principally

governing the forms of business organization in Thailand. The Civil and Commercial Code categorizes partnership into:
- unregistered ordinary partnership;
- registered ordinary partnership; and
- limited partnership.

- *Unregistered ordinary partnership:* an unregistered ordinary partnership is a partnership in which all partners are jointly and unlimitedly liable for all the liabilities, obligations and debts of the partnership. Each partner is required to make a contribution to the partnership in a form of monies, properties or services and, in case of doubt, the contributions are presumed to be of equal value. In addition, in the case where the partnership contract does not mention the sharing or division of profits or losses, the share of each partner in profits or losses of the partnership will be in proportion to his contribution. The formation of an unregistered ordinary partnership requires no legal formalities.
- *Registered ordinary partnerships:* an ordinary partnership may be registered. Upon registration, it becomes a juristic person, i.e. a separate and distinct legal entity apart from its partners. The advantages of partners to a registered partnership are that although every partner to the registered ordinary partnership has to be unlimitedly liable for all the liabilities, obligations and debts of the partnership, since the partnership is a juristic person separate from its partners, the creditors of the partnership must first claim for debt payments from the partnership and if the partnership is in default or if the partnership has no more assets to be enforced by the creditors, all partners shall be liable for payment of all debts incurred by the partnership. In addition, the liabilities of a partner for debts incurred by the partnership is limited to two years after the date his partnership terminates.

  Registration of a partnership must be made at the Registration Office of the province where the principal business office of the partnership is located. For Bangkok Metropolis, a partnership can be registered at the Office of the Bangkok Partnerships and Companies Registration, Ministry of Commerce.
- *Limited partnerships:* a limited partnership is a partnership which consists of two types of partners, i.e:

  (a) partner whose liability is limited to the amounts that he may have undertaken to contribute to the partnership; and
  (b) partner who is unlimitedly liable for all debts of the partnership.

A limited partnership is required to be registered at the Registration Office. Upon registration, a limited partnership is regarded as a separate legal entity.

A limited partnership should be managed by partner(s) whose liability is unlimited. If a limited partnership is managed by partner(s) whose liability is limited, said partner(s) will be required to be unlimitedly liable for all debts of the partnership. In addition, the name of a limited partnership may not contain any of the names of the limited partners, otherwise such limited partner(s) will be liable to third persons as though he (they) were partner(s) with unlimited liability. A limited partner may carry on any business of the same nature as that of the partnership and may transfer his share in the limited partnership without the consent of the other partners.

Creditors of a limited partnership are not entitled to take any action against limited partners unless the partnership is dissolved. In such an event, creditors can claim only the following amounts:
(a)   part of the undelivered contribution;
(b)   part of the contribution which has been withdrawn;
(c)   dividend or interest received in bad faith or contrary to the law.

Limited companies

Under the Thai laws, there are two types of limited companies, i.e. private limited company and public limited company.

–   *Private Limited Company:* private limited company is a company which is incorporated with capital divided into equal shares and having less than one hundred shareholders. The liability of the shareholders in a private limited company is limited to the amount unpaid on the shares held by them. The procedures to be applied in the formation of a private limited company can be summarized as follows:

(a)   *Filing of a memorandum of association*
        The promoters of the company (at least seven persons) must file a memorandum of association with the Bangkok Partnerships and Companies Registration Office, Ministry of Commerce. If the registered office is to be located outside Bangkok, the filing is to be made at the local Registration Office in the area where the registered office is located. Should the official be satisfied with the contents of the memorandum of association, registration of the same will be approved.
(b)   *Subscription to shares*
        After the registration of the memorandum of association, the promoters will arrange to have all shares subscribed to. A private limited company is not allowed to invite the public to subscribe to the shares in the company.
(c)   *Statutory meeting*
        After all the shares have been subscribed to, the promoters must call for a general meeting of subscribers, called 'a statutory meeting'. The following business should be transacted at the statutory meeting:

            (i)   adoption of the company's articles of association (by-laws);

145

(ii)   ratification of promoters' acts and expenses during the formation of the company;

(iii) fix the amount to be paid to promoters;

(iv)   establishment of preference shares, if any;

(v)   fix the number of shares to be alloted as fully or partly paid up by means other than in money, if any, and the amount by which they will be considered as paid up; and

(vi)   appointment of directors and auditors and establishment of the powers of the directors.

After the statutory meeting, the promoters will hand over the business of the company to the directors. The directors will request all subscribers to pay up each share in money in the amount of not less than 25 per cent of the value of the share.

(d)   *Registration of the Company*

After the payment of the minimum twenty five per cent and within three months after the statutory meeting, the directors must apply for the registration of the company. Upon registration, the company will have a juristic entity status. The articles of association of the company which have been adopted by the shareholders and registered at the time of registration of the company will govern the company's business and bind the directors and the shareholders of the company. The management of the company's business will be conducted by the directors. The directors will manage the company's business in accordance with the articles of association.

– *Public limited company:* public limited company is a limited company which has 100 or more shareholders and is established in accordance with the Public Company Act of 1978. The liability of shareholders in the public limited company is also limited to the unpaid amount (if any) of the par value of the shares. In addition, 50 per cent of the total shares issued and sold must be held by natural persons, each of whom holds shares equal to no more than 0.6 per cent of the total shares issued and sold.

The procedures required in the establishment of a public limited company are similar to that for a private limited company. However, there are certain important differences, being:

(i)   in a public limited company, there must be at least 15 natural persons as promoters;

(ii)   in a public limited company, there must be at least 100 shareholders;

(iii) a public limited company is entitled to issue debentures;

(iv)   a public limited company can invite the public to subscribe for shares;

(v)   subscribers to a public limited company must pay the full
      amount of each share.

Joint ventures

Under the Thai laws, there is no clear-cut meaning of 'joint venture'
although it is commercially recognized as a form of business organization.
The forms of business in the Thailand are principally governed by the Civil
and Commercial Code. However, the Code has not yet recognized a joint
venture as a unique form of business organization and there is no law
specifically governing a joint venture.
    Joint ventures in Thailand can be categorized into two major forms, i.e.
incorporated joint ventures and unincorporated joint ventures.

–   *Incorporated joint ventures:* when a joint venture is established in the
    form of a legal entity under the Thai law, it will have a legal status of the
    entity to which it is incorporated. Normally, it will be incorporated as a
    private limited company under the Civil and Commercial Code due to
    certain advantages over other legal entities.
–   *Unincorporated joint ventures:* in contrast to the incorporated joint ven-
    ture, this type of joint venture is established merely on a contractual
    basis without incorporation as a legal entity under the Thai law and the
    principles of contract law will govern a joint venture of this type.

CONTROLS ON ALIEN BUSINESSES

In general, aliens in Thailand have the same legal rights as Thai nationals
unless a right is particularly reserved to Thai nationals, or is specifically
denied to aliens.

The alien business law

Presently the most important law governing the participation of aliens
in business in Thailand is the Alien Business Law (National Executive
Announcement No. 281). The main objective of this law is particularly to
restrict aliens and/or majority owned enterprises from engaging in various
fields of business exclusively reserved for Thai nationals.

Article 3 of the Alien Business Law defines the word 'alien' as follows:

    'Alien' means a natural or juristic person who is not of Thai
    nationality, and includes:
    (a)   a juristic person of which half or more of the capital is owned
          by aliens;

147

(b) a juristic person of which half or more of the shareholders, partners or members are aliens;

(c) a limited partnership or registered ordinary partnership of which the managing partner or manager is an alien.

For the purpose of this definition, shares of a limited company with bearer certificate shall be regarded as shares of aliens, unless otherwise prescribed by the Ministerial Regulation.

Businesses controlled by the law
The controlled businesses are classified into three categories: A, B and C. Businesses in categories A and B are closed to aliens with the objective basically to reserve them for Thai nationals or enterprises with 51 per cent of equity participation owned by Thais. In the case of Category B, however, a foreign enterprise with the explicit approval of the Board of Investment (BOI) may initiate such an operation. In such a case, the foreign enterprise must have maintained the validity of BOI promotion, failing which, such privilege will subsequently be annulled.

Although the activities listed in Category C are open the laws require any new or existing foreign enterprise falling within this category to register with the Department of Commercial Registration. The license must be obtained prior to commencing business. A license issued is normally valid for a fixed period, but sometimes without limit and subject to some conditions.

List of Businesses Annexed to the Alien Business Law
(NEC 281)

Category A

Chapter 1 – Agricultural Businesses
(1) Rice farming
(2) Salt farming including salt mining except rock salt

Chapter 2 – Commercial Businesses
(1) Internal trade in local agricultural products
(2) Land trade

Chapter 3 – Service Businesses
(1) Accounting
(2) Law
(3) Architecture
(4) Advertising
(5) Brokerage or agency
(6) Auctioning
(7) Barbering, hair dressing and beautification

Chapter 4 – Other Businesses
(1) Building construction

Category B

Chapter 1 – Agricultural Businesses
(1) Cultivation
(2) Orchard farming
(3) Animal husbandry including silk worm raising
(4) Timber
(5) Fishing

Chapter 2 – Industrial and Handicraft Businesses
(1) Rice milling
(2) Flour making from rice and other cash crops
(3) Sugar milling
(4) Manufacturing of alcoholic and non-alcoholic drinks and beverages
(5) Ice making
(6) Manufacturing of pharmaceuticals
(7) Cold storage
(8) Timber processing
(9) Manufacturing of gold, silver, nielloware and stone inlaid products
(10) Manufacturing or casting of Buddha images and bowls
(11) Wood carving
(12) Lacquer-ware making
(13) Match manufacturing
(14) Manufacturing of white cement, portland cement and cement finished products
(15) Dynamiting or quarrying of rocks
(16) Manufacturing of plywood, veneer wood, chipboard or hardboard
(17) Manufacturing of garments or foot wear except for export
(18) Printing
(19) Newspaper publishing
(20) Silk spinning, weaving or silk fabric printing
(21) Manufacturing of finished products from silk fabric, silk yarn or silk cocoons.

Chapter 3 – Commercial Businesses
(1) All retailing except for items included in Category 'C'
(2) Ore trading except for items included in Category 'C'
(3) Selling of food and drinks except for items included in Category 'C'
(4) Trading of antiques, heirloom or fine arts objects.

Chapter 4 – Service Businesses
(1) Tour agency
(2) Hotel, except hotel management
(3) All businesses under the law governing places of service
(4) Photography, photographic processing and printing
(5) Laundering
(6) Dress making

Chapter 5 – Other Businesses
(1)   Domestic land, water and air transport.

Category C

Chapter 1 – Commercial Businesses
(1)   All wholesale trade except for items included in Category 'A'
(2)   All exporting
(3)   Retailing of machinery, equipment and tools
(4)   Selling of food or beverages for promotion of tourism

Chapter 2 – Industrial and Handicraft Businesses
(1)   Manufacturing of animal feeds
(2)   Vegetable oil refining
(3)   Textile manufacturing including yarn spinning, dyeing and fabric printing
(4)   Manufacturing of glassware including light bulbs
(5)   Manufacturing of food bowls and plates
(6)   Manufacturing of stationery and printing paper
(7)   Rock salt-mining
(8)   Mining

Chapter 3 – Service Businesses
(1)   Service businesses not included in Category 'A' or Category 'B'

Chapter 4 – Other Businesses
(1)   Other construction not included in Category 'A'.

IMMIGRATION

Generally speaking, an alien may enter Thailand either as an immigrant, if he would like to have a residence in Thailand or as a non-immigrant, provided he intends to stay in Thailand temporarily. Initially, such alien should meet the general requirement of obtaining a visa prior to entering the country.

Categories of visa

The Immigration Act of 1979 classifies the following categories of visa:
(a)   Diplomatic visa
(b)   Government Official visa
(c)   Non-immigrant visa
(d)   Tourist visa
(e)   Transit visa
(f)   Visa for resident
(g)   Visa for non-quota immigrant

Non-immigrant

It is only for the following purposes and periods that an alien may enter Thailand temporarily:

(a)   on diplomatic or consular mission, duration as necessity requires;
(b)   on an official mission, duration as necessity requires;
(c)   for tourism, duration not exceeding ninety days;
(d)   for sports, duration not exceeding thirty days;
(e)   for business purpose, duration not exceeding one year;
(f)   for an investment which has received approval from the concerned authorities, duration not exceeding two years;
(g)   for investments or other businesses in connection with investment under the Investment Promotion Act, duration as deemed suitable by the Board of Investment;
(h)   transit, duration not exceeding thirty days;
(i)   for the controller or crew of a conveyance entering a port or other locality in Thailand, duration not exceeding thirty days;
(j)   for study or observation, duration not exceeding one year;
(k)   to perform work of mass media, duration not exceeding one year;
(l)   for missionary work with approval from the appropriate governmental authorities, duration not exceeding one year;
(m)   for scientific research or teaching in a research or an educational institute in Thailand, duration not exceeding one year;
(n)   for work as a skilled worker or specialist, duration not exceeding one year;
(o)   other purposes as prescribed in the Ministerial Regulation, duration not exceeding one year.

A tourist visa is strictly to be issued for an alien who comes to Thailand for the purpose of pleasure. The issuance of a transit visa may be made for such an alien to permit entry into Thailand temporarily for sports, or transit, or as the controller or crew of a conveyance entering a port, station or locality in Thailand. A period of 60 days is normally to be granted for a tourist visa. Before the 60-day period expires, the tourist may apply at the Immigration Division to extend his stay for an additional 30-day period. Aliens who have obtained a transit visa will normally be allowed to stay for a period of two weeks, and renewal will be denied. Holders of both visas, according to the Alien Employment Law, are not permitted to work in Thailand.

A business visa may be issued for an alien who intends to work in Thailand. Simultaneously, dependent visas are usually granted to all members of his family. An application for such visa should initially be submitted to the Thai Embassy or Consulate in the country of origin of such alien. Normally, permission to stay for a period of 30 days will be granted. The alien, however, may apply at the Immigration Division to prolong his stay for an additional period of up to one year. The same applies to the members of his family. A holder of a business visa may apply for a long-term business visa, multiple re-entry and then, for permanent residence. He is entitled to obtain a work permit.

Immigrant

This annual immigration quota for each country is prescribed by the Minister of Interior. The quota, nevertheless, may not exceed 100 persons for each country and 50 for stateless immigrants. The colonies of a country or state are considered part of the parent country.

Accompanied by his personal history, an alien may submit an application for immigration at the Thai Embassy or Consulate in his country prior to taking off for Thailand. He may also do so after his arrival and after he has been permitted to stay in Thailand temporarily. A residence certificate is to be issued by the Immigration Division upon approval of the application and relevant documents. Within seven days of receipt of the residence certificate, in addition, the alien must apply for an alien certificate at the local police station.

The residence certificate is of unlimited validity. However, if a holder of a residence certificate leaves Thailand without a notification for a re-entry, his certificate becomes invalid. Despite such notification, if the resident immigrant does not return within one year, his residence permit automatically expires.

WORK PERMITS

An alien wishing to work in Thailand must first obtain a work permit in accordance with the Alien Employment Act of 1978.

The Alien Employment Act

This Act is administered by the Labour Department of the Ministry of Interior. As a general rule, with a few exemptions, natural persons not of Thai nationality are required to obtain work permits prior to commencing their work in Thailand. Aliens should submit applications for work permits to the competent authorities, namely the Director-General or his designees. The following factors are to be taken into account by the authorities in considering such applications:

(a) whether the applicant has residence in Thailand or has been permitted to enter Thailand on a tempoary basis pursuant to the immigration law, but not as a tourist or transitor;
(b) whether such alien is an unqualified or forbidden person according to conditions prescribed by the Minister in the *Government Gazette*.

Occupations closed to aliens

The holder of a work permit may not assume his engagement in all occupations. The Alien Employment Act lists the occupations which may be exclusively carried out by Thai nationals.

Exemptions

The following persons are exempted from obtaining work permits:

(a) member of the diplomatic corps;
(b) members of consular mission;
(c) representatives of member countries and officials of the United Nations Organization and its specialised agencies;
(d) personal servants coming from abroad to work exclusively for persons listed under (a), (b) or (c);
(e) persons who perform duties on mission in Thailand under an agreement between the Government of Thailand and a foreign Government or an international organization;
(f) a person who enters Thailand for the performance of any duty on mission for the benefit of education, culture, arts, sports or such other activities as may be prescribed by a Royal Decree;
(g) a person who is permitted by the Government of Thailand to enter and perform any duty or mission in Thailand.

Special application

An alien entering Thailand temporarily in accordance with the immigration law to conduct any work deemed to be urgent and essential will probably be granted a period of stay not exceeding fifteen days without a work permit. Such alien, however, may engage in his work only after a written notification has been submitted to the Director-General or other officials designated by him. It should be noted that this special treatment is available for all aliens regardless of types of visa. Consequently, a tourist visa holder may take advantage of this application and conduct his work in Thailand for the prescribed period.

Procedure

Normally, an alien should apply for a work permit himself. Alternatively, in practice, a prospective employer may on behalf of the alien apply for such work permit in advance. Issuance of the permit, however, will be withheld until the foreign employee is present in Thailand.

Duration and renewal

A work permit will normally be valid for one year. For a holder of a non-immigrant visa, related work permit will be valid for such period of time as the visa allows him to stay in Thailand. Where definite period of stay is not specified, a work permit granted to an alien who enters Thailand temporarily will be valid for 30 days from the date of issuance.

Prior to the expiry date of a permit, renewal can be made upon a yearly basis. However, renewal of a permit relating to a holder of non-immigrant visa should be in compliance with the renewed or extended visa. In the case of an alien entering Thailand without a fixed period of time, an additional 30 days might be granted.

Use of work permit

The law prohibits a work permit holder to undertake work other than that specified in the permit. Employers are required to notify the Registrar of the Labour Department within fifteen days after the date of employment of aliens. In the same manner, the employers are also required to notify the Registrar concerning the transfer and termination of work. In the latter case, within seven days of such termination, the permit should be returned to the Registrar.

Aliens are not prevented from working in more than one field or for a number of employers. Each work, however, will necessitate a separate work permit.

List of Occupations closed to Aliens under the Alien
Employment Act

(1) Labor
(2) Work in agriculture, animal breeding, forestry or fishery, or farm supervision (excluding specialised work)
(3) Masonry, carpentry or other construction work
(4) Wood carving
(5) Driving of motor vehicles or non-motorised carriers, except piloting international aircraft
(6) Shop attendant
(7) Auctioneering
(8) Supervising, auditing or giving services in accountancy except occasional internal auditing
(9) Gem cutting or polishing
(10) Hair cutting, hair dressing and beautician work
(11) Hand weaving
(12) Mat weaving or fabrication of wares from reed, rattan, kenaf, straw or bamboo pulp
(13) Manual fibrous paper fabrication
(14) Lacquerware fabrication

(15) Thai musical instrument fabrication
(16) Nielloware fabrication
(17) Goldsmith, silversmith, or other precious metal-work
(18) Bronzeware fabrication
(19) Mattress or padded blanket fabrication
(20) Alms bowl fabrication
(21) Manual silk product fabrication
(22) Buddha image fabrication
(23) Knife fabrication
(24) Paper or cloth umbrella fabrication
(25) Shoemaking
(26) Hat making
(27) Brokerage or agency work, except in international business
(28) Civil engineering work involving designing, drawing, calculation, organization, research, planning, testing, construction supervision or advisory work, except work requiring specialised skills
(29) Architectural work involving designing, drawing or estimating, and construction supervision or advisory work.
(30) Dressmaking
(31) Pottery or ceramics
(32) Manual cigarette rolling
(33) Tourist guide or tour organizing agency
(34) Hawking business
(35) Thai character type-setting
(36) Manual silk reeling and weaving
(37) Clerical or secretarial work
(38) Legal or litigation service.

TAXATION

The principal laws governing Thai taxation are the Revenue Code and the relevant Royal Decrees attached thereto.

General income tax liabilities

Under the Revenue Code, there are three classes of tax imposed upon income, namely:
(a) Corporate income tax;
(b) Personal income tax;
(c) Business or Sales tax.

Corporate income tax
This tax is applicable to companies (including foreign corporations and their branches), registered ordinary partnerships, limited partnerships, joint ventures, foundations and associations. Profitable businesses of foreign govern-

ments or their agencies also fall within the scope of this tax. The standard corporate income tax rate is 35 per cent of the net profit. Registered companies listed on the Securities Exchange of Thailand pay a reduced rate of 30 per cent (of the net profit). Income of foundations and associations excluding registration fees, subscription fees from members and donation of money or property are taxed at the rate of ten per cent Companies engaging in the international transportation business assume tax at the rate of three per cent of the gross ticket receipts collected in Thailand for transporting passengers, and/or three per cent of gross freight charges collected for transporting goods from Thailand, instead of a tax on the net profit.

For the purpose of tax computation, corporate entities are required by law to maintain books of accounts and supporting documents. Copies of the balance sheet and profit and loss statement certified by a licensed Thai auditor must be filed annually with the Registrar of Partnerships and Companies within five months after the end of the accounting period, and, in addition, with the Revenue Department within one month after approval by the General Meeting of Shareholders.

The company or partnership must file an income tax return within 150 days from the end of the accounting period. However, corporate income tax is payable in two installments within a year. The first installment must be paid on estimated net profit within 60 days from the last day of the first half of the accounting period (six months) and to be taken as a credit in the calculation of tax at the year-end tax payment. Any accounting period may be selected but not for a period of less than twelve months.

In addition to normal business expenses, depreciation allowances at rates ranging from five to twenty per cent as specified in the relevant Royal Decree are allowed as deduction in computing net profit. Net losses may be carried forward for five consecutive years.

Corporate income tax is applicable to all corporate entities established under Thai laws or those incorporated under foreign laws and are carrying on business in Thailand. Foreign corporations carrying on business in other countries including Thailand are taxed on the proportion of net profit arising from their business in Thailand. The definition of 'carrying on business in Thailand' is very broad and as a result pulls foreign entities into the fullest extent of Thai corporate income tax. Such definition is prescribed in Section 76 *bis* of the Code as follows:

'If a juristic company or partnership incorporated under a foreign law has in Thailand for carrying on its business an employee, a representative or a go-between and thereby derives income or gain in Thailand, such juristic company or partnership shall be deemed to be carrying on business in Thailand, and such employee, representative, or go-between whether a natural or juristic person, shall in so far as the said income or gains are concerned, be deemed to be the agent of the said juristic company or partnership and shall have the duty and liability to file a return and pay tax.'

Personal income tax

Every person, resident or non-resident, who receives assessable income as specified by the Revenue Code assumes personal income tax liability, whether such income is paid in or outside Thailand. A resident of Thailand is an individual who is present in Thailand more than 180 days in any calendar year. Residents may also be subject for the payment of tax on income derived from foreign sources, provided that such income is brought into Thailand.

Standard deductions of expenses allowed by the Code vary from ten per cent to 85 per cent depending upon the category of income but generally the taxpayer may elect to itemize expenses in lieu of taking the standard deduction.

The following annual personal allowances are allowed:

For taxpayer	Baht 13,000.–
For taxpayer's spouse	Baht 13,000.–
For each child (not exceeding 3 children)	Baht 6,000.–
For each child's education (only in Thailand)	Baht 2,000.–
For life insurance premiums	Baht 7,000.–
For interest on housing facilities	Baht 7,000.–
For taxpayer and spouse's contribution to approved provident funds (or actual contribution, if less)	Baht 7,000.–

A joint return may be filed by husband and wife whereby all income is to be attributed to the husband.

The net income after the above-mentioned deductions and allowances is to be taxed at the following rates:

Net income not exceeding:

Baht		40,000	–	7%
40,001	–	90,000	–	10%
90,001	–	150,000	–	15%
150,001	–	220,000	–	20%
220,001	–	300,000	–	25%
300,001	–	400,000	–	30%
400,001	–	550,000	–	35%
550,001	–	750,000	–	40%
750,001	–1,000,000		–	45%
1,000,001	–2,000,000		–	50%
2,000,001 up			–	55%

A personal income tax return for each tax year must be filed within the month of March of the following year.

Business tax

Business tax is a gross receipt tax levied on certain categories of business listed in the Business Tax Schedule of the Revenue Code. An additional surtax of ten per cent of the business tax is imposed as a municipal tax.

Summary of Business Tax Schedule

Category of Businesss	Rate	Taxpayer
(1) Sale of goods	1.5–50.0%	Seller, importer or manufacturer
(2) Rice and saw milling	3.5–4.0%	Operator
(3) Sale of stock	0.10%	Seller
(4) Hire of work	3.0–10.0%	Contractor
(5) Letting of movable property	2.5–3.0%	Lessor
(6) Warehousing	2.5%	Operator
(7) Hotel, restaurant and nightclub	2.0–15.0%	Operator
(8) Transportation	0.5–2.0%	Operator
(9) Pawn-Broker	2.5%	Operator
(10) Brokerage & Agency	5.5%	Broker/Agent
(11) Sale of immovable property	3.5%	Seller
(12) Banking	3.0–15.0%	Operator
(13) Insurance	2.5–3.0%	Insurer
(14) Entertainment	15.0–20.0%	Operator

Business tax is imposed upon any natural or juristic person or group of persons carrying on in Thailand the business listed in the Business Tax Schedule (Traders). A trader is required to file an application for business tax registration within 30 days as from the date of commencing the business. A monthly business tax return must be filed by a trader by the fifteenth day of the following month regardless of whether he has earned receipts during the taxable month.

Retailers are not liable for business tax payment on goods sold, since the business tax will be collected from the manufacturers and/or importers. Normally, business tax will be collected by the Revenue Department. However, in respect of imported goods, the Customs Department is responsible for collecting business tax at the time of importation.

Remittance tax

Remittance of assessable income out of Thailand to foreign companies or partnerships not doing business in Thailand is, after the deduction of the standard allowances ranging from ten to 40 per cent, subject to a withholding tax of 25 per cent. If the assessable income represents dividends paid to foreign shareholders, the rate is reduced to twenty per cent. Interest paid to foreign companies or partnerships engaging in banking, insurance or similar business activities is subject to withholding tax of ten per cent. Taxes withheld must be forwarded to the Revenue Department together with a return within seven days after the end of the month in which remittance is made.

A juristic company or partnership which remits out of Thailand funds representing profit, or which were set aside out of profits, from a business carried on in Thailand must, in addition to corporate income tax, pay twenty per cent tax on the sums remitted. A return must be filed and the tax paid within 7 days from the remittance date.

Income tax liabilities of foreign companies or juristic partnerships

Foreign companies or juristic partnerships carrying on business in Thailand are generally subject to tax in the same manner as a Thai company or juristic partnership. Special conditions apply to foreign companies having agents or representatives in Thailand and to those which do not carry on business in Thailand but derive assessable income from Thailand.

Foreign companies or juristic partnerships carrying on business in Thailand
(a) Foreign companies or juristic partnerships set up under foreign law carrying on business in Thailand must be taxed in accordance with the provision of companies and juristic partnerships income tax.
(b) Foreign companies or juristic partnerships set up under foreign law carrying on business in other countries including Thailand will be taxed on the net profits arising from business carried on in Thailand during any accounting period. The net profit will be calculated in the same manner as for Thai company or juristic partnership. In case of unascertainability, special methods of assessment may be applied.

For companies or juristic partnerships engaging in international transportation in countries including Thailand, the income tax payment is different, due to the difficulty in calculating net profits where the expenses of several branches are allocated between offices. The law therefore imposes a tax on the gross receipts before expenditures deduction as follows:

(i) in the case of carriage of passengers, fares, fees and any other benefit collectable in Thailand will be taxed at the rate of three per cent;
(ii) in the case of carriage of goods, freights, fees and any other benefits collectable in Thailand or abroad will be taxed at the rate of three per cent.

(c) Foreign companies or juristic partnerships having an employee, agent or representative assisting business transactions in Thailand and from which income or benefits are earned, will be deemed to have carried on business in Thailand and will be taxed. If the assistance of such

159

agent, etc., in Thailand results in income or benefits outside Thailand, no tax will be applied.

Foreign companies or juristic partnerships not carrying on business in Thailand

A company or juristic partnership set up under the foreign law which does not carry on business in Thailand will nonetheless be taxed on the following assessable income:

(i) income derived by post; or office of employment e.g. management and agency fees

(ii) income derived from goodwill, copyright and other rights which generally are royalty from patent, computer software, know-how and technical assistance

(iii) interest and dividends

(iv) benefit received from:
(a) hiring properties
(b) breach of a hire-purchase contract
(c) breach of an installment sale contract

(v) income derived from liberal profession, e.g. law, medicine, engineering, architecture and others as prescribed by Royal Decree.

Since such companies or juristic partnerships are not present in Thailand, the law requires a natural person, company, or juristic partnership, ministry, department, organization of government or other juristic persons to withhold tax on such incomes before remitting to the recipient.

International double taxation agreement

In order to promote trade between foreign countries and Thailand, the Government has entered into a number of Double Taxation Agreements with foreign countries in order to avoid the situation where a foreign individual or juristic person doing business in Thailand has to pay income tax on his income in two countries.

Thailand has signed international treaties with different countries to modify income tax laws between the Governments of the contracting countries. These countries are: Austria, Belgium, Canada, Denmark, France, Finland, The Federal Republic of Germany, India, Indonesia, Italy, Japan, South Korea, Malaysia, the Netherlands, Norway, Pakistan, The People's Republic of China, The Philippines, Poland, Singapore, Sweden and the United Kingdom.

It should be noted that international double taxation treaties relieve only income tax but not other taxes such as business tax since these taxes tend to be imposed by local authorities and are subject to frequent changes.

Income tax on the basis of residence or origin
The provisions of the general agreements specify taxation of certain incomes either on the basis of residence or on the basis of origin.

Income tax on a tax credit basis
While the country of source of income is entitled to levy income tax, the country of residence of the taxpayer is also entitled to do so, which will allow credit in respect of the tax paid in the country of source. Most agreements have provisions whereby dividends, interest and royalties payment will be assessed on a tax credit basis.

Tax exemption
The agreements also provide for the country of residence of exempt for tax collected in the country of source.

Privileges under international taxation agreements
International taxation agreements grant the following privileges to any person or juristic person residing in the contracting countries and deriving income in those countries:

(a) Net profit from business: under most agreements, a company of a foreign contracting state carrying out business in Thailand will be taxed on its profit only if it has permanent establishment in Thailand. The term 'permanent establishment' significantly limits the taxing jurisdiction of the Thai Government, since, in normal cases, the company will be taxed regardless of whether or not it carries out business through a permanent establishment in Thailand.

According to most international taxation agreements, 'a permanent establishment' includes:

   (i) a fixed location in which the business of the enterprise is wholly or partly carried on such as a building, office or facilities;
   (ii) having an exclusive agent habitually acting on behalf of, and in the name of the enterprise;
   (iii) cases where certain activities such as construction, installation and assembly are carried out.

(b) Income derived from international transportation: Income received from the international transportation business is exempted from taxation in Thailand. If derived from international shipping, it must be taxed at half the normal tax rate in Thailand. If there is no permanent establishment tax will be exempted.
(c) Interest, dividend and royalty: in general, most agreements provide for reduced rates of tax for income from interest, dividend or royalty payments received in Thailand, according to the details of each particular agreement.

161

ANEK

Tax clearance certificate

Before an alien may leave Thailand, he must first obtain a tax clearance certificate even if no income has been earned.

Departing aliens
The following aliens, whether or not they are liable to tax or duty, must file an application for a tax clearance within fifteen days prior to their departure:

(a) aliens holding Certificate of Residence;
(b) aliens entering Thailand to carry out business in the country regardless of what class of visa they hold, where they receive income (in or out of Thailand) and how many days they have stayed in the country;
(c) aliens entering Thailand on non-immigrant Category 'B' visas to carry out business in Thailand and each time stay more than fourteen days and altogether exceeding 90 days in any calendar year; and
(d) aliens entering Thailand on several occasions, and stay for a total of more than 90 days.

Exemptions
The following aliens are exempted from obtaining a tax clearance certificate:

(a) aliens in transit through Thailand, or who enter and stay in Thailand for not longer than 90 days and have no assessable income. This means those holding transit or tourist visas staying less than 90 days, since such visaholders will be presumed not to have worked. However, if a transit or tourist visaholder does derive income in Thailand, a tax clearance certificate must be obtained regardless of the length of stay;
(b) aliens entering Thailand on non-immigrant Category 'B' visas and each time stay not more than fourteen days and altogether not more than 90 days in any taxable year and derive no income. However, the following aliens are excluded:

(i) movie, radio or television actors, musicians, professional sportsmen or performers of any kind of entertainment;
(ii) where the Revenue Official has evidence that alien has taxable income under the Revenue Code;
(iii) officials or experts of the United Nations Organization or special organizations of the United Nations, who carry out duties in Thailand and who hold UN passports;
(iv) officials of an embassy, consulate general, consulate, diplomats, consular officials and persons who are regarded as diplomats according to agreements and who hold diplomatic passports;

162

(v)   persons not more than fourteen years of age, on the date of departure.

Types of tax clearance certificate
Tax clearance certificates may be classified in two types, as follows:

(a)   A short-term tax clearance certificate: this type is for aliens who want to leave Thailand temporarily for one trip. The certificate is valid for a period of fifteen days from the date of issuance, after which it expires, even if the holder has not departed Thailand within that period.
(b)   A long term tax clearance certificate: this type is for aliens who in connection with their occupation or profession make frequent trips in and out of Thailand in the normal course of business. This certificate can be valid for any period up to one hundred and eighty days from the date of issuance and cannot be extended.

Criteria for granting tax clearance certificate
Where an applicant has recently entered Thailand and is applying for a tax clearance certificate for the first time, or where tax is payable, a revenue official will summon the applicant for inquiry which will be recorded. If the inquiry shows that additional tax is due, the applicant must do the following:

(a)   For short-term tax clearance certificate: if tax is overdue, it must be paid. If this is not possible, the applicant will be required to provide a guarantor or collateral to secure the payment of additional tax. In addition, if the applicant has income tax due after departure, he may be requested to pay the tax in advance or to provide a guarantor or collateral to secure such tax payment before the tax clearance certificate will be granted.
(b)   For long-term tax clearance certificate: if any tax is overdue, or will be due after departure, in addition to demonstrating his need to frequently travel because of his business, the applicant must either show evidence of his property owned in Thailand or provide collateral to secure the tax payment.

EXCHANGE CONTROL

Under the Thai law, any and all matters involving foreign exchange are governed by the Exchange Control Act of 1942 and by Ministerial Regulations and notifications of the Bank of Thailand issued thereunder.

Generally, no person may remit Thai or foreign currency to a non resident outside the country, or hold foreign currency for more than a limited amount, or engage in any transaction involving foreign exchange without exchange control permission from the Bank of Thailand. The grant of these permissions is discretionary. However, in practice, there are few obstacles, should the applicant comply with the applicable procedures.

Import of foreign currency

Normally, there are no restrictions on importing of foreign currencies into Thailand. However, the procedures regarding the importation of foreign currencies must be complied with.

Non-Residents
Foreigners may bring currency and negotiated instruments into Thailand without limit. However, in the event of substantial amounts, they should be registered at the port of entry in order to avoid any problems at the time of departure since a person travelling abroad is permitted to take out of Thailand foreign currencies, foreign bank notes or coins in the amount not exceeding US$2,000 unless he registers the amount of money he brought into the country.

Residents
There are also no restrictions on the amount of foreign currency or negotiable instruments which a resident may bring into Thailand but, within seven days after he enters the country, all such currency and instruments must be sold to a commercial bank.

Remittance of foreign currency

In the event where foreign currency is to be remitted abroad for purposes other than payment of imports, the required EC Form (EC 31) must be filed with the Bank of Thailand together with documentary evidence indicating the nature of the remittance. Moreover, the Bank of Thailand may request other information before allowing the remittance.

Foreign exchange business transactions

Under the Act, in carrying out business activities in connection with foreign exchange, the following should be followed:

(a) a person intending to engage in the business activities in connection with foreign exchange must first obtain an authorization from the Minister of Finance;
(b) the authorized person must comply with the regulations prescribed by the Minister in respect of the buying and selling foreign exchange, a letter of credit and an international money transfer; and
(c) the authorized person must comply with the Ministerial Regulation or order promulgated by the Exchange Control Officer or by the Bank of Thailand.

Receiving foreign exchange as proceeds from exports

Exporters are required to obtain a Certificate of Exportation from an authorized commercial bank in order to clear export goods through Customs. This Certificate may be obtained after submission of documents such as the invoice, sales contract or evidence of sales negotiation, export permit (in case required), a copy of the letter of credit received and other relevant documents.

Export proceeds must be collected and sold to an authorized commercial bank:

- within fifteen days from the date of export if payment is made by a letter of credit;
- within 21 days from the date of export if a sight bill is drawn for collection;
- within fifteen days after the due date of an issuance bill, but not more than 180 days from the date of export;
- within fifteen days from the date of export in cases of other methods of payment.

Foreign investments and loans

Remittance of investment funds into Thailand, whether direct, portfolio or loans is free from any exchange control restrictions. However, the remittance of such investment funds and the returns therefrom requires approval to prove the inflow of respective investment funds. To facilitate the aforementioned procedure, the Exchange Control Officer at the Bank of Thailand has a Special Register in order to be informed about such evidence in advance, so that the application for the remittance can be readily approved.

Investment

Foreign investors may register their investment with the Exchange Control Office directly at the Bank of Thailand or indirectly through the commercial banks.

Applicants intending to register their direct or portfolio investment funds brought into Thailand must submit an 'Investment Funds Registration Form' together with all relevant documents.

In the event where the investor intends to remit funds invested and the returns therefrom, he must submit a required EC Form together with the relevant information and documents. The Exchange Control Official normally grants approval for the following types of remittance:

(a) transfer of profits or dividends after deductions of income or other tax and after appropriation to reserves;
(b) transfer of up to 50% of the estimated net profit for the first six months of the accounting year;
(c) remittance of investment funds upon liquidation of business in which

165

such funds have been invested or upon submission of evidence showing that the remitted funds are no longer required.

Loans

The remittance of international loans into Thailand is free from any restriction. However, to monitor the inflow of foreign loans, the Bank of Thailand requires that the loans are registered with the Exchange Control Official.

In the event where the loans are registered with the Exchange Control Official, the borrowers will be entitled to immediate purchase of foreign exchange to repay the loans at any commercial bank by submitting Form EC 31 together with the relevant documents, since the commercial banks are authorized to approve such application in the name of the Exchange Control Official.

In the event of unregistered loans, prepayment and registered loans without specific repayment dates, the Form EC 31 must be forwarded to the Exchange Control Official for consideration. An approval will be granted if it is shown that the funds originated from abroad.

Payment of imported goods

An importer must obtain approval before making foreign exchange payments for imported goods by submitting a Form EC 21/21 or EC 22/21 (for opening letters of credit) together with relevant documents and information to the Exchange Control Official through an authorized commercial bank. For advance payments of imported goods of not more than US$2,000. – or payment for imported goods by opening letters of credit with an expiry date over nine months, the Exchange Control Official may authorize an authorized commercial bank to approve it.

Transfer of securities, payable instrument and foreign currency

The transfer of share certificates, bonds, promissory notes, and cheques drawn against an account in a foreign country in the foreign currency requires an approval from the Foreign Exchange Official.

LABOR PROTECTION

Under the Thai laws, labor matters are generally governed by the National Executive Council Announcement No. 103 which is commonly referred to as 'The Labor Protection Law'. However, the Labor Relations Act of 1975 superceded NEC No. 103 in respect of labor relations. In addition, there is also the Labor Court and the Labor Court Procedure Act of 1979.

Labor protection law

NEC No. 103 establishes a framework for comprehensive labor regulations in order to protect employees' welfare and by which the employers are compelled to follow. The Minister of Interior has been empowered by this Announcement to issue Ministerial Regulations which are administered by the Labor Department.

Definition of 'employee'
The law defines an 'employee' to cover both permanent employees and temporary employees. 'Permanent employees' mean those whom the employer intends and agrees to employ on a permanent basis and 'temporary employees' mean those whom the employer intends and agrees to employ on an occasional or seasonal basis.

Under the law, temporary employees having worked for 120 days will have the same rights as permanent employees.

Working hours and holidays
The maximum working hours for industrial work are 48 hours per week, for transport work eight hours per day, for hazardous work 42 hours per week or not more than seven hours per day and for commercial work which is not industrial, transport or hazardous work 54 hours per week.

All employees are entitled to a free period of one hour after five consecutive working hours. However, less period may be agreed upon between the employer and employee provided that such period is not less than twenty minutes and in total not less than one hour per day.

A permanent employee is entitled to a minimum of one day's paid holiday per week as well as a minimum of thirteen traditional holidays per year including National Labour Day. Employees who have worked continuously for a period of not less than one year are entitled to a paid annual vacation of not less than six regular working days.

Sick leave and maternity leave
Full-time employees are entitled to paid sick leave not exceeding 30 regular working days per year; however, if an employee is absent for three or more consecutive days, an employer may require a medical certificate to be produced, except in cases of emergency. An employee may be dismissed for absence from work for three consecutive days without reasonable explanation.

Full-time employees who have worked with the employer for not less than 180 days are entitled to a 60-day maternity leave whereby the first 30 days will be with full pay. Those who have worked with the employer for a period less than 180 days are entitled to a 60-day maternity leave without pay.

Severance or termination pay
If the employer dismisses, fires, lays off or does not allow an employee to work for seven consecutive days without cause, the employee shall be entitled to severance pay as follows:

(a)   A permanent employee working for not less than 120 days but not more than one year will be entitled to not less than 30 days severance pay;

(b) A permanent employee working for more than one year but less than three years will be entitled to not less than 30 days severance pay;

(c) A permanent employee working for three years or more will be entitled to not less than 180 days severance pay.

The severance pay will be calculated basing upon the wages at the last effective rate. Permanent employees who, under the terms of their employment were employed for a specific period of time and whose employment is terminated at the end of that time and permanent employees whose employment is terminated during the probationary period are not entitled to severance pay.

For this purpose the probationary period shall not exceed 180 days.

An employer may terminate an employment with any employee without payment of severance on the following grounds:

(a) misconduct or intentionally committing a criminal offence against the employer;

(b) intentionally causing damage to the employer;

(c) violating the working regulations or rules or lawful orders of the employer after written warning has been given by the employer;

(d) abandoning work for three consecutive days or more without justifiable reason;

(e) negligently causing serious damage to the employer;

(f) being imprisoned by a final judgment.

Woman and child labor
Women may not be employed in work of a dangerous or strenuous nature or between midnight and 6 a.m. except in shift work. Unmarried women under eighteen years of age may be employed in a nightclub, dancing school, bar, massage parlour, hotel or such other places as prescribed by the Ministry of Interior.

Children under twelve years of age may not engage in any employment. Children between the ages of twelve and fifteen years may be employed in commercial concerns and any other light work, but not between 10 p.m. and 6 a.m.

Wages and overtime
Males and females must be paid equal wages and overtime for work of the same nature. Payment must be made in Thai currency unless the employee agrees to accept payment by cheque or in foreign currency. Overtime payment is additional to the regular wages and is paid for work done in excess of normal working hours or on weekly and traditional holidays or during annual vacations. Overtime rates differ and range from 1½ times (weekdays) to three times (weekly and traditional holidays) the normal wage. Employees engaged in executive and supervisory work and in certain other kinds of work prescribed by law are not entitled to overtime.

Workmen's compensation
Employees, with certain exceptions, are entitled to certain financial compensation for their injuries, sickness or death whilst engaged in their normal course of employment. Such benefits are guaranteed and in the event of a worker's death, compensation will be paid to the next-of-kin. The amount of compensation will vary according to the extent of the injury sustained.

Welfare and control
The law requires the employer to provide, at his own expense, clean drinking water, lavatories, first-aid and medical facilities and sanitary working conditions. The extent of which these facilities are required to be provided will depend upon the nature of the business and the number of employees involved.

Working rules and documents
Every employer with ten or more permanent employees must establish written rules and regulations regarding working conditions which must be made in Thai and contain the following particulars:

(a) working days, normal working hours and rest period;
(b) holidays and rules governing holidays;
(c) rules on overtime work and work on holidays;
(d) dates and place where wages, overtime payments and overtime payments for work on holidays are paid;
(e) leave of absence and rules governing the same;
(f) discipline and disciplinary measures;
(g) petitioning
(h) termination of employment.

A copy of the rules and regulations must be submitted to the Director-General of the Labor Department within the time specified and must be posted at the place of work.

The Labor Relations Act of 1975

This Act sets out the procedures for presentation of demands, negotiations between the employer and the employee, mediation by the Labor Department Officials and arbitration by a Labor Relations Committee. This Act also provides for the establishment of employers associations and labor unions and prohibits an employer from terminating employment or taking any action which may result in an employee, representative of employees, committee member of a labor union or labor federation being unable to continue working in certain circumstances.

169

The Labor Court and Labor Court Procedure Act of 1979

This Act provides for the establishment of a Central Labor Court in Bangkok and for regional and provincial labor courts.

The Labor Court has jurisdiction over disputes in connection with terms of employment, rights under NEC Announcement No. 103 and the Labor Relations Act and other labor disputes as referred to by the Minister of Interior.

INVESTMENT PROMOTION

As a developing country, Thailand recognized the need for foreign investment and technology, especially from private sectors. Thai laws pertaining to foreign investment, nevertheless, have been developed in a gradual process. The first investment legislation was the Industrial Promotion Act, enacted in 1954. One aim of this Act, *inter alia*, was to encourage the private sector to set up industrial ventures. Following the 1954 Act, several legislations concerning investment promotion were passed during the period 1960–1977.

Presently, the Investment Promotion Act of 1977 repealed and replaced such previous laws. This Act, however, still maintains the basic elements of investment promotion. It also represents the Government's policies toward current economic and social development of the country.

The Investment Promotion Act

The Act provides an outline of activities available for investment promotion. The Board of Investment has been established under this Act in order to process in procedure for approval of promotion. Broadly speaking, the activities which are eligible for promotion by the Board are the following:

(a) activities which are important and beneficial to the economic and social development and security of the country; or

(b) activities which are not available in the country, as not in sufficient quantity, or not produced by a modern process; or

(c) Activities which are economically and technologically appropriate, and have adequate prevention measures against damage to the environment.

Recently, in the extent of the above-mentioned aspects, the board prepared a list of activities which are basically eligible for promotion, and which can be grouped into six categories:

    (i)   Category 1 Agricultural products and commodities
    (ii) Category 2 Minerals, metals and ceramics
  (iii) Category 3 Chemicals and chemical products
  (iv) Category 4 Mechanical and electrical equipment

(v) Category 5 Other products
(vi) Category 6 Services.

In order to determine whether the investment project to which the Board may grant promotion be one which is economically and technologically appropriate, the Board utilizes the following guidelines:

(a) the existing number of producers and production capacity in the King-dom and the size of production capacity to be created under promotion compared with demand estimate;
(b) the prospect that such activity will expand the market for the products or commodities produced or assembled in the Kingdom and will en-courage the production or assembly in the Kingdom;
(c) the quantity and proportion of the resources available in the Kingdom, including the capital, raw or essential materials and labor or other services utilized;
(d) the amount of foreign currency which may be saved or earned for the Kingdom;
(e) the suitability of the production or assembly processes;
(f) other requirements which the board deems necessary and appropriate.

In the administration of investment promotion, the board maintains a policy of giving special consideration to investment projects which:

(a) significantly strengthen the balance of payments position especially through production for export;
(b) support the development of resources in the country;
(c) substantially increase employment;
(d) locate operations in the provinces;
(e) conserve energy or replace imported energy supplies;
(f) establish or develop basic industries which form the bases for further stages of industrial development;
(g) are considered important and necessary by the Government.

Collaterally, the Board of Investment issued the local shareholding require-ments for the exercise of its discretion for granting promotion in respect to joint ventures, as follows:

(a) for an investment project for manufacturing products mainly for domestic distribution, Thai nationals are required to own shares total-ling not less than 51 per cent of the registered capital;
(b) for an investment project in agriculture, animal husbandry, fishery, mineral exploration and mining, or services sector, Thai nationals must hold shares totalling not less than 60 per cent of the registered capital;
(c) for an investment project which exports at least 50 per cent of the output, the foreign investors may hold shares comprising the majority

of the registered capital, and comprising all registered capital if the production is totally for export.

Investment incentives

According to the Act, incentives are available for both local and foreign entities wishing to invest in Thailand in such fields of business as pointed out earlier. The potential investors, however, to avail of incentives, are officially required to register with the Board of Investment.

The incentives can be grouped, for convenience, into three categories:
(a)   tax incentives;
(b)   non-tax incentives;
(c)   additional incentives for investment in the designed investment zones and for investment in production for export.

Tax incentive

Probably the most important incentives affecting enterprises in their investment decisions are financial incentives, especially in the form of tax exemption. Tax incentives provided under the Investment Promotion Act of 1977 can be summarized as follows:

A promoted company may be granted exemption from corporate income tax for a period of three to eight years. Any losses incurred during the tax holiday period can be carried forward and deducted as expenses at any time within five years after the period of the income tax holiday.

Dividends derived from the promoted activities are also excluded from taxable income during the period of the income tax holiday.

A promoted company may be granted exemption or 50 per cent reduction of import duties and business taxes on imported machineries. In case of the purchase of locally manufactured machineries, exemption of business tax is given.

A promoted enterprise is entitled for a one-year period to a reduction of up to 90 per cent of import duties and business taxes on raw and essential materials. The same reduction of business taxes may be given on the purchase of domestic raw material.

Exemption from withholding taxes on goodwill, royalty and copyright for a period of five years in accordance with contracts receiving prior approval from the Board of Investment.

Non-tax incentive

Apart from the basic guarantees that there will be no nationalization and no new state enterprises to compete with promoted activities, non-tax incentives are offered under the Act as follows:

The existing state enterprises will be allowed to monopolize on the sale of products similar to promoted products. There will be no price controls on promoted products except when necessary in which case the prices will be set by the Board of Investment.

The promoted products will always be allowed to be exported.

To maintain the domestic market for promoted products, the government agencies or state enterprises will not be allowed to import similar products with exemption of import duties and busi ness taxes.

To give adequate protection, import duty surcharges, not to exceed 50 per cent of CIF prices, can be imposed upon similar imported products, and if the Board of Investment considers that this measure is inadequate the Ministry of Commerce will issue a ban on importation of such products.

Any tariff structure not compatible to investment promotion policy will be reviewed and revised without delay whenever the Chairman of the Board of Investment deems necessary.

To reduce administrative delay to a minimum, only fifteen days are allowed for various agencies concerned to resolve any legitimate problems or difficulties facing the promoted industries and to submit reports to the Chairman of the Board of Investment. If there should be any controversies the Chairman is empowered to make the final ruling for immediate implementation.

The promoted investors are allowed to remit abroad in foreign currencies:
- investment capital brought into Thailand and dividends or other benefits derived from such capital;
- external loans and interest thereof under contracts receiving prior approval from the Board of Investment; and
- goodwill, royalty or technical fees under obligations in accordance with contracts receiving prior approval from the Board of Investment.

Foreign limited companies registered in Thailand and under promotion are permitted to own land needed for their activities, in excess of limitations permissible under other laws.

Alien skilled workers, experts and their dependents essential to the promoted activities, are allowed to enter and reside in Thailand, in excess of the quotas, and shall receive necessary work permits, as approved by the Board of Investment.

The Board of Investment is empowered to grant entries into Thailand to aliens who have definite plans to explore investment opportunities or to perform other specific functions or tasks contributing to the performance of private investment.

Additional incentive
(a) Investment in the Designed Investment Zones
- reduction of up to 90 per cent of business taxes on sales of products for a period of not more than five years;

- reduction of 50 per cent of corporate income taxes for an additional five years after the normal income tax holiday or from the date of incoming earning for those without normal corporate income tax exemption;
- twice the costs of transportation, electricity and water supply allowed to be deducted from taxable corporate income;
- apart from normal depreciation, up to 25 per cent of the costs of infrastructural facilities installation allowed to be deducted from taxable corporate income at any time within the period of ten years from the date of income earning.

(b) Investment in Production for Export
- exemption of import duties and business taxes on raw materials for that portion used in products exported; also exemption of business taxes on the purchase of domestic raw materials;
- exemption of import duties and business taxes on re-exported items;
- exemption of export duties and business taxes on products of the enterprise;
- deduction from taxable corporate income of an amount equivalent to five per cent of an increase in income derived from export over that of the preceding year, excluding costs of insurance and freight.

INTELLECTUAL PROPERTY

The laws pertaining to Intellectual Property in Thailand consist of The Patent Act of 1979, The Trademark Act of 1931, and the Copyright Act of 1931.

The Patent Act of 1979

'Patent' means a document issued under the provision of law to grant protection for any invention or a design. 'Invention' means any innovation or invention which creates a new product or process, or any improvement of a known product or process. 'Process' means any process art or method of producing, maintaining or improving quality of a product, including the application of such process. 'Design' means any form or composition of lines or colours which gives a special appearance to a product and can serve as a pattern for a product of industry or handicraft.

In principle, a patent shall effectively and fully be protected by law upon registration in Thailand. If the owner of the said property does not apply for patent registration in Thailand, he will be granted protection in limited manners.

Registrable and unregistrable patent
The law provides that a patent may be granted only for an invention in respect of which the following conditions are satisfied (according to Section 6 of The Patent Act):

(a)   the invention is new;
(b)   it involves an inventive step; and
(c)   it is capable of industrial application.

An invention is new if it does not form part of the state of the art. The state of the art also includes one of the following inventions:

(a)   an invention which was widely known or used by others in the country before the date of the application for patent;
(b)   an invention the subject matter of which was described in a document or printed publication, displayed or otherwise disclosed to the public, in Thailand or a foreign country before the date of the application for patent;
(c)   an invention which was patented in Thailand or a foreign country before the date of application for patent;
(d)   an invention for which a patent was applied for in a foreign country more than twelve months before the date of the application for patent and a patent has not been granted for such invention;
(e)   an invention for which a patent was applied for in Thailand, but the applicant had abandoned such application. This provision shall not affect the rights of the joint inventor who did not jointly apply for a patent.

A patent shall not be granted (according to Section 9):

(a)   for food, beverage, pharmaceutical product or pharmaceutical ingredient;
(b)   for any machine particularly made for use in agriculture;
(c)   for any variety of animal or plant or any essentially biological process for the production of animals or plants;
(d)   for a scientific or mathematical rule or theory;
(e)   for a computer program;
(f)   for an invention the exploitation or publication of which would be contrary to public order or morality, public health, or welfare;
(g)   for any invention prescribed in a Royal Decree.

The provision of subsection (g) shall have no effect on an application which is filed before the issuance of such Royal Decree.
   Any patent granted under the prohibits of the law is invalid. The validity of a patent can be challenged by filing a petition to the Court by any person who has an interest in the patent or by the public prosecutor.

Patent for design
The law states that a patent may be granted for a new design for industry including handicraft. The following designs are not new:

(a)   the design which was widely known or used by others in Thailand before the filing of the application for a patent;

(b) the design which was disclosed or described in a document or a printed publication in Thailand or a foreign country before the filing of the application for a patent;

(c) Any design so nearly resembling any of the designs prescribed in a, b or c to be an imitation.

Right to apply

The inventor or designer shall have the right to apply for a patent. The right to apply for a patent may be assigned or transferred by succession. The assignment of the right to apply for a patent must be in writing and shall require the signature of the assignor and the assignee.

An applicant for a patent must be a national of Thailand or a national of a country which allows persons of Thai nationality to apply for patent in that country. Thailand is not a contracting member in International Convention providing international patent protection.

General rules of patent law in respect of employer – employee

Under the Thai Patent Act, where the invention of the employee is created under an employment contract or a contract for performing a certain work, the right to apply for a patent of such work shall belong to the employer or the hirer of the order to do the work, unless otherwise provided in the contract.

The right to apply for a patent shall also belong to the employer in the circumstances where an employment contract does not require the employee to exercise any inventive activity, but the employee has made the invention using any means, data or report that through his employment has been put at his disposal.

Therefore, an assignment agreement is not necessary in the matter. In order to promote inventive activities and to give a fair share to the employee in both circumstances as aforementioned, the employee-inventor shall have the right to remuneration other than his regular salary or payment. The right to remuneration may not be prevented by any contractual provision. A request for remuneration under such circumstances shall be submitted to the Director-General in accordance with the rules and procedures prescribed in the Ministerial Regulations. The Director-General shall have the power to fix such remuneration as he deems fit taking into account the employee's salary, the importance of the invention, benefits derived and expected to be derived from the invention and other circumstances as prescribed by the Ministerial Regulations.

Other than the foregoing, the right to apply for a patent shall belong to the employee who is an inventor. An assignment agreement will be necessary. The assignment of the right to apply for a patent will be acceptable in the Thai law where such assignment is made in writing and signed by both the assignor and the assignee.

Procedures

The application must be filed in the Thai language and under specific form prescribed by the Registrar. Such application will be examined and considered according to the receiving number and the Registrar will notify the applicant of the result of the consideration via registered post. This step normally takes about 3 months, but could be longer depending upon the Registrar's workload. Any amendment required must be made within 90 days from the date of receipt of notification from the Registrar. Any opposition must be raised within 180 days as of the date of publication whereby the applicant shall be required to file a counter-statement within 90 days from the date of receipt of the opposition. Time taken at this stage depends upon the circumstances surrounding the case.

If no objection is raised, the applicant has to file the application for examination within five years from the date of publication and pay the government fee.

It is worth noting that should the application be submitted to the Registrar without a complete set of documents the deadline for filing the additional documents shall be considered by the Registrar on a case to case basis. However, from past experience, the Registrar always allows not exceeding 60 days after the date of filing of the application.

According to the Thai Patent Law, design will be given patent right for seven years, whilst invention patent will be given right for fifteen years, effective from the date of submission of the application. The patent owner must pay the annuity (renewal) fees, starting from the fifth year to the seventh year for design patent and the fifteenth year for invention patent.

Revocation of the patent by the Board of Patent in Thailand
It is worth noting that at any time after the expiration of three years from the grant of a patent, if there is no production, sale or process of production of the patented products without any legitimate reason, any other person may apply to the Director-General for a compulsory license.

If no person applies for a compulsory license after the expiration of six years from the grant of a patent, the Director-General may request the Board of Patent to cancel the patent if it appears:

(a) that there is no production of the patented product or application of the patented process in the country without any legitimate reason; or
(b) that there is no product produced under the patent for sale in any domestic market, or there are some but they are sold at reasonably high prices or do not meet the public demand without a legitimate reason.

However, the order of the Board may be appealed to the Court within thirty days after the receipt of such order. If the patentee fails to do so within the said period, such order shall be final.

Patent infringement
Infringement of an invention or design patent can be easily detected and proved. The proprietor of the said patent or plaintiff may prove to the Court by showing the products which defendant sells or exhibits for sale in the market and explain to the satisfaction of the Court that such products aim

at intentionally or willfully infringing his patented rights. Infringement of a production process, on the other hand, is not so easily detected or proved. In many cases, the process could be differentiated and hence whether or not such process is deemed to be an infringement on plaintiff's patent remains a question. In this connection, proof must be provided to the satisfaction of the Court that an industrial secret has been stolen. Due to this fact, many countries have set forth the burden of proof in the opposite direction, i.e. in the case of production through a patented production process whereby the products are a novelty on the date of application of the patent for such process, the product of another party of the same type would be first assumed to derive from the process which has been patented. The result of this assumption is that the burden of proof falls on the defendant and not on the plaintiff.

The provisions which shall not be deemed an infringement:

(a) any act done by any person, shall not be deemed to constitute an infringement of the patent if it is done before the grant of the patent;
(b) the use of the patented product or application of the patented process particularly for the purposes of studying, researching, experimenting or analyzing;
(c) the manufacure of the patented product or application of the patented process, provided that the manufacturer or the user, in good faith, has manufactured or made serious preparations with a view to such manufacture before the publication of the application;
(d) the reproducing of the patented design particularly for the purpose of studying or researching;
(e) the sale or having in possession for sale of the product which the seller or possesser has acquired in good faith.

Patent application information
(a) Name and address of the applicant;
(b) kind of business of the applicant;
(c) name and address of the inventor or designor;
(d) profession of the inventor or designor;
(e) citizenship of the applicant, inventor and designor;
(f) priority:– the first filing date of patent application;
    – application number;
    – name of the country filing the application.

The Trademark Act of 1931

The Thai Trademark Act BE 2474 became effective in 1931. Thereafter a revised version of the Act was enacted in 1961. Protection is given to the registered trademarks. Applications for registration of trademarks and all matters relating thereto which conform with the requirements of the Trademark Act, Ministerial Regulations and the Rules of Practice of the

Trademark Division of the Ministry of Commerce, must be filed with the Trademark Registrar, Trademark Division.

Trademark definition
According to the Trademark Act, a 'trademark' is defined as including a device, brand, heading, label, ticket, name, signature, word, letter, numeral or any combination thereof, used or proposed to be used upon or in connection with goods of the proprietor of such trademark by virtue of manufacture, selection, certification, dealing with, or offering for sale. In order to be registrable, a mark must fall within the abovementioned definition.

Non-registrable mark
According to the Thai laws, the following cannot be used as a trademark or part of a trademark:

(a) royal or official arms or crests, the royal standards, official and national flags;
(b) royal name and royal monogram;
(c) representations of any of the Kings, Queens, Princes or Princesses of the reigning dynasty;
(d) royal and official seals;
(e) emblems and insignia of the royal orders and decorations;
(f) emblems of the Red Cross, or appellations 'Red Cross' or 'Geneva Cross';
(g) any mark which is contrary to public policy or morality;
(h) a device identical with, or similar to, the representation of a medal, diploma, or certificate awarded at an exhibition held by the Thai Government or by a foreign government or municipal corporation, unless such medal, diploma or certificate has been actually awarded for the goods bearing the representation of it;
(i) representation of a living person without his or her permission, or representation of a dead person without the consent of his or her ascendants, descendants and spouse.

Classification of goods
An applicant for registration of a trademark may apply for registration under one or more classes and for all the goods in one class or for specific goods in that class. However, if the same trademark is intended to be used for goods of different classes, a separate application should be made for each class of goods. The following is the classification of goods prescribed by the Act:
Class 1 Chemical substances used in manufactures, photography or physical research, and anticorrosives.
Class 2 Chemical substances used for agricultural, horticultural, veterinary and sanitary purposes.
Class 3 Chemical substances prepared for use in medicine and pharmacy.

Class 4   Raw or partly prepared, vegetable, animal and mineral substances not included in other classes.

Class 5   Unwrought and partially wrought metals used in manufacture.

Class 6   Machinery of all kinds, and parts of machinery, except agricultural and horticultural machines and their parts included in Class 7.

Class 7   Agricultural and horticultural machinery and parts of such machinery.

Class 8   All scientific instruments and apparatus for useful purposes; instruments and apparatus for teaching.

Class 9   Musical instruments.

Class 10   Horological instruments.

Class 11   Instruments, apparatus and contrivances, not medicated for surgical or curative purposes, in relation of men or animals.

Class 12   Cutlery and edge tools.

Class 13   Metal goods not included in other Classes.

Class 14   Goods of precious metals and jewellery and imitations of such goods and jewellery.

Class 15   Glass.

Class 16   Porcelain and earthenware.

Class 17   Articles manufactured from mineral and other substances for building or decoration.

Class 18   Engineering, architectural and building contrivances.

Class 19   Arms, ammunition and allied stores not included in Class 20.

Class 20   Explosive substances.

Class 21   Naval architectural contrivances and naval equipment not included in other Classes.

Class 22   Vehicles.

Class 23   (a) Cotton yarn.
           (b) Sewing cotton.

Class 24   Cotton piece goods.

Class 25   Cotton goods not included in other Classes.

Class 26   Linen and hemp yarn and thread.

Class 27   Linen and hemp piece goods.

Class 28   Linen and hemp goods not included in other Classes.

Class 29   Jute yarns and tissues, and other articles made of jute not included in other Classes.

Class 30   Silk, spun, thrown and sewing.

Class 31   Silk piece goods.

Class 32   Silk goods not included in other Classes.

Class 33   Yarns of wool, worsted or hair.

Class 34   Cloths and stuffs of wool, worsted or hair.

Class 35   Woolen and worsted and hair goods not included in other Classes.

Class 36   Carpets, floor-cloth and oil-cloth.

Class 37   Leather, skins unwrought and wrought, and articles made of leather not included in other Classes.

Class 38   Articles of clothing.

Class 39   Paper (except paper hangings) stationery and bookbinding.

Class 40   Goods manufactured from india-rubber and guttapercha not included in other Classes.
Class 41   Furniture and upholstery.
Class 42   Substances used as food or as ingredients in food.
Class 43   Fermented liquors and spirits.
Class 44   Mineral and aerated waters, natural and artificial.
Class 45   Tobacco, whether selected or unselected.
Class 46   Seeds for agricultural and horticultural purposes.
Class 47   Candles, common soap, detergents, illuminating, heating or lubricating oils, matches and starch, blue and other preparations for laundry purposes.
Class 48   Perfumery (including toilet articles, preparations for the teeth and hair and perfumed soap).
Class 49   Games of all kinds and sporting articles not included in other Classes.
Class 50   Miscellaneous
  (1)   Goods manufactured from ivory, bone or wood not included in other Classes.
  (2)   Goods manufactured from straw or grass not included in other Classes.
  (3)   Goods manufactured from animal and vegetable substances not included in other Classes.
  (4)   Tobacco pipes.
  (5)   Umbrellas, walking sticks, brushes and combs for the hair.
  (6)   Furniture cream, plate powder.
  (7)   Tarpaulins, tents, rickcloth, rope (jute or hemp) twines.
  (8)   Buttons of all kinds other than of precious metals or imitations thereof.
  (9)   Packing and hose.
  (10) Other goods not included in the foregoing Classes.

Search
It is worth bearing in mind that if a trademark is similar to a registered trademark and such mark is applied for registration, the Registrar will reject application. Therefore, before filing an application, a search at the Thai Register Office should be carried out in order to prevent any obstruction from the Trademark Registrar.

Registration procedure
The application for registration must be made on official forms and in the Thai language under the name of the proprietor of the mark who shall be either a person, persons or juristic person(s). If an application is filed under the name of a juristic person, the applicant may be required to submit the registration certificate (detailed) to the Registrar. The proprietor may file his own application or he may be represented by an agent. However, no application will be accepted unless the proprietor or his agent has a fixed place of business or an address for services in Thailand. A power of attorney

appointing an agent which must be executed by the applicant and notarized by a notary public is required for an agent to apply for registration on behalf of the proprietor. The Registrar will examine and consider the application and notify the applicant of the result via registered post within 90 days. If approval is granted, the Registrar will request a printing block and twenty prints to be submitted. The application will then be published in the Trademarks Journal and after a period of 90 days counting from the date of such publication if no objection is raised, then the trademark will be registered. The Registrar will issue a Registration Certificate for the applicant. Registration will be valid for ten years as of the date of application and should be renewed within three months before its expiration date.

Disclaimer
Where it is found that a trademark contains matter common to trade or otherwise of a non-distinctive character, the Registrar may require the proprietor to disclaim any right to the exclusive use of any part or parts of such trademark or of all or any portion of such matter, to the exclusive use of which the Registrar holds the applicant not to be entitled; or to make such other disclaimer as he thinks necessary for the purpose of defining the proprietor's right under such registration.

Appeal against the Registrar's order
If the Registrar rejects an application, the applicant has the right to appeal within 90 days as of the date of receipt of such order. The appeal must be filed either:
(1)   to the Thai Court; or
(2)   to the Trademark Appeal Committee.

If the appeal is filed with the Trademark Appeal Committee then the order of the said Committee shall be final and the matter cannot be taken to Court. However, if the applicant wishes to appeal the Registrar's order by filing a complaint with the Court of First Instance, the decision of this court can be appealed to the higher courts, i.e. the Court of Appeals and the Supreme Court in accordance with the court procedures.

Opposition
Within a period of 90 days from the date of advertisement in the Trademarks Journal, any person including a person who has not yet registered his trademark in Thailand may give notice of opposition to the Registrar against the registration of the advertised mark on the ground of, i.e. similarity, better title. If the opposition is made after the 90-day period, the opposition must be submitted either to the Trademark Appeal Committee or to the Court.

Cancellation of a registered trademark
A registration may be cancelled by the Registrar, the Trademark Appeal Committee and/or the Court. The Registrar may cancel registration of a

trademark if no application for renewal has been made within a period of three months from the date of expiration. Any interested person can file a complaint either to the Trademark Appeal Committee or to the Court for the withdrawal of a registered trademark. He must show that he has a better title to it than the person registered as the proprietor, or that the trademark has become common to the trade, or that it has been registered contrary to the provision of the Thai Trademark Act. If the interested person shows better title only for some of the goods of the class for which registration has been granted, the Trademark Appeal Committee or the Court will restrict the registration to the goods for which a better title has not been shown.

Associated trademarks
Two or more trademarks of the same description of goods, so closely resembling one another as to be deemed to deceive or cause confusion if used by a person other than the applicant, may if they belong to one and the same person, be registered as associated trademarks.

Assignment
A registered trademark may be assigned with the goodwill of business connected with the use of and symbolized by the mark. Associated trademarks are assignable or transmissible only as a whole and not separately. Neither a transfer of the right to a registered trademark, nor any change affecting the particulars already registered is valid in law unless registration thereof is made.

The Copyright Act of 1978

In 1931, Thailand had the Act for the Protection of Literary and Artistic Works which the protections thereof were similar to the protections of the copyrighted works. Since Thailand became a signatory to the Berlin Act of the Berne Convention in 1908, any foreign copyrighted work started to receive the protection in Thailand since 1931. Copyright in Thailand is now governed by the Copyright Act of 1978 which replaces the Act for the Protection of Literary and Artistic Works and the earlier legislation.

The work which will be protected according to the Copyright Act of 1978 as stated in Section 4 of such Act is a creative work in the form of literary, musical, audio-visual, cinematographic, sound and video broadcasting work, or any other work in the literary, scientific or artistic domain.

Period of protection
Generally speaking, copyright works according to the Thai Act shall subsist for life of the author of the work, i.e. the person who creates the work by his initiative idea, and continue to subsist for another fifty years from the death of the author. However, the following are the different terms of protection:

(a) the Copyright being a pseudonymous or anonymous work or the work created in accordance with the employment or direction or control of the copyright in photographic, audio-visual, cinematographic or sound and videobroadcasting work shall subsist for fifty years from the date of its creation but, if the work is published during the said period, the copyright shall continue to subsist for a period of fifty years from the date of its first publication;

(b) the Copyright in the work of applied art shall subsist for a period of twenty-five years from the date of its creation but, if the work is published during the said period, the copyright shall continue to subsist for a period of 25 years from the date of its first publication.

Copyright owners
The copyright is a personal right of the creator. In general, only a natural person can become the owner of a copyright. However, according to the law a juristic person is entitled to the copyright under the following conditions:

(a) the author shall be entitled to the copyright in the work he has created in the capacity of officer or employee unless it has been agreed otherwise in writing;

(b) the employer shall be entitled to the copyright in the work the author was specifically commissioned to make unless the author and the employer have agreed otherwise;

(c) in case of a work being by its nature an adaptation of the work copyrighted by virtue of the Thai Copyright Act with the consent of the owner of the copyright, the person making such an adaptation shall,, without prejudice to the right of the owner of the copyright in the work of the original author which was adapted, be entitled to the copyright by virtue of the Thai Copyright Act;

(d) in case of a work being by its nature a collection or composition of the works copyrighted by virtue of the Thai Copyright with the consent of the owner of the copyright, the person making such a collection or composition shall without prejudice to the right of the owner of the copyright in the works of the original authors which were collected or composed, be entitled to the copyright by virtue of the Thai Copyright Act.

According to Section 6 of the Act, the author shall be entitled to the copyright in the work he has created under the following conditions:

(a) in the case where the work has not been published, the author must be a Thai national or stay in the Kingdom at all times or most of the time during the creation of the work;

(b) in the case where the work has been published, the first publication must have been effected in the Kingdom or the author must be qualified according to that prescribed in (a) at the time of the first publication. In the case where the author must be a Thai national if he is a juristic person, such juristic person must be incorporated under the law of Thailand.

Publication of work as stated in the Act means a disposition of the duplicated copies of a work, regardless of its form or character, with the consent
of the author, by making duplicated copies available to a reasonable number
of the public having due regards to the nature of the work, but does not
include a performance or display of dramatic, musical or cinematographic
works, lecturing or delivering a speech on literary work, sound and video
broadcasting about any work, exhibition of artistic work and construction of
a work of architecture.

Therefore, the creator requires two conditions:
nationality: the creator must be a Thai national or must reside in Thailand
throughout or for most of the period of time of the creation of the work;
territorial: the publication must have been distributed first in Thailand.

International copyright work

Thailand was already bound by the Berne Convention according to the
Convention for the Protection of Literary and Artistic Works, works origi-
nating in one of the member countries shall be given the same protection in
each of the other member countries. In response to these commitments,
Thailand has a duty to comply with and uphold the conditions as agreed
upon. Therefore, Thailand has provided copyright protection to foreign
created works in the Copyright Act of 1978. In order to receive such
protection in Thailand, the following conditions must be complied with:

(a) work must have copyright under the law of the country of origin
    which must be a member country of the Convention of which Thailand
    is also member;
(b) the copyrighted works must be classified within the Thai categories to
    be accepted for protection;
(c) the country of origin of the work shall be considered to be:
    (i) in the case of unpublished works, the country to which the
         author belongs;
    (ii) in the case of works published simultaneously in more than
         one country in the Convention, the country the laws of which
         grant the shortest term of protection in a country outside the
         Convention and in a country, of the Convention, the latter
         country shall be considered exclusively as the country of
         origin;
(d) if the country of origin of the copyright work has prescribed conditions
    and procedures for copyrights to be granted then such conditions and
    procedures must be complied with;
(e) the law of country of origin must extend a reciprocal protection to the
    copyrighted works of the other member of the Convention; and
(f) Conditions must be complied with the Thai Royal Decree.

There is no requirement for copyright registration under the Thai law.
Therefore, if a work complies with the above-mentioned conditions, it will
be protected as a copyrighted work in Thailand. That is, Thai law gives the

same protection to foreign copyrights as Thai copyrights unless otherwise stated. So the foreign laws must treat likewise Thai copyrights in the host country (principle of national treatment).

It is worth bearing in mind that there is no provision in the Berne Convention or the Thai Copyright Act which specifies what category computer software comes under. Therefore, the matter of computer software will be excluded from the protection in the point of view of the Thai Courts.

Chapter 9

Hong Kong at the Crossroads: the People's Republic of China – Hong Kong Nexus and Its Impact on Business Transactions

Baker & McKenzie
Hong Kong

Introduction

In slightly over 140 years, Hong Kong has evolved from what Sun Yat-sen described as 'a barren rock' into what today is an oasis of capitalist activity. During that period, this small British colony has sat anomalously at the doorstep of China. Recently, the door has opened, and in just over nine years – on 1 July 1997, to be exact – China will resume sovereignty over Hong Kong.

Forecasting the effects that this change in Hong Kong's status will have is not merely an academic exercise. While forecasting is necessarily speculative and somewhat haphazard, it is nonetheless worthwhile to identify the issues involved; the change will not only affect the lives of those in Hong Kong and on the Chinese Mainland, it will also have a dramatic impact on investment and other economic activity in the entire Pacific Basin.

In this article, we focus on issues related to the legal aspects of doing business in Hong Kong and in using Hong Kong as a base for operations in the People's Republic of China (PRC). Business operations in the region are

187

already confronting complex and often confusing legal issues resulting from the interaction of the economies and policies of Hong Kong and the PRC. This is just the beginning of a process which, it is hoped, will ultimately lead to the harmonization of what today are vastly divergent systems. Over the next nine-year transition period, there will necessarily be significant adjustments in the legal framework for doing business in the region. To examine the issues involved, we have first set out in Part I a very brief overview of Hong Kong's history and economic development in order to give some sense of the broader context in which the issues arise. Part II discusses Hong Kong's current governmental and legal structures which regulate businesses operations. Special attention is given to the forms of doing business, taxation and intellectual property. With this as background, Part III turns to the economic and legal nexus between the PRC and Hong Kong and the impact that the growing economic interdependence has on business transactions today and the implications it has for business after 1997.

Overview

FOUNDING OF THE COLONY

Hong Kong is situated off the southeast coast of the Chinese Mainland in the mouth of the Pearl River. It comprises the island of Hong Kong, which was ceded by China to Great Britain in 1841, the district of Kowloon, which, together with Stonecutters Island, was obtained from China in 1860, and a larger area of the Chinese Mainland, called the New Territories, which was leased to Great Britain for 99 years in 1898. The island of Hong Kong, which is the hub of international trade and finance activity in the region, is less than one-tenth the size of the New Territories, having an area of only 32 square miles.

The island lies 76 miles southeast of Guangzhou, the capital of Guangdong Province, and an important commercial center for southern China. Hong Kong is therefore well-situated geographically as a trading center, and its modern history begins with the trading relations between China and the West, which from the end of the seventeenth century through today have been centered around Guangzhou.

It was commercial trading that first established the nexus between China and the West. First by the Portugese in the 16th century who settled at Macau, followed by the Spaniards, Dutch, French and English, all lured by the riches of Cathay. Because the British had already established a strong commercial position in the region through their centers in India, by the eighteenth century the British had a near-monopoly on commerce between China and the West.

In the eighteenth and nineteenth centuries, under the Qing Dynasty Imperial government, trade was tightly controlled. Westerners were allowed to have commercial dealings only with government approved groups of merchants referred to as Hongs. Commerce was strictly regulated through laws and decrees promulgated by the Qing government. These laws and decrees restricted foreign merchants freedom of movement within the country to certain commercial areas within Guangzhou – proto-types of today's Special Economic Zones. In addition, these regulations forbade foreign merchants direct access to the local government leaders, or Mandarins, and to the nineteenth century equivalent of 'end-users'. All communication with them had to take the form of a petition sent through the Hongs, and any reply came by the same channel. (It is interesting to note that the Chinese government's attitude toward foreign merchants has changed very little over the years.)

It was the foreign merchants' dissatisfaction with China's trade restrictions imposed on Guangzhou in the nineteenth century which eventually led to the founding of Hong Kong. The British merchants in Guangzhou believed that the Chinese would never ease the restrictions except by force, and they wanted to abolish the Hongs and have access to all of China. Negotiations between the Chinese Imperial government and the British government were out of the question. This would have assumed equality between the two nations – a concept which the Qing Emperor could not accept.

The opium trade, which the British continued to carry on in defiance of a Chinese government ban, exacerbated the situation. A special Imperial commissioner, Lin Zexu, was appointed to suppress the trade in Canton. In March 1839, he ordered all opium in the possession of foreign merchants to be seized. The British reluctantly complied with the order, withdrew to Macau, and requested military intervention from London. The Opium War began. The objective was commercial: to gain security for the merchants, either by territorial cession or by a commercial treaty with adequate guarantees of access to more ports. Soon, the British occupied Shanghai, and their troops arrived in Nanjing early in August 1842. To save the city, the Chinese accepted the British demands to open up other ports, and hostilities were concluded by the signing of the Treaty of Nanjing. One of the terms of the Treaty provided for the cession in purpetuity of the island of Hong Kong to the British.

Two important elements of Hong Kong's early history shaped its development and continue to play a key role in determining its future. The first of these elements is the significance of trade, the second is that the existence of a British Colony in Hong Kong was the product of what the Chinese perceive as a humiliating war, and an unequal treaty.

HONG KONG'S ECONOMIC DEVELOPMENT

Once established as a British colony, trade developed slowly. However, by 1866, foreign and Chinese communities on the island were flourishing. As the historian G.B. Endacott put it: 'Each [of the two communities] found the other economically useful; economic cooperation for mutual advantage was the essence of [an] unwritten compact.' The growth of the Chinese population increased domestic trade which in turn brought more Chinese from the mainland into the colony. Chinese emigration to various countries of the world stimulated the growth of Hong Kong's entrepot trade based on the need to supply Chinese communities abroad with products from their homeland. By the end of the 19th century, the colony had begun handling a large proportion of China's trade to the rest of the world. In 1890, 55 per cent of China's imports and 37 per cent of her exports passed through Hong Kong. Local industries and manufacturers began to develop, but shipping was the basis of local commerce.

The early twentieth century saw a period of relatively steady economic growth, although the aftermath of World War I brought about economic problems for the colony, with the dislocation of world trade and the decline of Britain's position in international commerce. At the same time, a new China was emerging. Having overthrown the Manchu empire and established a republic, Chinese leaders continued to struggle for unification. A new sense of Chinese nationalism engendered demands for the abrogation of 'unequal' treaties which the Qing Imperial government had entered, including the one which had given birth to Hong Kong. But such demands were interrupted by the Japanese invasion of China in 1937, marking the beginning of World War II. During the war, Hong Kong fell into Japanese hands bringing the territory's development to a halt. At the end of the war, the British resumed control, and industrial growth has been rapid ever since. Textiles, chiefly cotton and woolen-knitted goods and later man-made fibers, dominated the industry. Today, products of every sort, from state-of-the-art electronics and photographic equipment to plastic toys and footware, are part of an export and re-export industry valued at over US$35-billion.

The success of industry is the result of a combination of factors, including relatively low wages, and the intensive use of the most modern equipment run 24 hours a day. From the mid-1950s, the economic boom has continued virtually unbroken. Industrial expansion has been accompanied by a rapidly developing infrastructure: electric and gas companies, telecommunications and transport by sea, land and air, have all kept pace with the ever-increasing demand.

Hong Kong's development also has been fostered by a government policy of minimal interference with the economy. The Hong Kong government has given private capitalist enterprise near free reign to develop. This laissez-faire attitude of government has, in turn, created a business environment which continues to lure investment from around the world. Hong Kong has no foreign exchange controls and no restrictions on the holding of foreign currencies. Investment income can be freely transferred and capital freely repatriated. There are no anti-trust laws, nor are there any restrictions on foreign ownership of property.

Concurrent with the economic development, the political changes in the region have been equally rapid. Problems rooted in the historical fact that Hong Kong had been ceded to the British by what the Chinese considered to be an unequal treaty, had reached a critical turning point. In 1984, Great Britain and the People's Republic of China signed the *Joint Declaration on the Question of Hong Kong,* under which the PRC will resume sovereignty over Hong Kong in 1997. As of that date, Hong Kong will become a Special Administrative Region (SAR) of the PRC, to exist according to the principle, formulated by Senior Chinese Leader, Deng Xiaoping, of 'one country, two systems'. What this means, according to the *Joint Declaration,* is that Hong Kong will be directly under the authority of the Central People's Government in Beijing and shall at the same time enjoy a high degree of autonomy. Annex I of the *Joint Declaration* elaborates what can be expected from the principle of 'one country, two systems'. Most fundamental to this concept is that 'the socialist system and socialist policies shall not be practiced in the Hong Kong SAR and that Hong Kong's previous capitalist system and lifestyle shall remain unchanged for 50 years'.

In order to appreciate the potential impact of the 'one country, two systems' policy on business transactions and investment, it is necessary to first discuss Hong Kong's present governmental structure and legal framework regulating business operations.

Current Government and Legal Framework

GOVERNMENT

The head of Hong Kong's non-elected administration is the Governor, who is appointed by the British Government. The Governor holds office 'during Her Majesty's pleasure', which means he can be dismissed at any time, although the usual tenure is five years. The Governor's authority derives from the Letters Patent, and in theory he must follow instructions from London. In practice, London rarely interferes with Hong Kong's administration.

The Governor is served by two main advisory bodies – the Executive Council and the Legislative Council. The Executive Council is presided over by the Governor and consists of 5 ex-officio members, an additional official member, and 10 other unofficial members appointed by the Governor. The unofficial members are the representatives of the community. The Executive Council advises the Governor on major policy matters, although the ultimate decision on any matter rests with the Governor.

The main functions of the Legislative Council are to enact legislation and to control the expenditure of public funds. As a result of a White Paper issued by the Hong Kong Government in February 1988, the composition of the Legislative Council will be changed slightly this year to include the Governor, three ex-officio members, seven appointed official members, twenty appointed unofficial members, and 26 elected members from functional and geographical constituencies. The appointed official members are generally the heads of major government departments. In the past, industrialists, employers and professional interests have enjoyed far greater representation than employees and other interests among the elected members. In accordance with the White Paper, direct elections will be introduced for the first time in 1991 for ten seats currently filled by indirect elections. Thus, a more representative cross-section of the community may result.

An important sub-group of the government is made up of unofficial members of the Executive and Legislative Councils. Known by its acronym UMELCO, this group acts as a watchdog of the administration, handling public complaints and opinions on a wide range of government activity.

In addition to these formal bodies, the governments of Great Britain and China have established a joint liaison group to promote cooperation between the governments during the transition phase prior to 1997. While the group does not have a direct role in the administration of Hong Kong, its activities and responses are closely watched as a barometer of Hong Kong's transition.

Legal framework

Present system

As a British colony, Hong Kong falls within the common law family of legal systems. There are therefore two main sources of law in Hong Kong, legislation and case law. Legislation falls into basically three categories: parliamentary legislation, prerogative legislation, and local ordinances. Parliamentary legislation refers to that legislation enacted by the British Parliament which can extend to Hong Kong under certain conditions. Either the legislation may expressly provide that it applies to Hong Kong, or it may apply by 'necessary implication'. With the return of Hong Kong to Chinese sovereignty in 1997, such parliamentary legislation will lose it validity, unless the legislation has been integrated into local Hong Kong ordinances.

Prerogative legislation is legislation made by the Crown. It is commonly in the form of an Order-in-Council mad by the Queen with the advice of the Privy Council. Such prerogative legislation is only applicable to Hong Kong if the legislation specifically indicates so. The validity of prerogative legislation in Hong Kong derives from Hong Kong's present status as a British dependent territory, therefore after 1997 such legislation will no longer be valid.

The bulk of legislation in force in Hong Kong is local ordinances made by the Governor with the advice and consent of the Legislative Council. The Governor delegates rule-making powers to government bodies in order to promulgate more detailed regulations to supplement ordinances in force. In theory, however, all local ordinances and regulations can be overridden by Acts of Parliament made in the United Kingdom.

Case law is the other source of law in Hong Kong. By local ordinance, English common law and the rules of equity are in force in Hong Kong insofar as they are applicable to the circumstances of Hong Kong and its inhabitants. This latter proviso has been interpreted by Hong Kong's courts rather strictly to mean that English common law is inapplicable only if its application would cause injustice or oppression. When English law is not regarded as suitable and no other published law exists, the courts may also apply Chinese law and custom, a vague notion of local customary rules extant in Hong Kong in the 1840s.

Hong Kong's judiciary consists of inferior and superior courts with the High Court being the superior court of primary original jurisdiction. The Court of Appeal is the highest court which meets in Hong Kong and for most practical purposes is the final arbiter of Hong Kong law. Certain decisions of the Court of Appeal involving sums in excess of HK$500,000 or issues of great general or public import, may be appealed to the Privy Council in England, although only a few such cases arise each year.

It is remarkable that most legal proceedings in Hong Kong are conducted in English, despite the fact that the native tongue of 98 per cent of the inhabitants is Cantonese. Published law and court opinions are also published only in English. Recently, it has been decided to rectify this anomaly. Existing local ordinances will be translated into Chinese and future legislation will have both English and Chinese texts of equal authenticity. Moreover, the judges who interpret the law are increasingly Chinese rather than British. Indeed, the territory's first Chinese Chief Justice was appointed in March 1988.

Post-1997

Under the Sino-British *Joint Declaration,* all ordinances and legislation adopted locally will continue to remain valid after the establishment of Hong Kong as a Special Administrative Region. However, an important proviso to this is that such existing legislation will not be valid if it is contrary to what is called the Basic Law. The Basic Law is a document currently being drafted by a 59-member committee made up of representatives from both the PRC and Hong Kong. The Law will serve as a 'mini constitution' defining the respective authority of the Beijing government and the Hong Kong SAR government, as well as the rights and obligations of Chinese citizens living in Hong Kong. The Basic Law Drafting Committee met first in Beijing in July 1985. It is expected that the draft will be ready sometime this year, and its formal promulgation by the PRC's National People's Congress is expected to take place in 1990. Apparently to Beijing's chagrin, the British Parliament and the Hong Kong Legislative Council have both expressed intentions to debate the draft's provisions.

Based on the representations contained in the *Joint Declaration,* the Basic Law should contain the following salient assurances:

(a) the Hong Kong SAR government will be composed of local inhabitants. The chief executive, who will nominate principal officials, will be appointed by Beijing after elections or consultations held locally;
(b) the legislature, to whom the executive authorities shall be accountable, shall be constituted by elections;
(c) judicial power, which shall be exercised independently, shall be vested

in the SAR courts, and these courts shall possess the power of final adjudication;

(d) a prosecuting authority shall control criminal prosecutions free from any interference;

(e) the laws previously in force, other than those made in the United Kingdom but including common law and equity, shall be maintained unless they contravene the Basic Law, subject to amendment by the SAR legislature;

(f) the rights and freedoms of inhabitants shall be protected. Every person shall have the right to judicial remedies, confidential legal advice, access to the courts, and representation in the courts by lawyers of his or her choice. Every person shall have the right to challenge the actions of the executive branch of government in the courts;

(g) the social and economic systems in Hong Kong and the lifestyle of inhabitants will remain unchanged;

(h) until 30 June 1997, the government of the United Kingdom will be responsible for the administration of Hong Kong with the object of maintaining and preserving its economic prosperity and social stability.

Hong Kong's existing legal system has been structured to accommodate and encourage various forms of commercial activity. It is still too early to know with any certainty to what extent the legal framework for doing business will contravene the Basic Law. To appreciate the current and potential problems, we must first step back and examine the framework as it exists today.

FORMS AND CHARACTERISTICS OF BUSINESSES

At present, business operations in Hong Kong can be conducted through private or publicly held corporations, general or limited partnerships, sole proprietorships, or trusts.

Corporations

Corporations are governed by both common law and the Companies Ordinance. (In the Companies Ordinance, the term 'corporation' generally refers to corporations incorporated either within or without Hong Kong, whereas the term 'company' generally refers to corporations incorporated in Hong Kong. This distinction in terminology has not been followed in this article.)

(a) Incorporation of a Hong Kong company

To set up a private company in Hong Kong all that is required is at least two subscribers and a memorandum of association. Each subscriber must hold at least one share. A company may have fully or partly paid shares. If shares are partly paid, the shareholder's liability to the company and third parties is limited to the amount unpaid on the shares he holds. If shares are fully paid, a shareholder does not have any further liability.

The majority of companies in Hong Kong are established as companies 'limited by shares'. Under this form, shareholder liability is limited by the amount, if any, unpaid on shares held. A company may also be limited 'by guarantee', – a form frequently employed by social clubs – in which case liability is limited to the amount a shareholder undertakes to contribute to the company in the event of its being wound up. Unlimited companies are also permitted under Hong Kong's Companies Ordinance. As the name implies, under this form of incorporation, there is no limit on the liability of shareholders.

Unlimited companies and companies limited by guarantee are required to register their memoranda of association, as well as their articles of association. (These documents are the equivalent to what other jurisdictions refer to as a 'company charter' and by-laws', respectively.) For companies limited by shares, a statutory form of articles of association applies unless modified by the company on incorporation or at some later time. The articles of association as well as the memorandum of association are public documents, and can be altered only by a special resolution of shareholders passed by not less than three-fourths of the votes case at a general meeting.

(b) Certificate of incorporation
A certificate of incorporation issued by the Registrar of Companies is conclusive evidence that the company has met all registration requirements.

(c) Reservation of a company name
Prior to incorporation, an individual may apply to the Registrar for advice as to whether or not a particular name has been previously reserved or is already being used by an existing company. If accepted by the Registrar, a name may be reserved for a period of three months, and extended for an additional three months. Once reserved, no other party may register the same or similar name. It should be noted that registration of a company name does not afford trade name protection.

Certain words, such as 'royal' and 'imperial', are not permitted to be part of a company name in Hong Kong without the Registrar's special consent.

Generally, companies limited by shares or by guarantee must indicate this fact in their names as, for example, with the customary 'Limited' or 'Ltd.' in English or the Chinese equivalent.

(d) Private companies
A private company under Hong Kong's law is one which is limited to 50 shareholders, and which by its articles of association restricts the right to transfer its shares. In addition, private companies are prohibited from opening invitations to the public to subscribe for any shares or debentures. In Hong Kong, most wholly-owned subsidiaries of foreign entities are formed as private companies. Unlike public companies, private companies are not required to file either a prospectus or a statement in lieu of a prospectus.

(e) Shareholders
As indicated above, company must have at least two shareholders. This requirement is based on registered and not beneficial ownership, therefore

the use of a nominee for one share permits beneficial ownership of a company to remain only with one person, for example, a parent corporation.

There are no restrictions as to the nationality or residence of shareholders. A corporation, however, generally may not be a shareholder of a company which is its holding company.

(f) Registration of 'charges'

Under Hong Kong law, every security interest, referred to as a 'charge', created by a corporation registered in Hong Kong must be filed with the Registrar of Companies within five weeks after the date the charge is created. If it is not registered, the charge is void against a trustee in bankruptcy and any creditor of the corporation. When a charge becomes void, the creditor ceases to be secured or to have any priority of claim over the assets purported to be secured. However, there is no prejudice to any contract or obligation for repayment of the money secured. When a charge becomes void, the money secured thereby immediately becomes payable. The Registrar of Companies keeps a record of all charges and issues a certificate evidencing such registration. These records are open to inspection by any person on payment of a small fee. Once the debt is paid off, the Registrar may order that a memorandum of satisfaction be entered on the record. Every corporation must keep a record of charges in Hong Kong, and this requirement extends to any corporation incorporated outside Hong Kong which has an established place of business within Hong Kong.

(g) Management administration requirements

(i) Registered office

Companies incorporated in Hong Kong must have a registered office located in Hong Kong to which all communications and notices may be addressed. Registered office facilities are available from local service companies.

(ii) Shareholders register

Companies incorporated in Hong Kong must keep a register of shareholders which contains the names, addresses, and occupations of each shareholder. Confidentiality can be maintained through the use of nominees.

(iii) Annual Return to the Companies Registry

Generally, every company incorporated in Hong Kong and having share capital must file an annual return with the Companies Registry. A return is not required in the year of incorporation. The return must include a list of all the company's shareholders and those who have ceased to be shareholders. The annual return must also include the particulars of the directors and secretary of the company, as well as copies of the company's balance sheet, the report of auditors on each balance sheet, and a copy of the directors' company report.

(iv) Meetings and proceedings

196

A company is required to hold an annual shareholders meeting not more than 15 months after the last preceding meeting. The directors must convene an extraordinary meeting on the request of shareholders holding at least one-tenth of the voting shares.

Ordinary resolutions are adopted by a majority of votes cast at shareholders meetings A three-fourths majority of votes cast is required for certain actions, such as amendments to the memorandum of association or the articles of association. Resolutions in writing signed by or on behalf of all persons entitled to receive notice are treated as resolutions passed at the annual meeting.

Every company must maintain a minutes book into which is entered all proceedings of general meetings and directors meetings. The books containing minutes of shareholders meetings must be kept in Hong Kong and are open to inspection by shareholders during business hours.

(v) Accounting

All companies are required to maintain accounting records which must be kept either at the company's registered office or at such place as the directors think appropriate. Directors must annually present shareholders with a profit and loss statement and a balance sheet. Every company is required to appoint an auditor who must report to members of the company on the accounts and the financial statements.

(vi) Directors and managers

Companies are required to have at least two directors. Every company must also have a secretary, who may be one of the directors. The secretary must reside in Hong Kong or, if the secretary is a corporation, which is permitted under the law, it must have a registered office or place of business in Hong Kong. There are no restrictions as to the nationality or residence of directors. Every company must keep a register of the directors and secretary for public inspection in Hong Kong.

Establishing a branch or representative office

Opening a branch of a foreign corporation is a relatively simple process, requiring only registration with the Registrar and the Commissioner of Inland Revenue within one month of the establishment of the place of business. Registration with the Registrar may not even be necessary if the branch is not used to transact business that creates legal obligations in Hong Kong. This is true of a branch office which acts merely as a representative office or liaison office for the foreign corporation, although counsel should be sought to ensure that the scope of activities carried out by the office does not exceed the exemption.

In order to register a branch (other than a representative office), it is necessary to file an application with the Registrar together with the following documents:

(a) a certified copy of the instrument constituting or defining the constitution of the company;
(b) a list of the directors and secretary of the company;
(c) the names and addresses of one or more persons resident in Hong Kong authorized to accept notices and service of process on behalf of the company;
(d) the address of the principal place of business of the company in Hong Kong and the addresses of the principal place of business and the registered office of the company in the place of its incorporation;
(e) a power of attorney authorizing a named person to accept service of process and any notices on behalf of the company;
(f) a certified copy of the company's certificate of incorporation; and
(g) subject to certain exceptions, a certified copy of the latest accounts of the company.

The company is also required to annually register certified copies of its worldwide balance sheets and profit and loss statements as well as directors' and auditors' reports. The annual registration of documents is not required for a company, which, if incorporated under the Companies Ordinance would be a private company or which is considered to have substantially the same characteristics as a private company, and which is not required by the place of its incorporation to publish accounts or to register such documents.

Partnerships

Partnerships in Hong Kong are governed by the Partnership Ordinance. The Ordinance defines a partnership generally as the relationship which exists between persons carrying on a business in common with a view to profit. Excluded from the category of partnerships is the relationship between members of any company or association registered as a joint stock company, or formed or incorporated by or in pursuance of any other ordinance, or any act of Parliament or letters patent or royal charter. The Partnership Ordinance regulates the relationship of partners to third parties with whom they deal, the relationship of partners to one another and the dissolution of the partnership and its consequences. As in the United States, basic principles relating to partnership are derived from the concept of agency.

Limited partnerships

Limited partnerships in Hong Kong are regulated by the Limited Partnership Ordinance. Because corporations may be partners in ordinary partnerships, limited partnerships are seldom used. However, in some circumstances limited partnerships can afford significant tax and other benefits to US and Hong Kong taxpayers. Since corporations are permitted to be limited partners, some US and Hong Kong corporations find this an attractive option for combining limited liability with flow-through profits and losses. (This may be particularly advantageous for Hong Kong companies since consolidated filing of tax returns for group companies is not permitted).

Limited partnerships may not consist of more than twenty persons, one or more of whom are general partners liable for all debts and obligations of the firm. Limited partners contribute capital or property valued at the stated amount and are not liable for debts and obligations of the firm beyond the amount contributed. During the existence of the partnership, a limited partner is not permitted to withdraw any part of his initial contribution. If the initial contribution is drawn out, the limited partner remains liable for the debts and obligations of the firm up to the amount initially contributed.

Every limited partnership must be registered in accordance with the Limited Partnership Ordinance. Failure to do so may result in the entity being deemed a general partnership and every limited partner deemed a general partner. In order for a limited partner to maintain his status as a limited partner, he may not take part in the management of the firm and may not have the power to bind the firm. A limited partner may, however, inspect the books of the firm as well as other documents relating to the partnership business. In addition, a limited partner may consult with the general partners on business matters. If a limited partner takes part in the management, however, he is liable for all debts and obligations of the firm as though he were a general partner.

Limited partnerships in Hong Kong are required to file registration forms, notices of change in the partnership composition, a certificate of registration, notice of a general partner becoming a limited partner, and notice of assignment of shares. Notice must be published on any arrangement or transaction under which any person will cease to be a general partner of a firm and will become a limited partner. Until notice is published, the arrangement or transaction is deemed to be of no effect.

Sole proprietorships

A significant number of local businesses are operated as sole proprietorships in Hong Kong. Businesses operated as such enjoy reduced exposure to Hong Kong profits tax. A business carried on as a sole proprietorship must comply with the Hong Kong business registration requirements discussed below. Of course, operating as a sole proprietorship lacks the advantages of operating as a corporation, such as limited liability and continuity.

Trusts

Subject to statutory amendments, common law rules of equity relating to trusts apply in Hong Kong and trusts are commonly used in setting up businesses.

Business registration

Under the Business Registration Ordinance, every person or corporation (including a branch and representative office) which carries on any business

199

not registered under prior law or which is commencing any new business must register such business with the Commissioner of Internal Revenue. A 'business' is defined as including any form of trade, commerce, partnership, profession, craft or other activities carried out for the purpose of gain, and also includes social clubs.

The business registration requirement is purely related to revenue raising and information provided for the registration is not incorporated into a public register. Information provided under the Registration Ordinance cannot be divulged by officers of the IRD except in the performance of their duties.

Applications for registration must be made within one month after the commencement of any new business and should include the following:

(a) name and address of the branch's registered authorized representative for service of process in Hong Kong;
(b) date of registration under the Companies Ordinance;
(c) particulars of business carried on, such as:–

> (i) names under which business is carried on (this may be different from the name of the foreign corporation);
> (ii) address of principal place of business;
> (iii) addresses of all other places in Hong Kong at which business is carried on;
> (iv) description and nature of business;
> (v) date business commenced.

Business Registration Certificates are valid for a period of twelve months. Changes in the particulars of a business, as well as cessation of business activities must be reported to the Commissioner of IRD. A valid Business Registration Certificate must be displayed at the address of every place of business which has registered. Persons failing to make an application required under this Ordinance are subject to a fine of HK$2,000 (US$260) and to imprisonment for one year.

TAXATION

General overview

Tax in Hong Kong is levied under the Inland Revenue Ordinance (IRO) and its Rules (IRR). The Inland Revenue Department (IRD) is headed by a commissioner who is responsible for administering the IRO.

Employees of the IRD are required to keep confidential all matters relating to the financial affairs of any person that come to their attention in performing their duties. The penalty for a breach of the confidentiality requirement is a fine of HK$50,000 (approximately US$6,400).

Under the taxation scheme, tax is levied only on income (including interest) on profits 'arising in or derived from' Hong Kong, and on property. The key phrase here, as will be seen, is 'arising in or derived from'. Hong Kong is not a signatory to any bilateral tax treaties, although there is provision for limited tax relief on income chargeable in Hong Kong if it is also taxed in a commonwealth country other than the United Kingdom. Since Hong Kong is not a party to any tax treaties, exchange of information provisions included in most treaties do not apply. Hong Kong does not enforce judgments of foreign tax debts. (Issues relating to problems of double taxation are discussed in below.)

Types of taxes

There are four main taxes separately assessed in Hong Kong:

(a) Property tax
Property tax is levied at the current rate of 15.5 per cent of the net assessable value of land and buildings in the territory, with owner-occupied residences being specifically exempted. A corporation carrying on a trade, profession or business in Hong Kong which is liable to profits tax may apply to the Commissioner for an exemption from the property tax. An exemption must be applied for separately for each piece of property. Under this exemption, a corporation is defined as any company which is either incorporated or registered under any enactment or charter in force in Hong Kong or elsewhere, but the definition does not include a cooperative society or trade union.

(b) Salaries tax
After deduction for personal allowances certain expenses incurred for the production of income and holiday warrants, salaries tax is levied on income and pensions arising or derived from Hong Kong from any office or employment for profit. Salaries tax is assessed at progressive rates of three per cent to 25 per cent, but subject to a maximum effective rate of 15.5 per cent.

For the purpose of the salaries tax, income arising in or derived from Hong Kong from any employment includes all income derived from services rendered in Hong Kong, including wages, commissions, gratuities, perquisites, bonuses, leave pay, overseas allowances and tax reimbursement. Income derived from services rendered in connection with employment outside Hong Kong is generally not subject to the tax. (The specific issue of the source rule as applied to income derived in the PRC is discussed below.) In determining whether or not all services are rendered outside Hong Kong, services rendered in Hong Kong during visits not exceeding a total of 60 days in the 'basis period' for the year of assessment are ignored. Where the source of employment is 'fundamentally' in Hong Kong, the IRD will likely take the view that all remuneration for services, wherever rendered, is subject to the salaries tax. If all the employment services are rendered outside Hong Kong, the earnings are excluded from the tax. In determining where the 'fundamental' source of employment is, the Hong

Kong tax authorities consider factors in addition to the place of performance such as:

(i) the place where the employment contract is enforceable;
(ii) the nature and scope of duties and what remuneration is actually paid;
(iii) whether the employee holds an office in or is employed by a Hong Kong company;
(iv) who remunerates the employee and where the cost is ultimately borne;
(v) whether the cost of the employee's remuneration is treated as an expense by a Hong Kong company; and
(vi) whether the duties performed outside Hong Kong are merely incidental to those performed within Hong Kong.

Under a recently enacted amendment to the IRO, income derived from services performed outside of Hong Kong and taxed outside of Hong Kong is excluded from Hong Kong tax. However, directors' fees received from a company managed and controlled in Hong Kong are subject to taxation in Hong Kong, regardless of where services are rendered.

(c) Profits tax
The most significant of the four categories of income tax is the profits tax. Liability for the tax arises when the taxpayer is considered both to be carrying on a trade, profession or business in Hong Kong (so-called representative offices are exempt) and to have assessable profits arising in or derived from Hong Kong from such trade profession or business. (As further explained below, the courts typically apply the so-called 'operations test' to determine source, looking to place of performance, taking of orders, negotiation and signing of contracts.)

Direct sales made by a foreign corporation to Hong Kong will be taxable if the sale is considered to have been effected in Hong Kong through an agent or directly. If the contract is concluded outside Hong Kong – for instance, where an agent merely solicits orders for a foreign corporation which can accept or reject the order – no tax will be assessed.

For the purposes of the profits tax, no distinction is drawn between residents and non-residents. Branches of foreign corporations are liable for profits tax in the same way as local companies. There is no withholding tax on profits and Hong Kong does not impose a tax on capital gains or on dividends.

Losses can be carried forward indefinitely. Moreover, a change in ownership or business of a company does not prejudice the right of the company to carry forward losses to offset against future profits. As a result, there exists a market for companies carrying forward losses, although recent legislation proscribes the acquisition of a company for the sole purpose of tax avoidance.

Expenses incurred in the production of chargeable profits may be deducted, for example, interest payments, bad debts, capital allowances, repairs, registration of patents and trademarks, research and development costs, and contributions to approved retirement schemes. Depreciation allowances for capital expenditures are deducted with respect to qualifying industrial and commercial buildings and plant and machinery. No investment tax credits are available.

The current rate of profits tax is seventeen per cent for limited liability companies and 15.5 per cent for partnerships and sole proprietors.

(d) Interest tax

The interest tax is generally a withholding tax on Hong Kong source interest. The withholding tax, currently 15.5 per cent, is imposed on interest from loans, bills of sale, mortgages, and debentures, arising in or derived from Hong Kong, and on the interest element of annuities payable in Hong Kong. A significant exemption allows that interest from bank deposits in Hong Kong in any currency are *not* subject to the interest tax.

(e) Other taxes

There are no sales, value-added or purchase taxes in Hong Kong except for a first registration tax on motor vehicles. (Although there are reports that a sales tax may be introduced later this year). A stamp duty is applied in limited circumstances such as assignments of immovable property, an estate duty of six to eighteen per cent on the value of property situated in Hong Kong and certain lifetime gifts. There is no general tariff on imported goods. However, liquor, tobacco, methyl alcohol, non-alcohol beverages and concentrates, and cosmetics for local consumption are subject to tax whether they are imported into Hong Kong or manufactured in Hong Kong. Other miscellaneous taxes include a betting duty, air passenger departure tax, embarkation and berthing fees, entertainment tax, and tax on hotel accommodations.

Anti-avoidance legislation

Beginning on 1 March 1986, the Government issued new anti-avoidance provisions designed to counter transactions entered into solely with a view to tax avoidance. At the same time, a system for obtaining advance rulings was implemented to remove some of the uncertainties which might otherwise prevail. The lack of any severe sanctions for violation of these provisions makes it unlikely they will be an effective deterrent to tax avoidance schemes however.

INTELLECTUAL PROPERTY

Patents

Hong Kong does not have an indigenous patent law. Patent protection in Hong Kong can be obtained only if a patent has been obtained or is recognized in the United Kingdom. Hong Kong's Registration of Patents Ordinance provides that any person who has been granted a patent in the UK or holds a European patent may apply to have such a patent registered in Hong Kong. The application must be made within five years of the date of the grant of the British or European patent.

The Registrar of Patents in Hong Kong will issue a certificate of registration to the holder of a UK patent or a patent issued by the European Patent Office which designates the UK as a relevant jurisdiction, provided that the documents filed with the registrar are in order. A certificate of registration confers upon the holder privileges and rights as though the patent had been granted in the United Kingdom with an extension to Hong Kong. Once registered in Hong Kong, the applicant will enjoy patent protection as from the commencement of the term of the UK patent, but no action for infringement can be take in Hong Kong until the certificate of registration has been issued.

To apply for a certificate of registration, it is necessary to file with the Registrar a certified copy of the patent specifications, any drawings related to the patent and a certificate of the Comptroller-General of Patents, Designs and Trademarks in the United Kingdom giving full particulars of the grant of the patent.

The remedies available for patent infringement in Hong Kong are injunctions, seizure or destruction of infringing products and damages for lost profits. Pre-judgment remedial orders can be obtained in cases where there is strong evidence that the infringement is continuing, provided that the plaintiff makes the appropriate application speedily upon learning of the infringement. The application for a pre-judgment remedial order can be made *ex parte* and, in appropriate cases, a so-called *Anton Piller* order can be obtained. This is essentially a species of preliminary injunction, granted on an *ex parte* application which permits the plaintiff's representatives to enter the premises, search for infringing products and documents relating to dealings in infringing products and remove those products and documents into the custody of the plaintiff's solicitors. An order can also be obtained requiring the offender to provide details on affidavit as to his sources and sales of infringing products.

Trademarks

Hong Kong has its own trademark registration system governed by the Trade Mark Ordinance. A registered trademark confers a monopoly in the use of the registered mark in relation to goods to the same description as that described in the certificate of registration. Registration is granted initially for seven years and may be renewed thereafter without limit every fourteen years. Trademarks which denote a surname are usually unregistrable except upon evidence of prior use. Generic terms and those which are purely descriptive are also difficult to register.

No action can be taken under the Trade Marks Ordinance for infringment until the trademark in question has been registered. A trademark is infringed when another party uses an identical or substantially similar mark without consent of the registered proprietor, in connection with the same class of goods under which the trademark is registered.

Proceedings for trademark infringment can be brought either by the registered proprietor of the mark or a 'registered user'. A 'registered user' is a person licensed by the proprietor of the trademark to use the mark in Hong Kong.

The remedies available for trademark infringment are similar to those for patent infringement and interlocutory as well as final injunctions can be obtained. Furthermore, the Trade Descriptions Ordinance grants wide powers to the Customs and Excise Department to enable it to investigate and prosecute the offence of applying a forged trademark to goods. These powers include the power to enter premises, to board vessels and aircraft, to break open containers, and to seize goods. The Customs and Excise Department therefore can search and seize infringing goods coming into or leaving Hong Kong.

Without registering a trademark, it is still possible to obtain an exclusive right to use a mark in Hong Kong through the common law action of 'passing off'. In order to obtain the exclusive right to use an unregistered mark, it is necessary for the plaintiff bringing an action for passing off to prove that he has acquired an exclusive reputation in the mark through use. As a general rule, such use must have occurred in Hong Kong and be connected with a business conducted by the plaintiff in Hong Kong. Even when a foreign trademark is well known in Hong Kong to travelers and to people who are exposed to international media, it can be extremely difficult to persuade a Hong Kong court to give protection if the foreign mark has not been used in connection with a business activity in Hong Kong. In this regard, the rights flowing from registration of a trademark are stronger than common law rights. In other respects, common law rights are wider and more flexible than rights flowing from registration. A mark must be registered in respect of particular goods, and an action for infringement can only be brought if the infringer uses the mark in relation to goods in respect of which it is registered. For example, a mark registered for blutwurst would not be infringed if were used on shoes, although if the use on shoes amounted to a misrepresentation that the shoe business was associated with the blutwurst maker, the blutwurst maker may have a right of action in passing off quite independent of his registered trademark rights.

Since, at present, it is not possible to register service marks in Hong Kong, the availability of common law action for passing off is the only way to protect such marks. The Attorney-General of Hong Kong has indicated that legislation is being drafted which will extend trademark protection to service marks.

Copyright

Copyright law in Hong Kong is principally derived from the British Copyright Act 1956 which was extended to Hong Kong by the Copyright Hong

Kong Order 1972. In addition, Hong Kong has enacted local legislation dealing with copyright. Of particular importance is the Copyright Ordinance which provides for criminal sanctions for infringement. In addition, effective 1 February 1988, amendments to the British Copyright Act which extended copyright protections to computer software went into force in Hong Kong.

As in Britain, copyright in Hong Kong subsists in a work, subject to certain conditions, by virtue of its creation. No registration is required. The protection given by the Copyright Act continues for the life of the author plus 50 years. Foreign copyright works are also protected in Hong Kong by virtue of various Orders-in-Council which extend protection to works created in other countries which are signatories to international copyright conventions. In Hong Kong, copyright protection can be an important supplement to trademark rights. This is especially true where, for example, a logo has not been registered in Hong Kong and it lacks sufficient local reputation to succeed in an action for common law passing off. Under these circumstances copyright remedies might be available against an infringer who copies the logo.

The British copyright law, unlike that of most developed countries, also protects industrial designs. In addition to this, the United Kingdom Designs (Protection) Ordinance also extends the benefit of a United Kingdom design registration to Hong Kong. The scope of registered design protection is limited to the aesthetic elements of the design, that is, the features of the design that appeal to the eye, especially the eyes of the consumer. Protection for designs registered in the United Kingdom is extended automatically to Hong Kong, and there is no re-registration required. A design which clearly falls within the ambit of literary or artistic copyright is not registrable. No legal action can be taken against infringement of a registered design prior to registration, and while registration is not required in Hong Kong, the registration must be published in the Hong Kong Gazette in order to recover damages for infringement. The effect of the registration of the design is that the registered proprietor has an exclusive right to use the design for any purpose related to any sale, lease, or offer for sale of any article to which the registered design has been applied. Protection for registered designs lasts for 15 years.

OTHER REGULATIONS AFFECTING BUSINESS OPERATIONS

Import and export regulations

Hong Kong essentially maintains a free trade policy, adheres to the rules of the General Agreement on Tariffs and Trade ('GATT') and does not impose any import barriers. At the same time, Hong Kong respects restrictions imposed under international agreements. While Hong Kong itself adheres to a free trade policy, its exports have frequently been subject to trade restrictions unilaterally imposed by other countries. Restrictions on exports are most common in the area of textiles. Various agreements negotiated under the Arrangement Regarding International Trade in Textiles (the Multi-Fibre Arrangement) have resulted in the restriction or monitoring of certain exports. Export controls are administered locally to ensure that Hong Kong exporters comply with applicable export restrictions. Quotas are awarded on the basis of past export activities, and unused quotas may be traded.

Removal of Hong Kong's entitlement to preferential tariff treatment under the US's Generalized System of Preferences does not seem to portend significant adverse effects on Hong Kong exports next year when it takes effect, although, obviously, some Hong Kong companies will suffer thereby.

Employment regulations

Employment in Hong Kong is regulated by a variety of local legislation. The most significant is the Employment Ordinance which governs such issues as employment contracts, maternity benefits, holidays, payment of wages, severance payments, sickness, allowances, and protection against anti-union discrimination. The ordinance generally applies to all manual workers irrespective of their earnings, and to non-manual workers earning less than HK$11,500 per month. Hong Kong does not have a legislated minimum wage rate.

From the above description it is evident that Hong Kong's legal framework for business operations is the product of a legal culture firmly rooted in the common law tradition and imbued with what may be termed 'capitalist' virtues of private enterprise and free competition. The essential function of this framework has been to ensure the smooth operation of Hong Kong as a market place. As 1997 approaches, China has become an increasingly more important player in that market place. In the following section we will examine the PRC's growing involvement in Hong Kong's economy, the interfacing of the Hong Kong and PRC legal systems and the implications this has for business in the region.

The Economics Nexus and the Clash of Legal Cultures

THE 'MAINLANDIZATION' OF HONG KONG'S ECONOMY

Because of the geographic proximity, and a shared language and cultural background, Hong Kong and the PRC have always had very close economic and trade ties. Hong Kong has had to rely on imports to survive, having no natural mineral resources and very little arable land. China is Hong Kong's major supplier of agricultural produce. Recurrent water shortages on Hong Kong became so serious that in 1960 an agreement was signed to buy water from the PRC. The agreement has been renewed periodically and today between one-third and one-half of Hong Kong's water comes from across the border.

During the early years of the PRC's history when economic considerations in the PRC played a minor role behind that of politics, Hong Kong's involvement in the PRC's economy was erratic. China did not permit foreign investment, and China-owned businesses in Hong Kong remained relatively static. After Beijing announced its 'open-door' economic policy in 1978, economic activity between Hong Kong and the PRC developed rapidly. Imports and exports, tourism, and investment in China – especially in its Special Economic Zones in Guangdong province – have once again made Hong Kong a major doorway into the PRC. Between 1979 and 1984, the total trade value between Hong Kong and the PRC grew at an average annual rate of 23 per cent. China now figures prominently both as a source and market for re-exports and an estimated 80 per cent of Hong Kong's re-exports are presently China related. Hong Kong industries injected over US$3.5-billion of investment into China between January 1984 and June 1987 alone, making Hong Kong the largest so-called foreign investor in China. Hong Kong has become the largest market for China's exports. Hong Kong has also become the major source of foreign financing for China's modernization efforts. China has raised over US$14.5-Billion from Hong Kong, of which the Hong Kong branch of the Bank of China alone has supplied over 70 per cent. For the many international financial institutions which have shown an increased interest in PRC investments, Hong Kong has been chosen as a base for their PRC operations.

Concurrent with Hong Kong's increased activity in the PRC's economy has been the PRC's involvement in Hong Kong's economy. China is now the third largest foreign investor in Hong Kong's manufacturing sector after the United States and Japan. China accounts for about 18.4 per cent of all overseas investment in Hong Kong manufacturing industries, with HK$2,851-billion (US$365.5-million) committed to the territory. This figure represents only a small portion of China's total investment in the territory in relation to its investments made in banking, shipping and aviation. The Hong Kong Branch of the China International Trade and Investment Corporation (CITIC) has become a key player in Hong Kong's market. In 1986, CITIC acquired 95 per cent of Hong Kong's Ka Wah Bank to save it from collapse. Last year CITIC acquired 12.5 per cent of Hong Kong's major airline, Cathay Pacific, and became a shareholder in the company which will develop a second cross-harbor tunnel between Hong Kong and Kowloon. In addition to CITIC, there are currently about 1,500 (500 of which are officially approved by Beijing) business organizations directly owned by the PRC now operating in Hong Kong. Many of these, like CITIC, function as channels for PRC investment, having invested over US$4 billion in over 300 projects in Hong Kong. The Bank of China Hong Kong Branch (it has over 254 offices in Hong Kong), which is erecting Hong Kong's tallest and second most expensive office building for the new headquarters, its twelve sister banks, three insurance companies, the China Merchants Steam Navigation Company (which owns 200 companies and handles 30 per cent of the PRC cargo), and other transportation companies, and China Resources Holding Company (which handles 50 per cent of all PRC goods sold in Hong Kong) have played a growing role in Hong Kong's commercial sector, diversifying their investments into a variety of industries, such as real estate, public works, department stores and supermarkets.

Another important economic link between Hong Kong and China has been through China's Special Economic Zones. These are Shenzhen, across the border from Hong Kong, Zhuhai, located next to Macao, Shantou, in Guangdong province and Xiamen, in Fujian province. Of these Special Economic Zones, Shenzhen has developed most dramatically due largely to its geographic proximity to Hong Kong. Although the projects established in Shenzhen involve business entities from more than twenty countries, over 90 per cent of those entities have establishments in Hong Kong. Increasingly, Hong Kong and other companies have turned to the Special Economic Zones for processing and assembling work where, unlike Hong Kong, labor is plentiful and cheaper. Indeed, while unemployment in Hong Kong is currently at 1.5 per cent, over one million people in South China now work directly or indirectly for Hong Kong companies.

CONSEQUENCES OF THE HONG KONG-PRC NEXUS

As the two economies interact more and more, so, too, do the two legal systems. This interaction creates a unique and often confusing situation for business operations in the region. We have attempted to identify below a number of the more significant legal issues which businesses are confronting.

(1) Authority for Hong Kong-based PRC operations

Access to international financial and legal services, an efficient, modern infrastructure and the physical comforts which Hong Kong offers create an environment that the Chinese in the PRC recognize is very conducive to conducting international business transactions. This has resulted, as previously mentioned, in a growing number of PRC organizations setting up subsidiary operations in Hong Kong. While these subsidiaries are established in accordance with the Hong Kong Companies Ordinance, their authority to operate ultimately rests with their legitimacy under PRC law. For any PRC entity to legally conduct business abroad, including in Hong Kong, it must have the approval of the PRC Ministry of Foreign Economic Relations and Trade (MOFERT). Furthermore, if the organization's overseas activities include transactions involving foreign currency, this must be approved by the PRC State General Administration of Exchange Control (SGAEC). If a PRC subsidiary is operating without the necessary approvals, transactions which it has entered into become subject to certain legal consequences under PRC law. In the case of transactions involving foreign currency, the Penal Provisions for the Foreign Exchange Control Regulations not only impose heavy fines, but the foreign currency collected without approval can be confiscated by the PRC government and the subsidiary's business operations can be terminated. This can, needless to say, leave a foreign party to the transaction in the lurch.

The practical effect of this is that it is necessary for foreign parties to determine whether the PRC subsidiary is in fact a government-sanctioned operation. With an estimated two-thirds of the PRC companies operating unofficially, this is not an insignificant problem. Moreover, it is no simple matter to ascertain whether or not the subsidiary is operating with the required approvals. Neither MOFERT nor the SGAEC maintains public registries of approved organizations. Foreigners are generally left with no other alternative than to seek some type of informal confirmation through third parties, such as PRC law firms.

(2) Taxation

Another significant problem arising from the interfacing of the economic and legal systems of Hong Kong and the PRC is in the area of taxation, both of individuals and of companies.

(a) Individual income tax
Hong Kong's existing tax structure has attracted many multi-national corporations and smaller businesses to locate their Pacific Basin headquarters in Hong Kong or to use Hong Kong as the base for their operations in the PRC. For various business reasons (not the least significant of which is the high cost of maintaining permanent personnel in China), it has become quite common for companies to send their Hong Kong-based employees into the PRC for extended trips rather than stationing them there permanently. (Hong Kong Chinese employees, unlike their foreign colleagues, do not need visas to visit the PRC.) Until recently, a frequent consequence of this was that Hong Kong-based employees became liable to pay PRC individual income tax and Hong Kong salaries tax on the same compensation. In resolving this issue with other countries, the PRC has entered into bilateral tax treaties. However, because of political considerations, it was generally thought the problem of double taxation with Hong Kong should be solved through other means. The tax authorities in both the PRC and Hong Kong have shown an appreciation of the problem and a willingness to find a solution. Recently promulgated regulations by both PRC and Hong Kong tax authorities have essentially resolved a heretofore troubling issue.

Previously, one approach taken by companies with some success was the use of the so-called 'split' employment contract. Under this approach, an employer and his employee would enter into two employment contracts. One contract would cover only services to be performed in the PRC, and the other contract would cover only services to be performed in Hong Kong. The two contracts would issue from a single company, however, because of Hong Kong tax considerations it was often preferable to use two companies. Thus one company, incorporated in Hong Kong, would contract for the employee's Hong Kong services, and a non-Hong Kong company would contract for the PRC services. The use of a company incorporated outside Hong Kong reduces the possibility of the arrangement being audited by the Hong Kong IRD.

210

In an encouraging sign of cooperation between Beijing and Hong Kong tax authorities, the new tax rules in both jurisdictions now obviate the need for such split employment contracts. In addition to provisionally cutting its individual income tax rates 50 per cent last year, effective 1 January 1988, the PRC now taxes individuals only on income earned in respect of the number of days (over the applicable minimum) actually present in China. The Hong Kong tax authorities will similarly exclude income earned while working in China or elsewhere, provided proof of payment of a tax of substantially the same nature as the salaries tax can be provided.

(b) Corporate tax

Corporations based in Hong Kong with operations in the PRC are also confronted with the problem of double taxation.

In general, income is taxable in Hong Kong only if it has a source in Hong Kong. There is no statutory definition in the tax legislation of the term 'source'. As a result, the IRD looks to case law for guidance in ascertaining the source of income in any particular case. The case law definition of 'source' was, until recently, in conformity with the source principles of other jurisdictions namely, looking to the place where the taxable activity occurred. In the most common situation in Hong Kong, namely that of a trading or reinvoicing company, the tax authorities had taken the view that generally the determinative taxable activity was the execution of a contract. Therefore, if sales contracts were signed outside Hong Kong, no Hong Kong tax was levied because of the exemption for non-Hong Kong source profits. Recently, however, Hong Kong courts have begun to expand the scope of the definition of source. Hong Kong has been moving towards the notion that factors such as management and control of the operations should be considered in determining where profits arise. The IRD has developed the view that the locality of the source of an income should be determined, as we have noted, by the so-called 'operations test', that is, identifying the location of the operations from which the income substantially arises.

The recent Hong Kong case of *Sinolink Overseas Company* has expanded the source rule as it applies to a company's profits derived from its PRC's operations. In the *Sinolink* case, the company, incorporated in Hong Kong, carried on business as an importer and exporter of plywood. The company essentially conducted two businesses, one domestically within Hong Kong, and one in the PRC. The company did not maintain a permanent establishment in the PRC, but rather employed sales personnel to travel into China to solicit prospective customers. Sales contracts for the PRC sales were negotiated and executed within the PRC. Upon signing a sales contract, the company's PRC personnel would return to Hong Kong to fill the order. Orders were placed with overseas suppliers, and the products were directly shipped to the customers in China without passing through Hong Kong. The only participation of the Hong Kong office in the PRC sales was to liaise with European suppliers through correspondence and to handle after-sales paper work. In determining the source of the income from these PRC sales, the judge in *Sinolink* accepted the 'operations test' and concluded that the source was Hong Kong. In reaching this decision the judge looked to four factors to determine where the sales profits arose. The location where the sales contracts were executed, was, of course, one of the four factors considered. The other three were pre-contract preparation and management, the making of the purchase contracts with the suppliers, and post-contract performance and management. The Court upheld the imposition of the Hong Kong profits tax, emphasizing the importance of the location where sales support activities took place, and downgrading the actual selling activity.

The *Sinolink* court insisted that its ruling did not involve any change in the well-settled principles for determining source. The Court professed to be merely applying the 'operations test' to the particular facts of the case, but in doing so, it departed from previous practice by giving relatively less weight to the place of contract and more weight to other elements. Whether or not this change in the relative weight of factors to be considered amounts to a change in the law, *Sinolink* has undoubtedly prompted the IRD to take a more aggresive position. At present, the IRD generally will not seek to tax 'paper' reinvoicing companies (i.e. companies that only possess sales documentation). Apart from these companies, however, the IRD now scrutinizes any claim that sales profits are not taxable when the seller does not have a place of business outside Hong Kong and where the only operations taking place outside Hong Kong are negotiation and execution of sales contracts.

It is possible, however, at least for the present, to structure a company's sales operations in a way which avoids the negative tax consequences of *Sinolink*. This can be done through setting up two companies: one incorporated under Hong Kong law to provide support services in Hong Kong, and the other incorporated in another jurisdiction to act as the seller. The seller then contracts with the service company to provide the reinvoicing and other administrative paperwork needed to complete the sale for a minimal fee. Sales orders and acceptances would take place outside of Hong Kong through exchanging telexes. If structured properly, an arrangement of this type can avoid Hong Kong tax based on the *Sinolink* rationale because the seller itself would have no Hong Kong presence. Moreover, the seller would not have to file tax returns in Hong Kong since it is incorporated outside Hong Kong and has no direct or indirect presence in Hong Kong. Ideally, the seller is incorporated in a jurisdiction which imposes no, or only a minimal tax on sales profits. At present the IRD has accepted this type of arrangement. However, recognizing that this may only be a short-term solution, depending on the agressiveness of the IRD, a number of professional groups are currently lobbying the taxation authorities in an effort to find a long-term solution. Codification in the tax law of a more favorable definition of 'source' could have a lasting effect on business operations beyond 1997. The *Joint Declaration* between Britain and the PRC stipulates that the Hong Kong SAR will maintain an independent taxation system and Hong Kong will not bear any fiscal obligations to the Central Government in Beijing. However, questions remain as to how the Hong Kong SAR will fit into China's individual and corporate tax structure after 1997. If the problem of double taxation can be resolved prior to 1997, and codified in local Hong Kong legislation, this will help guarantee Hong Kong's position as an attractive base for PRC operations.

(3) Dispute resolution

Taking advantage of its geographical location, and a developed network of transportation and communications facilities, the Hong Kong International Arbitration Centre (HKIAC) was established in 1985. The Centre operates under a committee composed of business and professional people of many different nationalities and with a wide range of skills and experience. Several PRC owned institutions, including the Bank of China, made financial donations towards the establishment of the HKIAC. In addition, officials from the China Council for the Promotion of International Trade, which runs an arbitration centre in Shenzhen across the border from Hong Kong, have also begun to support the idea of arbitration in Hong Kong. They have, for example, provided the Hong Kong Centre with the names of Chinese experts who are available to serve as arbitrators under the offices of the HKIAC.

Hong Kong's arbitration law, under which the HKIAC operates, is based upon the same law of the United Kingdom. However, Hong Kong has been able to make significant improvements to that law which gives arbitrators greater independence and support. In our practice, we are seeing with increasing frequency contracts between foreign parties and Chinese in the PRC provide for arbitration of disputes to take place at the HKIAC. An obvious issue is the wisdom of choosing the Centre for arbitration of disputes which arise after 1997. While today there is considerable confidence in the independence and professionalism of the Hong Kong Centre, there is some uncertainty whether such attributes will be preserved after 1997.

Prior to 1997, enforcement of arbitral awards from the HKIAC in the PRC will be facilitated by multilateral convention. The PRC has recently acceded to the 1958 New York Convention on the Recognition and Enforcement of Arbitral Awards, which permits a foreign party to enforce a foreign arbitral judgment in China as long as the judgment originates in a country that is also a member of the Convention. The Convention also currently applies to Hong Kong. As to post-1997 awards, section XI to Annex 1 of the Sino-British *Joint Declaration* states, that 'the Central People's Government shall take the necessary steps to ensure that the Hong Kong SAR shall continue to retain its status in an appropriate capacity in those international organizations of which the PRC is a member and in which Hong Kong participates in one capacity or another'. It appears therefore, that in principle, the New York Convention should still be effective in enforcing Hong Kong arbitral awards in the Mainland after 1997.

Enforcing foreign court judgments, other than arbitral awards, including those from Hong Kong courts, presents a different problem. As of 1986, no foreign judgment had been enforced in China through judicial procedures. (Certain Eastern block judgments have been enforced through diplomatic channels). Under the PRC's 1982 Civil Procedure Law (Chapter XXIII), a PRC court can be entrusted by a foreign court to take certain legal actions, including execution of a final foreign judgment, in accordance with international agreements or principles of comity. A case may be rejected by the PRC court 'if it violates the sovereignty...of the PRC' or violates the basic principles of the laws of the PRC or China's national and social interests. Although these limitations may be analogously compared to so-called public policy objections in other jurisdictions, the absence of any judicial assistance agreement like that recently concluded with France or foreign investment agreements which China has signed with seventeen countries, obscures the enforceability of a Hong Kong judgment in the PRC now or after 1997. The PRC's curious requirement that the foreign court – and not the foreign judgment holder – request the PRC court to enforce the judgment further complicates this issue because Hong Kong, like many other jurisdictions, has no established procedure for a litigant to request the court to assist in enforcing the judgment in a foreign jurisdiction.

(4) Security interests

Somewhat akin to the enforcement of a Hong Kong judgment in neighboring China is the difficulty in enforcing a lien created under Hong Kong law in respect of an asset owned by a joint venture in China. In a recent case in which we were involved, Chinese authorities refused to permit enforcement of a lien in favor of a Hong Kong bank in respect of assets contributed by the Hong Kong party to a PRC joint venture. Although a security agreement evidencing the lien was executed by the Hong Kong party's director, who was simultaneously the vice-chairman of the joint venture company, the Chinese authorities insisted that actual knowledge, evidenced by written notice to the Chinese party as well as to the foreign parties, was required to perfect the Hong Kong Bank's lien. (The PRC does not currently have a public system for filing liens.)

Recent PRC legislation, effective 1 March 1988, prohibits the contribution of assets encumbered by liens. Thus, this thorny issue may not be a serious problem for future transactions. But for assets subject to liens contributed to joint ventures prior to 1 March 1988, lien holders' security interests may not be so secure. Such lien holders would be well-advised, if possible, to issue prompt written notice to the relevant Chinese parties.

(5) Intellectual property issues

The Hong Kong Government is currently considering what changes should be made to the patent system in light of 1997. There is a consensus that continued registration of patents in the UK after 1997 would be inappropriate. No decision has been reached on whether to set up a registration system in Hong Kong. One possibility being considered is to provide a system of registering in Hong Kong patents granted by an established patent office elsewhere.

More and more companies marketing their products in Chinese-speaking markets are recognizing the importance of selecting a Chinese trademark. A particular problem arises when selecting a Chinese trademark for a product which will be marketed on both the Hong Kong and PRC markets. The official national language of the PRC is Putonghua (Mandarin), a language based on the northern dialects of China. In Hong Kong and neighboring Guangdong province, the native dialect is Cantonese. A person who knows only Cantonese cannot understand a person who speaks only Putonghua, and vice-versa. The characters in which Chinese is written generally carry the same meaning in all dialects. However, because the characters are pronounced differently from one dialect to another, a problem can arise with trademarks. A trademark which has a pleasant sound in Putonghua may sound unpleasant in Cantonese. For example, the mark CHILLO for water coolers, could be transliterated in Putonghua using the character Qi Lou ('7th Floor'). In Hong Kong this sound has the colloquial meaning of 'Lunatic'. There is no problem when a Hong Kong-Cantonese speaker sees the characters for the mark (which are pronounced in Hong Kong as Chut Lo), but when a CHILLO salesman in Hong Kong uses the Putonghua pronunciation to introduce himself, people become wary. The problem can also arise in radio advertising and television audio without the character visuals.

Another problem in the area of trademarks is the form of the Chinese characters chosen. Chinese in Hong Kong use the traditional, more complicated forms of characters. In the PRC, however, a system of simplified characters is used. In the PRC, trademarks in traditional characters are accepted for registration, however, some people regard them as 'old fashioned', while others considered them elegant or 'high class'. There may be instances where it is preferable to choose traditional characters instead of the simplified version for a PRC trademark, perhaps to suggest a degree of sophistication or a link with the past. On the other hand, some traditional characters are so different from the simplified form that they may not be recognized or understood by people who have been taught only the simplified form. In Hong Kong simplified characters are generally acceptable for trademark registration, although to date most Chinese trademarks in Hong Kong are written in traditional characters. Some of the products made in the PRC and sold in Hong Kong bear simplifed character marks, and most Hong Kong people seeing a product marked in simplified characters would tend to associate it with the PRC.

It is desirable to choose a single Chinese trademark which can be used in both Hong Kong and the PRC, however, great care must be taken in the choice of the mark to ensure that it is compatible with both dialects.

As we have seen, both Hong Kong and the PRC have developed very comprehensive legislation dealing with trademarks. However, the criteria for registrability, and more importantly the mechanisms for dealing with counterfeiting and infringement are quite different in the two jurisdictions. A recent case involving registration of a well-known trademark of a multi-national corporation in the PRC provides an instructive precedent for the interplay between Hong Kong and PRC law. In that case, an Australian shell company had misappropriated the multinational's mark and registered in the PRC under China's first to file rule. Since China did not then recognize a bad faith argument (new regulations now seem to), the multinational could only argue that the Paris Convention protected well-known marks. The problem, however, was that the mark should be well-known in the signatory's country, that is, in China. Despite nearly world-wide recognition of the multinational's mark, it was not well-known in China. But it was well-known in Hong Kong. The PRC trademarks authorities apparently placed considerable, if not determinative, weight on this factor, and ruled in favor of the multinational corporation.

Unfortunately the economic cooperation between Hong Kong and the PRC has not extended to other illegitimate commercial endeavors. Counterfeiting operations which have found it more difficult to operate in Hong Kong recently – where counterfeiting can be stopped swiftly with injunctions and seizures of counterfeit goods – have frequently moved their operations across the border into China where detection of the schemes may not be as quick, or where means of stopping the infringement may not be as accessible.

The area of copyright protection presents an area of greater uncertainty than trademarks. As previously noted, it is by virtue of various Orders-in-Council that the British Copyright Act 1956 extends to Hong Kong protecting works created in Hong Kong as well as foreign copyright works. Unless the copyright law is codified in Hong Kong's local legislation, the copyright protection currently available will become a nullity after 1997. On the PRC side, no copyright law has yet been promulgated nor has the PRC acceded to the Universal Copyright Convention or the Berne Convention. Without the PRC or Hong Kong being members of an international convention, Hong Kong and PRC works cannot be guaranteed protection in foreign countries and foreign works would have no protection in Hong Kong or the PRC. However, the PRC is currently drafting a copyright law, which is expected to be promulgated within the next few years. If they follow the same course as with their patent law, then it can be expected that their application for membership in one or both of the international conventions is not far off. It will be interesting to see to what extent the PRC copyright law is compatible with Hong Kong's present system of protection as this may give some indication of how the PRC will handle other differences and conflicts between PRC and Hong Kong law.

Reconciling the Hong Kong and PRC systems of intellectual property protection and methods of dealing with infringement presents a formidable problem which the authorities on both sides, not to mention foreign investors, have a strong economic incentive to resolve.

(6) Other issues

Other legal and economic issues will surely arise as the PRC and Hong Kong systems converge and global economic relations become more interdependent.

One such legal issue that already has been a subject of debate in Hong Kong is the question of who will have the power to interpret the Basic Law. As noted, the Joint Declaration provides that Hong Kong's legal system will remain intact and its independent judiciary will be permitted to continue. According to newspaper reports, the latest version of the first draft of the Basic Law provides that the power of interpretation of the Basic Law shall be vested in the Standing Committee of the National People's Congress. Lawyers in Hong Kong are concerned that delegation of this power to Beijing will conflict with the Joint Declaration's assurance that 'except for foreign and defence affairs, which are the responsibilities of the Central People's Government, the Hong Kong Special Administrative Region shall be vested with executive, legislative and independent judicial power, including that of final adjudication'. Many Hong Kong lawyers have voiced concern not only of the prospect of a legislative body interpreting the law but also that the Chinese legislature, its view colored by the PRC socialist system, will interpret the Basic law in a way wholly inappropriate to the markedly different conditions existing in Hong Kong.

Trade issues are also a current subject of discussion. Recently, actions were taken by both the United Kingdom and the PRC to ensure that Hong Kong will continue as an independent member of GATT after 1997. The PRC is also applying for membership in GATT but whether membership will be granted is uncertain. If the PRC does succeed in becoming a member, China would, in theory, have two votes in GATT after 1997. In such a case, the anomalous possibility of China and Hong Kong voting on different sides of trade issues exists. If the PRC's bid to join GATT fails, China may use Hong Kong to provide a back-door entry into members' markets. At this stage, of course, it is impossible to predict what will happen.

Changing world conditions and particularly trade relations with the West also portend change in Hong Kong. The Hong Kong Government faces increasing pressure from the United States to uncouple the Hong Kong dollar from its official peg to the US dollar. The United States insists that the currency is undervalued and should be allowed to rise with the currencies of Hong Kong's other Asian neighbors, Taiwan, Korea and Singapore, which have appreciated considerably over the past two years. A Hong Kong dollar unleashed from the currently sinking US dollar could have a significant impact on Hong Kong-produced exports.

Conclusion

The Hong Kong-PRC nexus has created a wealth of opportunities for business. As 1997 approaches, the opportunities increase, but so do the risks and uncertainties. The growing linkages between the two economies and the concurrent interactions of the two legal systems is evolving daily into a unique, sometimes confusing business evironment. Because the continued stability of that environment is in the interests of all, we are likely to see greater effort at harmonization of the two systems. Different areas of the law are more likely to be harmonized than others and those areas dealing with international trade are likely to be the principle focus of any harmonization effort. The symbiotic relationship which has developed between the PRC and Hong Kong suggests a future for Hong Kong where the economic status quo is largely preserved and there is some convergence of two disparate legal systems.

Chapter 10

The Forms of Foreign Investment in the People's Republic of China

by Owen D. Nee

Coudert Brothers
Hong Kong

Introduction

The possibility that foreign business concerns could participate in China's economic growth through direct and indirect equity investments was first rumored in the press during 1978. By the end of 1986, just eight years later, more than 7,500 Chinese-foreign equity and contractual joint ventures had been approved by the Chinese government. Of this number 3,233 were equity joint ventures with investment totalling US$4.7-billion, 40 were offshore oil exploration, development and exploitation contracts with total committed investment of approximately US$2.5-billion, and 4,274 contractual joint ventures with a total planned investment of approximately US$9.7-billion. Additionally China had authorized 120 wholly-owned foreign enterprises to commence operation in China. By any standards, such figures represent remarkable success in attracting foreign investment, particularly when one remembers that China had existed in self-reliant isolation for over thirty years and began the process with untrained officials and a legal system inimical to private ownership of the means of production.

At the end of 1986, however, China's foreign investment program was stalled. The investment figures for 1986 were lower than those of 1985, the first reversal for China's investment program since the beginning of the Open Door Policy. On 11 October 1986, the State Council adopted a series of preferential measures in order to encourage more foreign investment with the stated goal of achieving an annual foreign investment commitment of US$20-billion each year during the remaining four years of the Seventh Five-Year Plan. Whether such a goal can be achieved depends on the resolution of a number of problems discussed in this paper.

This paper describes the forms of investment used by the People's Republic of China to attract foreign investment and provides an analysis of the problems encountered by foreign companies in implementing such investments over the last seven years.

The Legal Framework

The legal system of the People's Republic existing prior to 1979 did not provide any basis for foreign investment in China. The 1978 Constitution described the country as 'a socialist state of the dictatorship of the proletariat' with two kinds of ownership of the means of production: 'socialist ownership by the whole people and socialist collective ownership by the working people'. Nor did the system of state-owned enterprises through which China implemented its ownership by the whole people of the means of production offer a vehicle into which foreign investment could be readily assimilated. State-owned enterprises logically could not be half-owned by the whole people and half-owned by The Coca-Cola Company.

Clearly some new category of enterprise had to be created as the legal conduit through which foreign investment could flow. *The Law of the People's Republic of China on Joint Ventures Using Chinese and Foreign Investment,* which was adopted on 1 July 1979, created such an entity called most frequently a 'joint venture', but probably more accurately translated as a 'joint investment enterprise' – thereby recognizing the distinct and separate status of this new form of enterprise from the conventional state-owned enterprise.

The problem was larger than just a new name for a new type of enterprise, however, and quickly the Chinese realized that a host of new laws and regulations would be required in order to properly define the position of this new type of enterprise within the Chinese economic system. Tax laws, accounting rules, foreign exchange regulations, labor regulations and rules on registration would all be necessary. Such a massive legislative program could only take place gradually, however, if major errors were to be avoided.

In order to make progress with its foreign investment program and to avoid waiting on the slow process of drafting a complete legislative framework, the Chinese authorities adopted three strategems: (1) adopting new laws and regulations in a piecemeal fashion, correcting prior mistakes as they went along; (2) trying out new proposed laws and regulations through internal

guidelines that are made available to Chinese officials responsible for conducting foreign investment negotiations or on occasion adopting such new
laws only in Special Economic Zones as an experiment; and (3) adopting
model forms or precedents of foreign investment contracts that can be used
with minor variations for many different investments. Although only the
published laws and regulations are legally binding, the bureaucratic structure of the Chinese government and the foreign investment approval process
are such that the unpublished guidelines and model forms are treated by
Chinese negotiators with much the same regard as law.

Thus, the practical framework for the regulation of foreign investment in
China is much more than just China's published laws and regulations. It also
includes future laws that are expected to be published (but appear only as
'internal' guidelines available to Chinese negotiators); it includes legislation
from the Special Economic Zones, which is applied by 'analogy'; and it
includes model contract forms that have been drafted or approved in prior
transactions by the controlling ministry or government agency. A textual
analysis of only China's published laws and regulations therefore would lead
one to believe that there is both more uncertainty and greater flexibility
within the system than in fact exists once one reaches the negotiating table.

THE BIFURCATION OF THE CHINESE LEGAL SYSTEM

The difficulty of understanding China's laws governing foreign investment is
complicated by the fact that China has two separate legal systems, rather
than one. In most countries that seek to encourage foreign investment, there
is a set of regulations that sets forth the procedures under which a foreign
company can apply to invest in the host country. Such legislation may grant
incentives or impose terms restricting the form and types of investments that
are permitted. But once approval is obtained, the foreign investor and the
company he establishes are regulated by the general laws of the host country, such as the corporations law, foreign exchange control law, tax laws and
laws related to labor relations. In other words, the foreign investment
enterprise established after approval of the foreign investment application is
governed by the same laws as those applicable to domestic enterprises.

In China, the situation is quite different. First, China's foreign investment
laws not only establish the procedures and conditions under which foreign
investment is permitted, they also stipulate the form of the enterprise
created and have special laws to regulate foreign exchange, tax, labor
matters and a large number of other issues that would normally be governed
by the general laws of the host country. Therefore, in analysing any legal
question in China related to foreign investment, the first inquiry is always to
determine whether there is a law or regulation on the subject that specifically relates to foreign investment enterprises. Since such laws are specifically
designed for foreign investment enterprises, Chinese partners to joint ventures are generally not familiar with such rules and are of little help in
providing information.

221

Second, if there is no specific law in China stipulating how a foreign investment enterprise is supposed to handle a particular legal problem, the domestic laws in China relating to domestic enterprises are applied. Joint ventures or cooperative enterprises in China are Chinese legal persons and therefore are subject to Chinese laws of general application. For example, when a joint venture contracts with a foreign company for the supply of goods, that supply contract will be governed by China's *Foreign Economic Contracts Law,* which is similar to generally accepted international contract law principles. However, when the same joint venture contracts with a Chinese enterprise, that domestic contract will be governed by the *Economic Contracts Law* of China, which is a law drafted to regulate contractual dealings between two state-owned enterprises.

The differences between the two laws are substantial. Under the *Foreign Economic Contracts Law,* if there is a breach of contract, the defaulting party should pay damages to the non-defaulting party so that the non-defaulting party receives the benefit of the original bargain. Under the *Economic Contracts Law,* however, if the default is caused by a change in the State Plan, such as an order to the Chinese enterprise to supply its goods to some other enterprise than the joint venture, then no damages can be paid and the contract must be amended or cancelled. If the default is not due to change in the State Plan, but simple non-performance, then the non-defaulting party has the right to insist upon contract performance and the courts may order the defaulting party to perform. In addition to specific performance of the contract, the penalties stated in the contract for non-performance must also be paid.

Foreign investment enterprises are therefore subject to two separate sets of legislation, the first of which is designed to approximate the legal relationships found in Western free-market economies and the second of which has been formulated to regulate contracts used as a method to implement socialist State Planning. In general, the rules related to the formation of a joint venture and its internal operations are of the first category, but once the joint venture is in production or operation, its contractual relations are governed by the second system.

It is therefore extremely important for foreign investors to look past the set of laws that relate solely to foreign investment projects and examine the domestic regulations affecting their industry.

Forms of Investment

This section describes the principal forms of investment that China has developed during the past eight years to absorb foreign investment and technical expertise. The description of the forms will differentiate between what is required by the published laws of the People's Republic of China and the broader framework applied by Chinese negotiators in the negotiating process.

There are three forms of investment enterprises in China: equity joint ventures, cooperative joint ventures and wholly-foreign owned enterprises. Each is discussed below.

EQUITY JOINT VENTURES

The equity joint venture in China has the most complete set of published laws and regulations regarding its creation and operation. The Joint Venture Law of 1 July 1979 sets forth the general principles governing the establishment and operation of joint venture enterprises and served as necessary enabling legislation legitimizing the numerous joint venture contract negotiations already in progress at the time of its promulgation. The Joint Venture Law's provisions deal with approval procedures, capital structure, management, profit distributions, labor relations and dispute settlement, among other important issues. The JV Implementing Regulations take the fifteen articles of the Joint Venture Law and expand on them in great detail while correcting some errors in prior legislation.

In all, there are approximately 270 pages of published statute law and regulations relating to equity joint ventures. Scholarly commentators have generally found the published laws and regulations to be unobjectionable and some have gone as far as to publicly applaud the draftsmen's efforts. Yet no one who has completed an equity joint venture in China would claim that it was an easy process, no matter how much law there is. Examining some of the important issues encountered by investors attempting to complete equity joint ventures in China will make this clear.

(1) Organization and status

Documents required
The Joint Venture Law provides that joint ventures formed pursuant to its provisions should take the form of a limited liability company to exist for a stated duration to be agreed upon in the contract. Joint ventures are created by the parties agreeing upon the text of a joint venture contract and articles of association, which are submitted to the Ministry of Foreign Economic Relations and Trade ('MOFERT') or, within the monetary limits set by the State Council, submitted to the appropriate local examination and approval authority authorized by MOFERT for approval. If the contract is approved, MOFERT issues a certificate of approval. Once approved, the joint venture company must register with the local bureau of the Administration of Industry of Commerce in order to receive its business license. The date of the business license is the official commencement of the corporate life of the company.

The JV Implementing Regulations specify certain matters which must be covered in the joint venture contract. In addition to such standard matters as the names of the parties, their addresses, the name of the joint venture company, and its address, the JV Implementing Regulations require that the contract contain provisions describing the purpose of the venture, its scope and scale of production, the total amount of investment, registered capital, the method of contributing capital, the composition of the board of directors, the responsibilities and powers of the management staff, the main production equipment and technology to be utilized by the venture, the means of purchasing raw materials and selling finished products, the ratio of domestic and export sales, principles for finance, accounting and auditing of the venture, matters concerning labor, the duration of the venture and the procedure for its termination and liquidation, liabilities for breach of contract and the method for settling disputes.

Similarly, the JV Implementing Regulations contain a laundry list of matters which must be dealt with in the articles of association. While several of these matters repeat what appears in the joint venture contract, repetition is required by the law.

Fortunately, the task of negotiating a joint venture contract and articles has been simplified by the issuance of a model form of joint venture and articles by the Foreign Investment Bureau under MOFERT. While these forms leave much to be desired, they do establish a framework for the negotiations and address all of the matters which are required to be included in the contract and articles.

It is important to note that the principal document which creates a joint venture is the joint venture contract and not the joint venture 'agreement'. The JV Implementing Regulations contemplate that the parties may enter into a joint venture agreement on some of the main principles and provisions of the joint venture before taking the final step of negotiating the definitive joint venture contract. Only the contract and not the agreement is binding and only the contract can receive a MOFERT approval that permits the registration of a joint venture company.

While not required by the law, it is quite common in industrial joint ventures to also have as attachments to the contract, a technology transfer agreement, trademark license agreement and distribution agreements.

Limited liability company

The entity created once the joint venture contract and articles are negotiated and approved is a limited liability company. Article 4 of the Joint Venture Law and Article 19 of the JV Implementing Regulations make clear that the company is to be a limited liability company and the parties are only liable up to the amount of capital for which they subscribe. The limitation on liability applies to third parties that deal with the joint venture corporation. The limitation does not apply to the legal liability of the investing parties between themselves arising out of the obligations and duties set forth in the joint venture contract. It is typical for a joint venture contract to require that an investing party, which defaults in the performance of one of the obligations set forth in the joint venture contract, be responsible for all economic losses caused by the breach of contract. While the *Foreign Economic Contracts Law* establishes some limits for such liability, joint venture contracts normally contain rather broad obligations applicable to the foreign investor relating to the transfer of technology, training of management personnel, arranging finance for the venture or exporting its products. Such obligations are too frequently assumed by the foreign investor during the negotiation process without a full appreciation of the potential liability that could subsequently be assessed in favor of the Chinese investor if the business failure of the venture can be attributed in whole or in part to the foreign investor's inadequate performance of these obligations.

Shareholders
A rather unusual fact about Chinese joint ventures is that there is no role for the shareholders in the management of the venture. There are no annual shareholder meetings or any requirement that any matter be referred to the shareholders for decision. Instead, the members of the board of directors who are appointed directly by the parties to the venture are supposed to represent both the interests of the company and the interests of the shareholder that appointed them.

Investment certificates
Yet another unusual feature of the entity created by the joint venture contract and articles of association is that Chinese joint venture companies do not issue stock certificates as evidence of the ownership of corporate capital. Instead, a Chinese venture is supposed to issue an 'investment certificate' once the investment provided for in the joint venture contract has been injected. The investment certificates, which are only issued once a Chinese accountant has issued a report verifying that the contributions have in fact been made, lists the name of the joint venture, the date of establishment of the venture, the names of the partners, the investment contributed and the date of contribution, and the date of issuance of the investment certificate. The JV Implementing Regulations establish pre-emptive rights in regard to transfers of investment certificates and require the consent of the other party for any transfer of an interest in the venture.

As with other aspects of equity joint venture law, the Special Economic Zones are experimenting with a more flexible attitude toward corporate capital. At the end of 1986, the Guangdong Provincial government adopted regulations permitting joint ventures in the Special Economic Zones to issue stock to the public.

Scope of operations
The scope of a joint venture company is also much narrower than the modern notion of a Western corporation, which by its constituent documents is most often formed for any lawful business purpose. A joint venture enterprise in China is formed for a single specific purpose, such as constructing and operating a hotel on a specific site or operating a specific service enterprise. Moreover, a general purpose such as to cooperate in a particular industry has not been acceptable on the grounds that the approving authorities were unable to determine the feasibility of the venture, unless a specific project was proposed and evaluated. Certain powers such as the right to trade in Chinese goods in order to balance foreign exchange income and

expenses (as permitted by the foreign exchange balancing regulations) must be specifically mentioned as being within the scope of the venture's operations, if the right to trade is to be exercised. Any amendment or expansion of the venture's original purpose has to be approved by the same formalities as the original joint venture documentation.

(2) Capital contributions

The Joint Venture Law specifically allows the contribution of capital either in cash or in kind. In kind capital contributions may include industrial property rights and know-how, land usage rights, buildings, plant, equipment, and trademarks. Capital contributions in kind (other than the site) are to be appraised and agreed upon values specified in the joint venture contract and articles of association. In accordance with the ratio of the mutually agreed contribution values, the parties are to share in venture's profits, risks and losses.

Required amounts of equity
China did not have any published regulations specifying the amount of equity capital that the joint venture must receive from the investing partners until 1987; but starting in September of 1985 there was an internal directive from the State Council to the national and local authorities that approve joint ventures to the effect that they should not approve any joint venture unless it met a specified debt/equity test. The directive used the concept of 'total investment', which is the total cost of all expenses to be incurred by the venture prior to achieving production at the rate stipulated in the feasibility study for normal production.

In March of 1987, the internal directive was converted into a law known as the *Provisional Regulations Concerning the Ratio of Registered Capital to Total Investment of Joint Ventures Using Chinese and Foreign Investment*. These regulations provide that the registered capital of equity joint ventures must be as follows:

Total Investment	Equity	Permitted debt
$ 1 to $3,000,000	70%	30%
$ 3,000,000 to $ 4,200,000	$2,100,000	Remainder
$ 4,200,000 to $10,000,000	50%	50%
$10,000,000 to $12,500,000	$5,000,000	Remainder
$12,500,000 to $30,000,000	40%	60%

226

Total Investment	Equity	Permitted debt
$30,000,000 to $36,000,000	$12,000,000	Remainder
$36,000,000 and above	33%	67%

If a joint venture encounters special circumstances and cannot comply with these regulations, a joint approval of MOFERT and the State Administration of Industry and Commerce is required. Although joint ventures that have previously been approved by MOFERT are not subject to these regulations, if such a joint venture decides to increase its capital, then at the time of the increase, it should come into conformity with the regulations.

Appraisal of capital contribution values
Appraising capital contributions has proved quite difficult, partially due to inherent problems of the Chinese economic system and partly due to internal guidelines applied by the Chinese to the process. If the Chinese contribution consists of existing plant and equipment, the carried cost for such property in the state-owned enterprise method of accounting is seemingly difficult to compute, either due to an absence of accurate records or a reluctance to produce those records for foreign inspection. Moreover, since the assets of state-owned enterprises are owned by the government, there is not a free market mechanism for their transfer and market values cannot therefore be determined.

Pursuant to the JV Implementing Regulations it is now possible to appoint a third party agreed upon by the joint venture parties to evaluate the respective worth of each party's contribution.

The most common procedure to date for determining equity shares has been to proceed exactly in the reverse of the method contemplated by the Joint Venture Law and JV Implementing Regulations. Rather than appraising assets to be contributed and setting the investment ratio based on a comparison of values, the first letter of intent or memorandum of agreement states what the investment ratio should be and the types of assets the parties will contribute. For example, the memorandum of agreement may call for a fifty-fifty joint venture with the foreign side contributing all necessary foreign equipment, technology and raw materials and with the Chinese side contributing a building and an initial inventory of locally available raw materials. After exhaustive negotiations to determine the true market value of the foreign supplied capital items, during which the Chinese act more as buyers than joint investors, the Chinese contribution is then mutually assumed to be of an equal value in order to maintain the fifty-fifty investment ratio. Occasionally this method leads to out-of-date plant and equipment in China being appraised at values higher than new plant and equipment in the investor's own country.

227

Value of land contributions

One of the most common forms of Chinese investment to a joint venture is the contribution of the land use rights for the property on which the joint venture is to be constructed. Land may either be contributed as part of the Chinese partner's capital contribution or rented by the joint venture for a stipulated annual land use fee. Most major cities and provinces in China now have local regulations that specify what the standard land use fees for their area are. There is normally one rate for industrial projects, another for hotels and apartment buildings and a third for service enterprises. The local regulations normally contain rules as to when land use fees must be paid, whether there is an exemption for the period of construction and how frequently the land use fee can be increased by the local authorities. As part of its attempt to improve the investment environment in China, the *Provisions of the State Council of the People's Republic of China Regarding the Encouragement of Foreign Investment* adopted in October of 1986 provide that technologically advanced or export enterprises should pay a maximum land use fee of RMB 20 Yuan per square meter per year.

If the land is to be contributed by the Chinese partner to the venture, the Chinese partner will arrange for the local land bureau to issue to the joint venture a 'Land Use Certificate' which entitles the venture to use the land for the full term of the joint venture. The Chinese partner does not in fact prepay the land use fee for the full term of the venture, but instead is liable to pay such fee out of its share of the profits derived from the joint venture each year.

When the Chinese side contributes the land usage rights to the joint venture, the value of the contribution is determined by multiplying the area of the site times the length of the joint venture times the standard land use fee for the particular area.

When evaluating joint venture projects, it is important to review not only the land use fee applicable in the area, but also whether a site development fee is imposed. Many municipal governments have had to invest heavily in the improvement of the local infrastructure in order to attract foreign investment and the municipalities like to recover this investment by charging a site development fee, which is separate from the land use fee, to new joint venture projects within their area.

Shanghai, Shenzhen, and Hainan Island have each adopted regulations in the past six months which permit joint ventures and other foreign investment enterprises, as well as domestic enterprises, to purchase land. In the case of Shanghai, the maximum period of ownership is 70 years from the date of the grant of the land. It is likely that in the future, the purchase of land by means of the grant system will become increasingly common in China.

Technology contributions

The contribution of technology as part of the foreign investor's capital contribution is specifically permitted by the Joint Venture Law and JV Implementing Regulations. It is seldom, however, that foreign investors

228

elect to contribute their technology. There are several reasons for this reluctance. First, the experience of foreign investors has been that determining the capital contribution value of their technology is quite difficult. Second, a capital contribution of technology normally means that there is no contract governing the transfer of the technology and consequently there is no document establishing the restrictions on the use of the technology or the protection of its confidentiality. Finally, the contribution of technology means that the foreign investor cannot receive a royalty on the continuing use of the technology by the venture, since the ownership of the technology has been contributed.

For these reasons, it is more common for foreign investors to increase their cash contribution to the joint venture and enter into a separate technology transfer contract with the venture. Frequently, a portion of the foreign exchange capital contribution of the foreign investor is repaid to the investor by the joint venture to cover the initial upfront fee for the transfer of the technical documentation. Using this method permits the foreign investor to both increase its capital contribution without increasing its risk and also allow the licensor to receive a running royalty for the continuing use of the technology.

Timing of capital contributions
Because many joint ventures were approved by MOFERT and, for various reasons, the foreign investor never made its promised capital contribution, MOFERT adopted strict regulations on the timing of capital contributions that came into effect on 1 January 1988. The *Several Provisions on Capital Contribution by Parties to Joint Ventures Using Chinese and Foreign Investment* require that capital contributions of cash or industrial property rights must be owned by the contributing party, which technically prohibits use of a special purpose corporation to make an investment in China, and the property contributed must not be subject to any form of encumbrance. If the joint venture contract provides that the capital will be contributed at one time, then the date of contribution must be within six months of the issuance of the business license. If installment contributions are contemplated, then fifteen per cent of the capital must be contributed within three months of the issuance of the business license and there should be a clear schedule as to when the remainder of the capital will be injected.

The regulations also provide that if the capital is not contributed for three months after the due date, then after the delinquent party is warned about its default, the defaulting party's contributions to date will be transferred to the performing party and the defaulting party held liable for damages. It is difficult to imagine that these provisions will ever be applied to the Chinese party to a joint venture, but it is clear that they will be strictly enforced against the foreign investor.

The regulations make no allowances for conditions placed on the duty to invest. It is frequently the case that the foreign investor will condition its obligation to contribute to the registered capital on the receipt of a ruling that the venture is entitled to certain benefits, such as being qualified as a technologically advanced enterprise or a tax ruling as to the period of tax exemption and reduction. It is also frequently the case that investment capital is conditioned upon receiving the commitment of a bank or banks to make a loan to the joint venture for the remaining portion of its total investment above the amount of registered capital. Such conditions do not appear to be legitimate grounds for delaying the contribution of capital to the venture. The regulations therefore greatly increase the risks inherent in agreeing to invest in China.

(3) Management and control

Board of Directors
The Joint Venture Law and Implementing Regulations provide that the venture is to be managed by a Board of Directors, which is to be the 'highest authority' of the venture, the composition of which is to be specified in the joint venture contract and articles of association.

The chairman must be Chinese, and the vice chairman a foreign appointed director. The Board of Directors is empowered, according to the Joint Venture Law, to discuss and determine all important issues concerning the joint venture. While the amendment of the articles of association, decisions on termination of the venture, approvals for the increase or assignment of registered capital and the merger of the joint venture must be approved by the board unanimously, the articles of association may state the required number of votes necessary to approve any other matter.

The Joint Venture Law makes clear that the chairman of the Board of Directors is the legal representative of the venture. While the law does not specify the powers and duties of this position, two powers should be noted. First, as legal representative, the chairman must sign all legal documents related to the commencement and prosecution or defense of legal proceedings with third parties. Second, the chairman convenes and presides over meetings of the Board of Directors.

Operating officers
Beneath the Board of Directors, offices for a general manager, deputy general manager, chief engineer, chief accountant and auditor are referred to in the Joint Venture Law, together with the stipulation that the positions of the general manager and deputy general manager shall be assumed by the separate parties to the venture, just as each party appoints its own designated number of directors. Article 39 of the JV Implementing Regulations confers considerable power on the general manager: 'The general manager shall, within the scope empowered him by the board, represent the joint venture in outside dealings, have the right to appoint and dismiss his subordinates, and exercise other responsibilities and rights as authorized by the board...'.

What is not apparent in the Joint Venture Law or Implementing Regulations is the system of managers and deputy managers, that appears in most joint venture contracts. The management staff is effectively doubled by the

Chinese requirement that each foreign appointed manager have a deputy to act as his counterpart. Since the vast majority of the labor force will be Chinese, the system of deputies makes some sense in order to ensure that the foreign manager's instructions are carried out by the workforce. The deputy system, however, has two faults: first, the Chinese negotiators would prefer to have each manager's decision arrived at jointly by the manager and his deputy; second, the deputy system undermines the authority of the appointed managers, since the workforce naturally tends to follow the instructions of the Chinese deputy who will remain in China long after the expatriate advisor has returned home.

The deputy system is symptomatic of another problem experienced in operating joint ventures. Too many decisions are made by committees, where equal numbers of foreign investor appointees and Chinese appointees are supposed to negotiate and decide all issues. While such a management principle corresponds to the much valued Chinese maxim of equality in all things, it is a difficult and time consuming way to run a business. This is particularly true since Chinese members of lower level committees do not wish to make decisions unless they have instructions from their own higher level authorities, which in turn means many decisions of a routine nature are referred to the Board of Directors.

The Board of Directors is not the easiest place to make management decisions either. First, the Board is supposed to act for the benefit of the investing parties and on a basis of equality when handling any important matter, rather than deciding issues in the interest of the venture itself. Second, on the Chinese side, there is always a great reluctance to go further than or act on any matter outside the basic premises of the joint venture contract, since Chinese bureaucrats know that under their system such actions should first be approved in writing by higher authorities. Board meetings can last several days, even when the parties thought the agenda and issues were settled before the commencement of the meeting. Issues that are not decided are held over until the next meeting and those that are decided are memorialized in the vaguest of language in order to avoid problems with higher authorities that monitor the venture's progress.

In one recent well-publicized case, an American-Chinese joint venture adopted at a Board of Directors meeting a proposal to substantially expand the scope of business of the venture. When the joint venture ran into problems, there was much embarrassment arising from the fact that the Board resolution had not been submitted to MOFERT for approval. Thus, Board meetings should be handled with a reasonable degree of care for the legal niceties.

(4) Operational matters

The Joint Venture Law contains only a few scant provisions relating to operational matters. The venture's production and operation plans are to be filed with the authorities concerned and implemented through economic contracts. The venture is supposed to give priority to the sourcing of its raw materials and supplies in China, though it may also purchase such items from abroad if it has the foreign exchange to do so.

State planning
The paucity of direction provided by the Joint Venture Law in regard to the planning for construction, purchasing of local raw materials and the sale of finished products has to a large extent been remedied by the JV Implementing Regulations. These regulations solve the interesting problem of how a profit motivated company, the joint venture, fits into a state-planned economy like China's. The system used is that for state planning purposes, the joint venture becomes a unit of the 'department in charge', which is the parent organization of the Chinese partner. For example, pursuant to Article 54 of the JV Implementing Regulations, the joint venture must develop a capital construction plan in accordance with the plans contained in the feasibility study. This plan, once developed, becomes part of the 'department in charge's' capital construction plan. The significance of this provision is that in China construction materials are allocated in accordance with the state plan. By including the joint venture's construction plan within that of the Chinese parent unit, the joint venture's needs for construction materials becomes a small part of the overall national planning process.

Similarly, the joint venture must work out annual production and operating plans. After being approved by the joint venture's board of directors, this plan is incorporated in the annual plan of the department in charge and in turn becomes part of the overall national planning process. Materials which are under planned distribution in China are allocated to the joint venture through the incorporation of its annual production plan into that of the department in charge. Other necessary materials that are not under the national distribution plan can be purchased at state enterprise prices from the commercial departments, from the local markets or, if necessary, imported.

Once finished products are produced, the joint venture sells its products in much the same way. If the product is one that is under planned distribution in China, the output is incorporated in the annual plan of the department in charge and the national economic planning mechanism handles its distribution by allocating the output to specified end-users or for sale by the Ministry of Commerce through the national distribution system. If the product is one that is handled exclusively by the commercial departments in China, the commercial department will enter into annual purchase contracts with the joint venture to purchase its output. Output that is either not under planned distribution or handled by the commercial department, or output in excess of the planned amounts, can be sold by the joint venture itself through its own sales efforts. This latter method of sale is used in more than 90 per cent of all joint ventures.

Local raw materials
In purchasing goods of Chinese origin, the joint venture is under certain constraints. Gold, silver, platinum, petroleum, coal, and timber used by the

venture in the production of export products are priced at international market levels (rather than the lower Chinese prices) and paid for in foreign currency or Renminbi. More troublesome is that when the joint venture needs materials that China presently exports, it must negotiate a price based on the international market price and pay foreign currency for the purchase. Because balancing the foreign exchange account is frequently difficult, the added burden of paying for such commodities in foreign exchange frequently is a hardship to the foreign investor. The Chinese authorities justify this result by pointing out that if the joint venture had not purchased the product, it would have been exported anyway so it is only fair that the price be paid in foreign exchange. Other than the above, by law (but not always in practice) joint ventures are supposed to pay the same prices as state-owned enterprises for their raw materials.

(5) Labor

The Joint Venture Law states that the employment and dismissal of workers should be provided for in the joint venture contract in accordance with law. Regulations on labor management, however, extensively amplify and correct the Joint Venture Law by mandating the use of a labor contract and the formation of a joint venture trade union, stipulating minimum wages to be paid and procedures for hiring and firing workers. The first of these regulations were adopted in 1980: *Regulations on Labor Management in Joint Ventures Using Chinese and Foreign Investment*. Subsequently, additional rules were found to be necessary and in January of 1984, China issued *Provisions for the Implementation of the Regulations on Labor Management in Joint Ventures Using Chinese and Foreign Investment*. Local governments have entered the movement to 'clarify' labor laws for joint ventures and in March of 1986, the Beijing Municipal government issued *Supplementary Rules of Beijing Municipality for the Implementation of 'Regulations on Labor Management in Joint Ventures Using Chinese and Foreign Investment'*.

Though there are certainly problems with these regulations, the most constant source of frustration related to labor matters is the internal guideline to the effect that Chinese counterparts must receive the same basic pay as expatriate staff on the basis of equality. This guideline is memorialized in the Beijing *Supplementary Rules* as the 'principle of equal ability and contribution, equal remuneration'. No rational means for avoiding this requirement has been discovered to date other than hard bargaining at the negotiating table, during which the foreign investor is put in the embarrassing position of having to argue that the senior Chinese staff – that is, the same people with whom he is negotiating – are worth less than the expatriates to be imported.

Joint ventures are also supposed to maintain a bonus and welfare fund for workers and staff members out of the after tax profits and before distributing net profits to the investing partners. This fund, together with the Chinese negotiating preference that bonus payments should be based on the profitability of the enterprise and go equally to the workers, cause consternation with investors interested in promoting worker productivity. Such a system does avoid the problem of worker envy of higher paid fellow workers, which seems the justification for the equal bonus system.

Labor costs

While the take-home pay of workers is low by international standards, the various additional costs imposed by labor regulations can drive the price up so that Chinese workers are no less expensive than those of competing Asian countries. Based on the Beijing *Supplementary Rules* and assuming that a worker in a state enterprise in the same industry has take-home pay of RMB 120 Yuan per month, the following chart lists some of the more common additional labor charges and their costs to joint ventures:

Cost Item	Percent of Standard	Renminbi	US Dollar (¥3.70 = US$1.00)
Basic wages	120–150% of state enterprise worker's wage	¥180.00	$48.65
Medical fees	7.5% of Basic Wage	13.50	3.65
Old-age support fund	20% of Basic Wage	36.00	9.73
Education fund	1.5% of Basic Wage	2.70	0.73
Government subsidies for housing, food, health, eduction	n.a.	70.00	18.92
Labor Union Funds	2.0%	3.60	0.97
Total:		¥305.80	$82.65

As with many other aspects of investing in China, the new *Encouragement of Foreign Investment Regulations* of October have helped to alleviate the problem of excessive labor costs by allowing the local governments to legislate uniform rates for pension plans, unemployment insurance and housing subsidies and that such rates will apply equally to state-owned enterprises and joint ventures.

There is also the required welfare and bonus fund drawn from the after-tax profits of the joint venture. This fund, according to the JV Implementing Regulations, is to be decided each year by the Board of Directors, but internal guidelines indicate that it should not be less than five per cent of after-tax profits.

Because labor charges can mount up rapidly, one of the new incentives being considered by the central government is a limitation on total labor costs to between 2.4 to 2.7 times the take-home pay of a worker in a state enterprise. While such an amount is actually more than that stipulated by the Beijing regulations, it is considerably less than what is normally paid in most joint ventures.

(6) Foreign exchange balancing and banking

Forex balance

China's foreign exchange regulations contain specific provisions relating to joint ventures. All receipts of a joint venture in foreign currencies must be deposited with the Bank of China (or other banks approved by the Bank of China) in special foreign exchange accounts, while the receipt of Renminbi must be deposited in the venture's Renminbi account. Payments of foreign currencies are to made out of the foreign exchange account, while payments to local entities should be made from the venture's Renminbi account. Both the repatriation of operating profits after tax and payments upon termination of the venture should also be made from the foreign exchange account.

The requirement that each joint venture must earn adequate amounts of foreign exchange by exporting its own products in order to cover all of its foreign exchange expenditure – which is referred to as balancing the foreign exchange account – has severely limited the number and type of joint ventures that can be done in China. In order to provide additional means of balancing the foreign exchange account, besides the joint venture exporting its own products, the State Council in February of 1986 adopted new regulations suggestion various methods that can be used to balance the foreign exchange account. Additionally, in October 1986, the State Council promulgated its Encouragement of Foreign Investment Regulations which permit approved joint ventures to sell products produced in China on the export markets, thereby allowing joint ventures to engage in trading activities to balance their foreign exchange requirements.

Banking

Although the Joint Venture Law and Implementing Regulations indicate that joint ventures can deal with foreign banks directly to obtain financing, the Chinese partner has in most cases raised numerous obstacles. First, since the finance is coming from abroad, the Chinese partner frequently says that the foreign investor should provide the loan itself, as the Chinese partner does not wish to deal with banks it does not know. Second, although financial security devices are now being used experimentally in China, foreign investors have found that to negotiate standard credit documents such as mortgages, pledge of shares, or assignments of receivables, is extremely difficult.

Partly because of the uncertainty of foreign investors as to the political stability of China, many early joint ventures had high debt-equity ratios. As mentioned above, a State Council regulation now limits the permissible amount of debt that a venture can incur during its start-up period. Projects which generate large amounts of foreign exchange, such as hotel projects, have been and continue to be successful in arranging foreign bank financing supported by guarantees provided by local Chinese financial institutions such as the Chinese trust and investment companies; joint ventures in other areas have been less successful in arranging debt since their lower amounts of foreign exchange revenue provide too low a cashflow debt service coverage ratio in foreign exchange.

(7) Duration, termination and liquidation

Duration
The term of the joint venture must be stipulated in the joint venture contract after negotiation between the parties. The JV Implementing Regulations suggest that the normal term for a joint venture is between ten and thirty years, but also recognizes that in special situations it may be necessary to have an even longer term. An amendment to the JV Implementing Regulations of January 1986 opens up the possibility of 50-year joint ventures. Although the negotiated term of joint ventures has been moving up from the ten to fifteen year range to the fifteen to twenty year range, no one so far has achieved a 50-year venture.

The JV Implementing Regulations also recognize that the parties may wish to extend the term of the venture, but to do so an application must be filed with the original approving authority at least six months before the scheduled termination date for the venture.

Termination
The JV Implementing Regulations refer to a number of specific circumstances under which a joint venture can be brought to an early termination: an inability to continue operations due to heavy losses; an inability to continue operations due to force majeure; an inability to achieve the desired objectives for which the joint venture was formed and no reasonable prospects for development; or a breach of the contract by one of the parties causing the joint venture to be unable to continue operations. Additionally the regulations permit the parties to stipulate in the contract other grounds for termination.

In such cases, the board of directors may decide to terminate the venture. Any early termination of a joint venture, whether due to breach of contract or by mutual agreement of the parties, must be approved by the original approval authority. If one of the parties has caused the termination by defaulting on its contractual obligations, that party is liable for the losses so caused.

Liquidation
If there is a decision by the board of directors to terminate the venture or upon the scheduled termination date, the board of directors is required by the JV Implementing Regulations to appoint a liquidation committee. Although the regulations are not entirely clear on the subject, it appears that the liquidation committee acts as its name implies; that is, assets are sold to satisfy the outstanding debts and liabilities of the venture and the remaining property is distributed in kind to the investors in accordance with the capital contribution ratio.

Most foreign investors would prefer to see the venture sold to the Chinese side for some stipulated price that took into account the future profits of the venture appraised as a going concern. While the regulations do not approach the subject in this way, recent joint ventures have in fact been documented so as to give the Chinese side a right of first refusal to buy the venture as a going concern. If the Chinese side elects not to purchase, then the venture is liquidated, the assets distributed and the business ends in the manner contemplated by the JV Implementing Regulations.

(8) Governing law and dispute settlement

All Chinese joint ventures are governed by Chinese law; the JV Implementing Regulations do not permit any other alternative.

Disputes, however, may be settled by third country arbitration, even though the JV Implementing Regulations reflect a bias toward Chinese arbitration. The most frequently selected country is Sweden, since the Chinese prefer it, but other places that have been chosen are Switzerland, the United Kingdom or Hong Kong, and in some cases, Beijing under arbitration conducted in accordance with the UNCITRAL Rules. Since China is now a signatory of the New York Convention, foreign arbitral awards are enforceable in China.

CONTRACTUAL JOINT VENTURES

Through the end of 1986, there were 4,274 contractual joint ventures in China with a planned total investment of approximately US$9.7-billion. Both in number and amount of investment, the contractual joint venture has proven to be more popular than the equity joint venture.

In April of 1988 a *Law of the People's Republic of China on Chinese-Foreign Contractual [Cooperative] Joint Ventures* was presented to the National People's Congress for adoption. In some means that is not too clear, the law has been tentatively adopted, but formal promulgation is to await ratification by the Standing Committee of the National People's Congress. The new law is the result of a long period of drafting and revision. The first draft of the Cooperative Enterprises Law was first circulated in 1983 and later was replaced by a more lengthy version in 1985. The 1985 version contained 64 separate articles and considerable detail as to the operation and management of contractual joint ventures. The new Contractual Joint Venture Law is only 28 articles long and it is thought that MOFERT will issue implementing regulations in much the same way as was done with the JV Implementing Regulations under the Joint Venture Law.

It is highly likely that the Contractual Joint Venture Law will reverse past practice, so that in the future the equity joint venture will be more popular than the contractual joint venture. The new law lacks substance and, where it contains substance, its provisions are unattractive to foreign investors. Previously, the primary reason for the popularity of the contractual joint venture was that it served as an alternative to the rigid rules of the equity joint venture law. For example, if the two parties were discussing an equity joint venture and the Chinese side discovered that it did not have enough capital to invest in order to make up its share of a 50/50 joint venture, then the parties would elect to do a contractual joint venture where it was possible for the Chinese side to contribute less than the foreign side and still take one-half of the profits, just so long as the contract so stipulated. In all other respects the venture was the same as an equity joint venture, except for where the contract specifically changed the rules. This flexibility was particularly attractive to Hong Kong Chinese that had many ingenious ways of contributing capital and sharing profits and losses.

Now, however, the new law creates a legal framework for contractual joint ventures that eliminates much of flexibility that used to be applied to these ventures. While it is still true that the Chinese can invest less and take more of the profits, the new law creates a number of onerous burdens on the foreign investor which will probably mean that the contractual joint venture loses its past appeal.

(1) Organization and status

Contractual ventures as legal persons
In the 1985 draft of the law, two types of contractual joint ventures were specifically recognized. One type, which was called a cooperative, was very similar to an equity joint venture, but the parties could change any provisions in the equity joint venture law that did not appeal to them. The entity created was a Chinese legal person, just like an equity joint venture was, and it was possible to stipulate that the cooperative would have limited liablility.

The second type of venture was the true contractual joint venture. No new legal entity was created. Instead, each of the parties stipulated in the contract their respective rights and obligations and the sharing of output or profits and the sharing of expenses and liabilities. Such a creature was similar to the common law partnership.

The new Contractual Joint Venture Law cannot make up its mind on the organization and stauts of the contractual joint venture. The law provides that a contractual joint venture which meets the conditions for being considered a legal person under Chinese law shall acquire the status of a Chinese legal person in accordance with law. Although this would seem to imply that if a contractual joint venture does not meet the conditions for being considered a legal person, then it is not one, there is some doubt. First, all of the provisions related to the true contractual joint venture of the common law partnership type have been eliminated from this draft of the law indicating that the true contractual joint venture may now be in disfavor. Second, the State Administration of Industry and Commerce has been hesitant to register the foreign investor partners to true contractual ventures since the law was released. Third, and most importantly, in the few cases of true contractual joint ventures to date, the Chinese authorities have shown an unwillingness or reluctance to deal with the registered foreign investor and have instead preferred to treat the enterprise as a legal entity and deal with the enterprise. In essence, the Chinese regulatory authorities realize that it is easier to manipulate and control legal entities formed under Chinese law, wherein Chinese citizens are part of management, than it is to legislate or administratively restrict the rights of a foreign company doing business in China.

Absence of limited liability

One of the most attractive features of a contractual joint venture has always been that the foreign investor could provide that its capital was returned to it during the term of the venture. In equity joint ventures, registered capital, once contributed, cannot be reduced or returned to the investor until the termination of the venture.

The new law provides in Article 23 that if a foreign investor is to receive its capital contribution back during the term of the venture, then at the end of the venture all of the fixed assets of venture must belong to the Chinese party. This provision, although more strict than prior practice, is not unfair.

The same Article goes on to provide, however, that if the foreign party is to recover its investment during the period of the venture's operation, the Chinese and foreign parties shall, as provided by the relevant laws and the contractual joint venture contract, be liable for the debts of the venture. This probably means that there is no limitation on the liability of the foreign investor, although possibly the detailed regulations will 'clarify' this section of the law.

In the past, it has been common in contractual joint venture contracts where a legal entity was established to provide that the liability of the parties was limited to their original contribution to capital; if capital was recovered during the term of the venture, then the party that had recovered a portion of its capital contribution was liable to repay the same to the venture if the venture could not meet its obligations. The foreign investor was never required to pay a fixed percentage of any debts of the venture, except in the case of a true contractual joint venture where a partnership was created.

(2) Capital contributions

Forms of capital contributions
Previously, the form of capital contributions to contractual joint ventures was considerably more flexible than in the equity joint venture. For example, natural resource mining rights were a recognized form of contribution, as were labor services. The new law, however, in Article 8 provides that capital may be contributed 'in cash or in kind, or may include the right to the use of a site, industrial property rights, technical know-how or other property rights'. This seems little different from the similar provisions in the Joint Venture Law and may constitute a narrowing of the permissible forms of capital contribution.

Return of capital
The most striking difference between equity joint ventures and contractual joint ventures is that the contractual joint venture contract may stipulate a time period for the repayment of the foreign investor's capital. Such a return of capital is not permitted under the Joint Venture Law, though it is possible to specially provide for a reserve fund to repay the foreign investor's capital upon termination of the venture. The method for the return of capital normally stipulated in the contract is for the cashflow applicable to the depreciation of the foreign investor's fixed asset contribution or the total fixed assets of the venture to be paid directly to the foreign investor at such time as the depreciation is recognized as an expense in the venture's accounts.

The new law has added a rather onerous burden to this early return of capital, since if the contract provides that the foreign investor gets back its capital contribution during the term of the venture, then at the end of the venture all assets of the contractual joint venture must be turned over to the Chinese partner without charge.

Division of profits
Profits arising in a contractual joint venture are to be distributed in the ratio stipulated in the contractual joint venture contract. Normally, this means that the Chinese party contributes less of the capital, but takes more of the profit.

It is also possible in contractual joint ventures to provide that the output or production of the venture is divided between the parties or that the gross revenue earned is divided between the parties. In either case, however, some arrangement must be stipulated in the contract for the payment of the contractual joint venture's operating expenses and taxes by each of the partners.

(3) Management and control

Contractual joint ventures are to have either a board of directors or a joint managerial institution which shall, according to the contract and articles of association of the venture, decide on all major issues concerning the venture.

One interesting feature of the new law is that Article 12 permits the foreign side to appoint the chairman of the board of directors, so long as this is stipulated in the contractual joint venture contract. It has been suggested, however, that the only reason this increased freedom was given to contractual joint ventures is that since the venture does not enjoy limited liability, it might be a good idea to make a foreigner the legal representative of the company.

It is specifically permitted by the new law that the contractual joint venture may enter into a management contract with a third-party and turn over management of the venture to the third-party.

(4) Operational matters

The new law contains almost nothing about how the venture is to be operated within China's economic system. Prior experience with contractual joint ventures has indicated that they are treated in the same way as equity joint ventures; that is, the department in charge is the organization responsible for incorporating the venture into the Chinese state planning system.

(5) Taxation

The new law does not say anything about the taxation of contractual joint ventures. It is therefore uncertain how they will be taxed in the future, but it is likely that the prior practice of separate taxation of the partners will continue. In an equity joint venture, the joint venture is the taxpayer and pays a tax of approximately 33 per cent. In contractual joint ventures, each partner pays his own tax separately; the foreign investor at rates which range from 30 per cent to 50 per cent depending upon the amount of profit earned and the Chinese investor at a flat rate of tax of 55 per cent.

In the case of equity joint ventures, when the foreign investor repatriates profits, he must pay a ten per cent withholding tax. Contractual joint venture investors, however, have been able to avoid a withholding tax on their profits, since such transfers are treated as inter-company transfers and not subject to withholding tax.

JOINT DEVELOPMENT

Joint development is similar to the true contractual joint venture and to date has been used solely for the granting of cooperative offshore oil exploration, development and exploitation contracts.

Unlike the true contractual joint venture, where it is common for both sides to contribute capital during the investment phase of the contract, in projects for joint development, the exploration stage is funded at the sole risk of the foreign investor. If oil is found in commercial quantities worthy of development, both the Chinese side and the foreign oil company invest in the joint development of the resources. Once production has begun, the recovered oil is divided between the parties as stipulated in the joint development contract.

The Model Contract proposed by the China National Offshore Oil Corporation ('CNOOC') for its dealings with foreign oil companies in the cooperative development of China's oil resources is the best example to date of how a 'model' contract can take on certain attributes of a law. Negotiators that have successfully concluded oil contracts with CNOOC acknowledge the reasonableness of China's desire for uniformity with all oil companies, and have (after lengthy negotiations) grown to appreciate the benefits of CNOOC's treatment of the draft as a law unto itself. To the extent that the contract has the effect of a law, the parties' rights and obligations are fixed permanently.

The Model Contract provides that a fixed percentage of the recovered oil must first go to the Chinese side in payment of the Consolidated Industrial and Commercial Tax and as a royalty or fixed share, thereafter a specified percentage of the oil is divided between the parties in order to recover the capital invested in exploration and development together with accrued interest charges, and finally the remaining percentage of the oil is divided between the parties pursuant to a sliding profit formula that is determined during the bidding and contract negotiation process. Although Joint Development probably affords the greatest flexibility of any of the presently available forms of investment, its usefulness has so far been limited to the offshore oil area. Moreover, it is not at all certain that Joint Development contracts will not be regulated in the future by new laws applicable to enterprises operating in China.

Foreign capital enterprises

In April of 1986, the National People's Congress added a third form of foreign investment enterprise to the available forms of investment in China by the adoption of the *Law of the People's Republic of China Governing Foreign Capital Enterprises* (12 April 1986). Most often referred to as the 'wholly foreign owned enterprise law', the new statute permits foreign investors to establish wholly-owned subsidiaries in China.

Prior to the law's promulgation, China had approved 120 wholly foreign owned foreign enterprises. Most, if not all, of these enterprises are located in China's Special Economic Zones which for a number of years have allowed foreign industrialists to come to China and establish their own wholly-owned plants. Additionally in Shanghai, 3M and W.R. Grace of the United States have established wholly foreign owned plants which are being watched as bell-wether projects.

The law gives scant guidance on how such Foreign Capital Enterprises will actually be approved and function within China's economic system and the past experience in China's Special Economic Zones may not be applicable when dealing in other parts of China under the new law.

(1) Application and approval

At the moment, it is known that an application must be filed with MOFERT for the approval of any wholly foreign owned investment. The central government has not so far delegated any of its approval powers for Foreign Capital Enterprises down to the local economic relations and trade commissions, as has been done in the case of equity and contractual joint ventures. MOFERT is still working on the form of application that should be used, but some of the more important items included are very similar to those found on a feasibility study for a joint venture – that is, the amount of the planned investment, the type of enterprise to be established, the products to be produced, the work force to be employed, and local raw materials required for production. The application must also state how the enterprise will balance its foreign exchange income and expenditures, and the expected profits to be earned by the enterprise.

Some Chinese officials, when discussing the idea of wholly foreign owned plants have argued that the approval process will be much more cumbersome than joint ventures or cooperatives, but this may be due to the fact that such officials saw direct equity participation in a joint venture as more financially rewarding to their cities than sponsoring an application for a foreign investor to establish a plant owned entirely by foreign interests.

(2) Organization and supply

Articles of Association for the Foreign Capital Enterprise must also be filed. As a Chinese corporation, such articles are important for the enterprise, as there is no corporation or companies law to describe the inherent powers of the Foreign Capital Enterprise as a Chinese corporation. The books of account of the Foreign Capital Enterprise must be kept in China and its accounting statements, audited by a Chinese accounting firm, must be filed with the Administration of Industry and Commerce and the local bureau of taxation. Labor is to be recruited and hired on a basis similar to that found in joint ventures; that is, there is to be a labor contract approved by the local labor bureau to which each employee will be a signatory. The Foreign Capital Enterprise is on its own in arranging for the supply of local raw materials necessary for production. There does not appear to be a system similar to that of joint ventures whereby the department-in-charge will be responsible for arranging the necessary raw materials as part of the state planning process.

(3) Foreign exchange

While subject to China's general laws on foreign exchange control, the law specifically states that the Foreign Capital Enterprise is solely responsible for balancing its own foreign exchange needs and expenditures – the state will not undertake an obligation to bail out a Foreign Capital Enterprise that is unable to balance its own foreign exchange needs with its foreign exchange income. Thus, such enterprises will necessarily have to export some portion of their production.

(4) Duration and liquidation

Foreign Capital Enterprises, just like joint ventures and cooperatives, must have a specific duration, which is to be stated in the application form. At the end of this period or in the case of an early termination of its business activities, the Foreign Capital Enterprise must go through liquidation procedures that the law does not define, but which are assumed to be similar to those applicable to joint ventures and cooperatives.

(5) Scope of business

It was originally thought that Foreign Capital Enterprises would be limited in scope to productive enterprises establishing manufacturing plants in China. This original conception may not be correct, however, since several recent real estate projects appear to be proceeding on a wholly-owned basis.

(6) Management autonomy

Not until a number of these enterprises are established and operating will one know with any certainty how they will operate in China and whether they are a worthwhile investment vehicle for other foreign investors to consider. At the moment, however, their principal attraction appears to be that, if under a joint venture or cooperative scheme, a foreign investor must discover a way to balance the foreign exchange requirement, why should a foreign investor also pay the high cost of management inefficiencies in having a Chinese partner as well? The Foreign Capital Enterprise at least affords the management of the enterprise with the freedom and discretion to make its own, unilateral decisions as to how to manage the new company.

Foreign Investment Approval Process

The approval process for foreign investment proposals is as important as the published laws and regulations governing such investments, since the approval process determines how the investment project will be integrated within the Chinese economic system.

(1) State planning

State planning of the national economy is required by the Chinese constitution. The State Council is responsible for ensuring the proportionate and coordinated development of the national economy as a whole through the national economic planning mechanism, supplemented by market regulation in limited areas. The compilation of the annual and five year State Plans is a process of adjusting and consolidating at the national level the economic plans of the ministries, provinces, municipalities directly under the control of the State Council and autonomous regions. The Seventh Five Year Plan (1986–1990) was presented to the National People's Congress in 1984, where it was adopted along with long range economic planning goals that extend into the 21st century.

Once approved, a foreign investment project (other than a wholly foreign owned enterprise) becomes part of the State Plan with both its planned production and necessary inputs of raw materials and utilities accounted for within the plan. Since the state planning process predicts future economic needs and goals and since at any particular point the Chinese authorities are operating with an existing State Plan, a major foreign investment project that is not contemplated in the exisiting plan will be subject to lengthy delays before it can be implemented. Any major foreign investment project therefore that will require the utilization of substantial power, utilities, transportation or raw material supplies should be part of the existing State Plan before a foreign investor spends time and money pursuing the project.

(2) State planning and the approval process

The approval process for foreign investment projects is meant to ensure that the requirements for overall national economic planning are met before the investment program is implemented. What is normally thought of by the foreign investor as a non-binding letter of intent is, in fact, the initial stage of the foreign investment approval process. Under the Chinese system, the Chinese party is supposed to submit a written proposal on the project to the appropriate authorities at the provincial, independent municipality, autonomous region or State Council levels. The proposal should include information on the foreign partner, the object of the proposed investment, sphere of operation, scale of production, total amount of investment, technology to be employed, sources of raw materials, fuel, power and equipment, market studies, economic effects and basic terms of the joint venture. Most letters of intent touch on many, if not all of these subjects; and, even though the foreign investor may consider that all subjects are left open for further study, refinement and possible amendment, since the relevant higher authorities act on the written approval and authorize negotiations based on the signed proposal, it becomes very difficult to change the terms stated in the initial letter of intent, even though such terms are not legally binding.

The level to which the initial written proposal must go for final approval is still subject to confusing interpretations. As a general rule, it has been stated that the Provinces of Guangdong and Fujian may approve investments up to any level without hight approval, that independent municipalities directly under the State Council such as Beijing and Tianjin may approve investments up to US$10,000,000 without higher approval and

Shanghai may approve investments up to US$30,000,000; and that Ministries and certain coastal provinces have authority to approve investments between US$3 and 5-million without higher approval; all other investments must go to MOFERT for prior approval. Even in the areas where the lower level economic authorities have apparent approval power, they must report to the higher level organizations for the record (and the higher level authority can intervene with an objection, if it chooses) and, in cases where the national economic system is to be called upon to support where the national economic system is to be called upon to support the venture through the supply of raw materials or utilities or where a national level organization is necessarily involved (such as the China National Offshore Oil Corporation in offshore oil matters,) the lower level economic authorities must receive the central government's approval.

(3) Feasibility studies

Once the initial approval is received, the Chinese party and the foreign investor are supposed to jointly conduct an economic feasibility study. This study should include all technical aspects of the project and predict future income and expenses. Again this feasibility study is supposed to be submitted for approval through the relevant chain of command.

It is this stage of the negotiation process that frequently creates the greatest difficulties. The foreign investor will by now have studied Chinese laws and regulations governing foreign investment and trade and learned something of the likely operating expenses to be incurred in China. In order to achieve an acceptable return on investment, the foreign investor will want to write into the feasibility study tax concessions or holidays, reduced customs duties on imports, favored treatment as to the pricing of Chinese supplied raw materials or utilities, lower land use costs or reduced local or consolidated taxes. But since the original letter of intent said nothing about such concessions, the Chinese side will be very reluctant to go beyond the initial mandate granted by the higher level economic regulators. The Chinese side has certain additional responsibilities in the second stage of the approval process beyond preparing the 'joint' feasibility report. The Chinese party sponsoring the investment must separately report on the concrete arrangements that it has made for performing its portion of the proposed investment. Under current practice this may include such matters as initial commitments from Chinese financial institutions like the Bank of China or the People's Bank of China to lend the Chinese party its portion of the equity investment, proof that the required raw materials and utilities necessary for the venture are available in the locality and that the sources of supply have been confirmed, and that the percentage of the production to be sold locally can be distributed efficiently and absorbed by the local market. Normally this secondary report prepared by the Chinese side is not shown to the foreign investor.

(4) Contract and articles of association

Once the 'joint' feasibility report and secondary report are approved by the higher level economic regulators, the Chinese side is authorized to negotiate the investment contract and related legal documents. The Joint Venture Law indicates that once negotiated and signed, such documents are submitted to MOFERT for approval within three months. While this was the system in China in 1979, the early experience led to a modification of the system since the foreign investment control authorities found that they must either re-negotiate the contracts causing delays longer than three months or approve contracts that did not fully conform to China's internal guidelines. Therefore, now before any contract which constitutes a final and binding legal document can be signed, it must be submitted to and approved by MOFERT as a matter of policy.

Nevertheless, MOFERT must also review and approve the contract after it is signed, even though it has given preliminary approval to authorize the signing.

Once MOFERT or the relevant lower level authority has approved execution of the contract, it is signed but then must be formally resubmitted in technical compliance with Article 3 of the Joint Venture Law. The formal submission in the case of an equity joint venture is supposed to include (1) an application for the establishment of the joint venture, (2) copies of the contracts and articles of association, (3) the feasibility report, (4) name list for the joint venture's Chairman, Vice-Chairman, general manager and deputy general manager and (5) comments on the joint venture from the province, municipality, autonomous region or ministry proposing the venture.

(5) Approval certificate

A formal approval certificate is supposed to be issued by MOFERT within three months of the formal submission, but recently (because the ventures are subject to approval prior to signing) this procedure has been shortened. After the formal approval is granted, the joint venture is required to register with the Administration of Industry and Commerce or its agency in the locality where the joint venture is situated, according to the special provisions on registration applicable to equity joint ventures.

Chapter 11

Technology Transfer to the People's Republic of China

by Dr. Arthur Wolff

Law Offices of Arthur Wolff
Vienna, Austria

Introduction

Since the end of the 1970s, the government of the People's Republic of
China ('PRC') increasingly realized the importance of technology transfer
from abroad.[1] The policy of readjustment of 1980–81 led to the insight that
the acquisition of foreign technology and know-how for the production of
such things as machinery and equipment may in the end be cheaper than
buying the hardware and thus save foreign exchange. The business of transferring technology and know-how to the PRC since then definitely shows a
decisive upward trend: Prior to 1978 the import of 'pure' technology (i.e. in

---

1. For a general discussion of transferring technology and licensing to the PRC, *see*, e.g. St.
   Lubman, 'Technology Transfer to China: Policies, Law and Practice', in: M.J. Moser (ed.),
   Foreign Trade, Investment and the Law in the People's Republic of China (Hong Kong-New
   York-Oxford 2nd. edn. 1987) p. 170–198; although written prior to the issuance of the 1985
   legislation on technology transfer (*see* in the text p. 253), still illuminating, in particular as
   to practical problems, Ch. Kamm, 'Practice of Licensing with China', in: R. Goldscheider
   & Arnold (eds.), *The Law and Business of Licensing*, Vol. 3, 3 F-13-44 (reprint from *Les
   Nouvelles*, Volume 15, Number 4).

the form of licenses) to the PRC made up only 2.3 per cent of total imports and import of equipment 90 per cent. In 1984, the former rose to 59.9 per cent and the latter fell to 40.1 percent.[2]

Technology transfer to the PRC takes various forms, including licensing of patents and know-how, countertrade, contribution of technology to non equity and equity joint ventures.[3] Although technology transfer and license arrangements with the PRC sometimes follow international practice, in recent years some peculiarities typical for such agreements with Chinese partners developed.

They show that the Chinese often try to interpret the oft-quoted principle of 'equality and mutual benefit,'[4] to their advantage. The long-awaited 'Regulations of the People's Republic of China on the Administration of Technology Import Contracts' referred to in more detail below as the first law directly addressing technology transfer[5] were therefore of great interest to the practitioner.

In the following, an outline of the legal framework for technology transfer/licensing to the PRC is given combined with a discussion of areas of particular concern to the foreign licensor. The discussion focusses on licensing transactions with occasional reference to the joint venture legislation regarding technology transfer and follows in a loose form the steps one might take in a technology transfer transaction, i.e. from pre-negotiation considerations to the questions of the applicable legal framework, the legal requirements for the contract and the clauses typically found in such a transaction.

As to terminology, the expressions 'Supplier' and 'Recipient' are used for 'Licensor' and 'Licensee', as they are also used in the relevant Chinese laws.

---

2. Cf. the *Journal of International Trade* published by the Ministry of Foreign Economic Relations and Trade, 1985, No. 4, p. 45.
3. C.C.-M. Chan gives in the *Information Bulletin of the European Association for Chinese Law*, Vol. iv, No. 1 (April 1988), p. 3, a detailed table illustrating the importance of the technology trade to the PRC for 1981 to 1986, broken down in the categories: complete plant, technical licensing agreement, technical consultancy, technical service, cooperative production, key equipment, others.
4. *See* e.g. Articles 1 and 6 of the Law of the People's Republic of China on Joint Ventures Using Chinese and Foreign Investment, adopted on 1 July 1979, at the Second Session of the Fifth National People's Congress and promulgated on 8 July 1979. It is supplemented by the Implementing Regulations for the Law of the People's Republic of China on Joint Ventures Using Chinese and Foreign Investment, promulgated by the State Council on 20 September 1983, and other pertinent legislation. *See also* Article 3 of the Foreign Economic Contracts Law of the People's Republic of China, adopted at the Tenth Session of the Standing Committee of the National People's congress on 21 March 1985, effective as of 1 July 1985.
5. Articles 5 and 7 of the Joint Venture Law (*see* above note 4) and Chapters iv and vi of the Implementing Regulations for it (*see* above note 4) address technology transfer only in connection with contributions to the capital of, respectively the importation of technology by a joint venture.

Ascertaining the Authority of the Chinese Party and Project Authorization

Over the last few years, foreign trade has been decentralized.[6] With the resulting reorganization of the foreign trade structure and the many entities now involved in foreign trade, the questions of the authority of the Chinese party to negotiate and sign the contract and of whether (and by whom) the project has been authorized are of considerable importance. Before entering into negotiations consuming more often than not much time and money, the foreign party should therefore seek confirmations as to the following matters:

IDENTITY, NATURE AND AUTHORITY OF THE CHINESE PARTY

The foreign party should confirm the identity, legal status and authority to engage in the contemplated transaction of the Chinese entity with which it will be contracting, preferably by reviewing the latter's business license and, if available, its articles of association.[7] If the foreign party is not dealing with one of the Foreign Trade Corporations, it should establish the authority of the Chinese party to deal directly with foreigners and to expend foreign exchange. Article 3 of the Detailed Rules referred to below provides in this respect that a Chinese entity not having 'the power to engage in the foreign technology import business shall, when importing technology, entrust and issue a power of attorney' to entities that have such power 'to sign technology import contracts with foreign parties'. In view of the problems in practice to establish these facts – the Chinese parties in the past were usually not willing to provide appropriate documentation, when requested so to do – the foreign party will have to rely on the assurances of the Chinese party or advice of the Department of Treaties and Law of the Ministry of Foreign Economic Relations and Trade ('MOFERT'), the China Council for the Promotion of International Trade ('CCPIT') or the legal opinion of a Chinese law firm.

PROJECT AUTHORIZATION AND FEASIBILITY STUDY

The foreign party should also make sure that the relevant PRC planning authorities have authorized the proposed project. The monetary value of the

---

6. For a discussion of the PRC's foreign trade system *see* J.P. Horsley, 'The Regulation of China's Foreign Trade', in: M.J. Moser (ed.), *Foreign Trade* ... (above note 1), pp.5–41.
7. For a detailed discussion as to how to establish corporate (and signing) authority of a Chinese entity *see* C.J. Conroy and M.J. Moser, 'Selected Legal Aspects of Financing Transactions with the People's Republic of China, in: M.J. Moser (ed.), *Foreign Trade* ... (above note 1) p. 381 (at pp. 383–384).

transaction will determine which level of government planning agency has the power to authorize the project. Projects involving lesser amounts may be authorized by provincial or municipal planning commissions. Preferably the foreign party should ask actually to see the required feasibility study prepared by the Chinese party and the project authorization certificate.

The Legal Framework and the Applicable Law

FOREIGN ECONOMIC CONTRACTS LAW

The Regulations on the Administration of Technology Import Contracts referred to below address only questions typically related to technology transfer contracts with foreign technology suppliers. For other questions their Article 5 refers to the Foreign Economic Contracts Law ('FECL') and 'other relevant laws' of the PRC. The FECL, however, does not contain provisions, which in civil law countries would be part of the 'general law of obligations' (such as provisions regarding the formation of contracts, agency, error, time limits, time and place of performance, warranties). The FECL contains a number of provisions which are of specific relevance to technology transfer/licensing contracts, which are here only listed without further discussion:[8]

- Articles 19–22, 24: damages for breach of contract;
- Articles 26 and 27: assignment of a contract;
- Articles 9 and 10: void contracts;
- Article 29: (unilateral) recission of a contract;
- Articles 31, 35 and 36: termination of a contract;
- Articles 37 and 38: arbitration and litigation;
- Article 5: choice of law (*see* below).

Article 5 FECL allows the parties to a contract involving foreign interests, including a technology transfer contract, to choose the law to govern their relations under the contract with the exception of joint ventures, cooperative ventures and natural resource development contracts.

One common way to deal with the problem of choosing respectively not being able to agree on the law applicable to the contract is to omit a governing law clause and leave the matter for resolution by the arbitrators, if a dispute arises. They will determine the proper law of the contract in the light of all the circumstances and the conflicts rules in force at the seat of the

---

8. For a discussion of the FECL, *see* J.A. Cohen, 'The New Foreign Contract Law', *The China Business Review*, July—August 1985, p. 5., P.R. Torbert, 'Contract Law in the People's Republic of China', in: M.J. Moser (ed.), *Foreign Trade* ... (above note 1), pp. 321–342.

arbitration. If the arbitrators sit in the PRC, they will have to look at Article 5 FECL, which provides that, in the absence of an applicable law clause, the law of the country with the closest connection to the contract is to be applied.

THE TECHNOLOGY IMPORT CONTRACTS LAW

There exist several specific national and local laws dealing with technology import, including tax laws. The provisions in local legislation are similar to the national rules, but contain sometimes not so minor differences in emphasis and detail. The relationship between the national and the local legislation is unclear, in particular the question whether local legislation pre-empts national legislation or to what extent the latter has superseded the local legislation.

In this paper, only the national legislation is discussed in more detail. Provisions in local legislations and joint venture legislation are, however, occasionally referred to in order to illustrate similarities or divergencies. The foreign party will, of course, have to look at applicable local rules in detail.

(1) The national technology import contract laws

Technology transfer/licensing into the PRC is governed by the Regulations of the PRC on the Administration of Technology Import Contracts ('TICR'), promulgated by the State Council on 24 May 1985, and according to their Article 13 effective as of that date. They aim to expand economic and technical cooperation with other countries and to upgrade the scientific and technological standard of the PRC in order to promote the national economy's growth (Article 1). In view of these aims, it is not surprising that the responsibility not only for their interpretation, but also for formulating detailed rules for their implemention, rests with MOFERT (Article 12).

They apply in principle to all acquisitions of technology by companies, enterprises, organizations or individuals within the PRC from transferors outside the PRC, except where the technology is contributed as capital to an enterprise with foreign investment. They were preceded by two sets of local provisions, the provisions on technology import contracts of the Special Economic Zones of Shenzhen and Xiamen referred to below.

In addition to these specialized regulations, the Joint Venture Law Implementing Regulations of 1983 contain some provisions on technology transfers to equity joint ventures. Regarding technology transfer between Chinese entities, rules were promulgated on 10 January 1985.[9]

The TICR were supplemented by the 'Procedures for Examination and

---

9. For an analysis of the 'PRC Domestic Tech-Market', *see* Chi Shaojie, *Les Nouvelles* 1987, No. 4, p. 150.

Approval of Technology Import Contracts' promulgated by MOFERT on 18 September 1985.

To further rationalize and reaffirm the PRC's reliance on technology import, MOFERT on 20 January 1988 (and effective from that date) promulgated a new set of rules, the 'Detailed Rules and Regulations for the Implementation of the Regulations on Administration of Technology Import Contracts' ('Detailes Rules') which repealed the 'Procedures for Examination and Approval of Technology Import Contracts'. The Detailed Rules clearly show the PRC's continuing interest in the import of modern technology, while at the same time reflecting the perceived need to critically examine all transfers of technology. They do not, however, add significantly to the requirements already in the FECL, the TICR and the standard form contracts, but clarify the application and approval procedures for technology import contracts. Much of their effect will depend on the discretion exercised by the approval authorities in the approval process, in particular with respect to the special approval required for restrictive terms, which are discussed below.

(2) The local technology import laws

The TICR which are to be applied nationally, were preceded by the following sets of local provisions:

- the Interim Provisions of the Shenzhen Special Economic Zone for the Import of Technology (the 'Shenzhen Regulations'), promulgated by Guangdong Province on 8 February 1984;
- the Provisions of the Xiamen Special Economic Zone for the Import of Technology (the 'Xiamen Regulations'), promulgated by Fujian Province on 14 July 1984;
- the Interim Regulations of the Guangzhou Economic and Technological Development Zone Concerning the Introduction of Technology promulgated by the Municipal People's Government on 9 April 1985.

The first two sets of regulations are occasionally referred to in the following to illustrate accordance with or divergencies from the national regulation.

Scope of Technology Import Legislation

The TICR do not cover the transfer of technology in general, but only technology import into the PRC, i.e. the acquisition of technology by companies, enterprises, other organizations and individuals within the PRC ('Recipients') from companies, enterprises, other organizations or individuals outside the PRC ('Suppliers') through trade or economic and technological cooperation.

The TICR therefore – and according to their Article 4, also the Detailed Rules – govern also technology transfer contracts by Chinese-Foreign Joint

Ventures, by Chinese-foreign cooperative ventures and wholly foreign-owned enterprises (hereinafter referred to as 'Foreign Investment Enterprises') established in the PRC, whether they involve the foreign partner or a third-party foreign entity or individual. They do not apply, when the technology forms part of the foreign party's capital contribution to a Joint Venture. In that case, the Joint Venture Law and its Implementing Regulations will apply.

The TICR give no definition of a technology import or licensing contract. By way of example, their Article 2 lists the following Technology Transfer Contracts:

– acquisition or licensing of patents or other industrial property rights;
– supply of technical know-how in the form of drawings, technical documents and specifications, such as process specifications, formulae, product design, quality control and management skills;
– tendering of technical services.

The Detailes Rules are more specific, their Article 2 requiring that the following six types of 'technology import contracts' be submitted for examination and approval:

– contracts for the assignment or licensing of industrial property rights, i.e. contracts involving the assignment or licensing of patents for inventions, utility models or designs, or the assignment or licensing of trademark rights, but *excepting* contracts that involve only the assignment of trademark rights;
– contracts for the licensing of proprietary technology, i.e. contracts for the supply or the imparting of knowledge relating to the manufacture of a certain kind of product or the application of a certain technique, as well as of product design, technological processes, formulae, quality control and management that has not been made public and is not protected by industrial property law;
– technical service contracts, i.e. contracts under which the Supplier utilizes its technology to provide services or advice to the Recipient in order to reach specific objectives. These include contracts under which the Recipient entrusts the Supplier with carrying out, or carries out jointly with the Supplier, a feasibility study on a project or an engineering design; contracts under which a foreign geological exploration team or engineering team is hired to provide technical services; contracts under which the Supplier is entrusted with the provision of services or advice on an enterprise's technological transformation, improvement of production technology or product design, and quality control and enterprise management; but *excepting* contracts under which a foreigner is engaged to assume a position in a Chinese enterprise;
– contracts for cooperative production or design that include the assignment or licensing of industrial property rights, the licensing of proprietary technology, or the provision of technical services;

- contracts for the importation of complete sets of equipment, production lines and key equipment that include the assignment or licensing of industrial property rights, the licensing of proprietary technology, and the provision of technical services;
- other technology import contracts that the examination and approval authority deems shall be subject to examination and approval.

The catch-all category listed as last category allows the Chinese authorities to exercise their discretion and insist on the examination and approval of contracts that do not clearly fall into the other categories listed, thus creating some uncertainty, e.g. as to whether a computer software license will be considered a technology import contract.

Requirements for Transferable Technology

The past several decades have witnessed an increasing preoccupation with the nature of technology imported by developing countries. It has been argued that much of this technology is not suited to their economic conditions and is backward. It comes, therefore, as no surprise that one of the purposes of the Chinese technology transfer legislation is the exercise of government control over the quality and effects of imported technology, as witnessed by the requirements for transferable technology discussed below.

ADVANCED AND APPROPRIATE TECHNOLOGY

In conformity with standard contract practice and current policy in the PRC and the provisions of other legislation,[10] Article 3 TICR requires the technology to be acquired to be 'advanced' and 'appropriate', which is identical to the phrase used in the Joint Venture Law. The TICR, however, do not specify what will be deemed to constitute 'advanced' and 'appropriate' technology.

The Xiamen Regulations also do not define what is 'advanced' technology, but Article 6(1) does provide that, if the technology is examined and certified by state scientific research departments as being of an advanced world level, the Chinese Recipient may enjoy unspecified preferential treatment stipulated by the Xiamen Municipal People's Government and may apply to a state bank located in the Xiamen SEZ for low-interest loans or financial assistance to acquire such technology. Similarly, Article 6 of the Shenzhen Regulations provides that, if imported technology is certified by

---

10. Cf. Article 5 of the Joint Venture Law (*see* above note 4), providing that the 'technology ... contributed by a foreign participant (in a joint venture) as investment shall be truly *advanced and appropriate* to China's needs' (emphasis added). Its Article 7 provides for tax advantages, if 'up-to-date technology by world standards is contributed'.

the Shenzhen Municipal Science and Technology Development Center to be
of an advanced world standard, both parties to the technology transfer
contract may apply for preferential tax and land use fee treatment.

In the absence of a definition, Article 44[11] of the Joint Venture Law
Implementing Regulations and the aims of the TICR as set forth in their
Article 1[12] indicate that the requirements of the technology being 'advanced'
and 'appropriate' will be met, if marked social and economic results are
achieved domestically or competitive capacity in the international market is
enhanced.

The type of technology viewed as advanced and appropriate is constantly
changing. The absence of a definition in this respect is therefore unlikely to
be an oversight, but gives the Chinese the required flexibility in determining
the scope of this term. For example, the original definition of advanced
technology in the Joint Venture Law indicates that world state-of-the-art
technology is required. An additional test is that advanced technology must
be able to be successfully integrated into the particular Chinese industry.
Technology of the 1970s rather than that of 1988 may thus be viewed as
advanced. When determining whether technology is 'advanced and
appropriate', the Chinese should therefore – at least for the time being –
more emphasize the appropriateness of the technology to be acquired and
not so much advancement. The criteria for technology transfer should be
based on market demand: Technology salcable in the PRC should be viewed
as appropriate and therefore acceptable. When negotiating with the
Chinese, the prospective foreign technology Supplier must therefore con-
vince the Chinese party that the technology is suitable for the Chinese
situation, yet, also advanced.

As Chinese law provides that the Recipient will usually be entitled to use
the technology at the end of the contract term (*see* below), the Supplier will
also often be reluctant to supply its very latest technology or at least insist
on a cut-off date earlier than the end of the contract term, if it is under an
obligation to pass on improvements.

EIGHT REQUIREMENTS

Apart from the two components of transferable technology discussed in the
preceding paragraph, Article 3 TICR lists eight additional requirements as
fundamental objectives: The technology must also be capable of fulfilling
'one or more' of the following requirements, i.e. to:

11. 'Technology imported by joint ventures shall be appropriate and advanced, enabling the
    resulting products to display marked social and economic results domestically or to have
    capacity on the international market.'
12. Expansion of China's international economic and technological co-operation, upgrading of
    its scientific and technological standard, promotion of its economic growth.

- develop and produce new products;
- improve the quality and performance of products, reduce production costs and conserve energy or materials;
- further the full utilisation of China's natural resources;
- increase product export and foreign exchange earnings;
- further environmental protection;
- improve safety in production;
- further the improvement of management and administration; assist in raising the level of science and technology.

The list seems to flesh out the third general requirement for imported technology: that it have 'significant economic benefits', a requirement referred to in both the Shenzhen and the Xiamen Regulations.

As it is doubtful, whether provisions regulating the nature of imported technology are likely to produce favourable results for the host country, the degree of the beneficial effect of these provisions will depend on the skill of the economic experts in the approval authorities and the detail of the econometric background.

The Use of Standard Form Contracts

As in other socialist countries, standard form contracts are widely used in the PRC to ensure that the state's interests are adequately protected. This is in principle also the case for technology transfer/licensing transactions. As such transactions, however, frequently require more flexibility, the Chinese party does not always insist on using a standard form contract, but is agreeable to drawing up an appropriate contract together with the Supplier or at least to change certain clauses, if it is sufficiently interested in the particular contract. Even such modifications have been accepted that, pursuant to Article 9 TICR, need a special approval.

The form contracts tend to be lacking in detail about many important aspects of the technology transfer and seem to be derived from simple sales contracts. They are thus more appropriate to a one-off discrete transaction and are neither specific nor flexible enough to work out an ongoing, complex technology transfer relation.

Scope of the Contract

The scope of technology transfer often goes beyond the transfer of mere product or process technology: The Chinese Recipient will often want to define as broadly as possible the scope of the contract and the technical documentation the Supplier should provide. Thus, it may, e.g., request basic know-how regarding product development. The Supplier should therefore agree to supply documentation only 'as readily available', as even in a large company with thorough documentation much has become general knowledge no longer available in a form that can easily be documented. The Recipient's concern with documentation can be particularly vexing, where it wishes to list types of documents which the Supplier does not ordinarily supply to licensees or which concern e.g. components the Supplier itself sources from third parties. The prospective Recipient will also often request know-how regarding the installation of a plant or organisation of a production process. All these aspects make technical training by the Supplier's personnel and appropriate provision in the contract very important, as it substitutes for non-existing and supplements not readily understandable documentation.

Requirements as to Content of Contract

Over the years the PRC has negotiated so many technology transfer/ licensing contracts that the Chinese are well familiar with the usual contents of such contracts. The TICR do not deviate in this respect from international practice:

They stipulate that the contract must comply with the relevant provisions of the Foreign Economic Contract Law – its Article 12 gives provisions generally to be included in foreign economic contracts – and other relevant laws of the PRC.

The contract must also set forth:

– the content, scope and the requisite description of the technology to be acquired and a list of patents and trademarks, if such are involved;
– the technical objectives to be achieved using the technology and the time requirements for their achievement;
– the amount, form and method of remuneration to be paid to the Supplier.

The Detailed rules also specify the essential clauses and terms that must be included in the contract as follows:

– the name of the contract;
– the contents, scope and requirements of the technology to be imported;
– the standards, time periods and measures for realizing, checking and inspecting the objectives for the technology to be imported, and the undertaking of risks and liabilities;
– the obligation to maintain the confidentiality of the technology to be imported, and the ownership and sharing of improved technology;
– the price or the total amount of the remuneration and the price of each item, and the means of payment;
– the method for computing the amount of compensatory damages for breach of contract losses;
– the method for the settlement of disputes;
– the interpretation of expressions and terms.

Even though Article 7 does not purport to impose any standard for the parties to follow, they, nevertheless, do not have full discretion to negotiate these clauses as many of them are restricted by other articles.

Prohibition of Certain Restrictions

The PRC has for a long time been a staunch supporter of UNCTAD's endeavors to formulate and agree on an international code of conduct on the transfer of technology. This support and the experiences of developing countries with restrictive clauses in technology transfer contracts are reflected in Chinese legislation on technology import:[13]

The Joint Venture Law Implementing Regulations provide that unless otherwise agreed, there should be no restrictions on the quantity, price or region of sale of products that are to be exported.

In a general statement, Article 9 TICR provides that the Supplier may not require the Recipient to accept unfair restrictive conditions. It then lists nine restrictive provisions, which may not be included in the contract without special approval from the approval authority. This requirement seems to preclude the possibility of regarding a contract as having been approved by the approval authority not having made a decision within 60 days (Article 4), if a contract contains any of the following provisions listed in Article 9, i.e. provisions:

- requiring the Recipient to accept additional conditions unrelated to the technology acquired, such as requiring the Recipient to purchase 'unnecessary technology, technical services, raw materials, equipment or products' (Article 9(1), *see* below);
- restricting the Recipient's freedom to purchase raw materials, (spare) parts and components or equipment from sources other than the Supplier (Article 9(2), *see* below);
- restricting the Recipient from developing and improving the technology acquired (Article 9(3), *see* below);
- restricting the Recipient from acquiring similar or competing technology from other sources (Article 9(4), *see* below);
- nonreciprocal terms of exchange of improvements of the acquired technology (Article 9(5), *see* below);
- restricting the quantity, type and the sales price of products manufactured with the acquired technology (Article 9(6), *see* below);
- unreasonably restricting the Recipients' distribution channels and export markets (Article 9(7), *see* below);

---

13. Thus expressly the Chinese delegate to UNCTAD'S 5th session on that subject matter in October 1983, *see* UN Doc. TD/Code TOT/SR. 18, 24 October 1983, p.4.

- restricting the use of the acquired technology by the Recipient after the expiration of the contract (Article 9(8), *see* below);
- requiring the Recipient to pay for or take on obligations with respect to patents that will not be used or that have been declared invalid (Article 9(9)).

This list reads like a checklist of areas in which PRC legislators believe foreign Suppliers have taken advantage of their Chinese partners and where they feel they have to correct the abuses arising from previous negotiations. It is *grosso modo* familiar to Western lawyers/licensors, because Western antitrust laws often contain partly similar provisions and so do technology transfer control laws in many developing countries. The list makes it easier for the Chinese to negotiate for more favorable terms respectively less restrictive provisions, because they can refer to this list as 'the law', thus increasing their bargaining power.

The prohibited arrangements often providing a major inducement to foreign companies to transfer their technology, the list poses a serious problem for potential Suppliers. Depending on the transaction, the contracting parties may have sound economic reasons to agree to provisions that fall within Article 9. Although the TICR do allow for special approval of such provisions, Article 9 clearly indicates that such provisions are presumed undesirable. A party feeling such provision is essential to its interests must therefore persuade both its negotiating partner and the PRC authorities of its acceptability. Article 21 of the Detailed Regulations offers the parties in this context the opportunity to explain the reasons why the contract contains restrictive terms listed in Article 9 TICR. It is to be hoped that this may increase their chances for approval.

In the following, the prohibition on restrictive provisions is discussed in some detail with the exception of Article 9(9), which provision is unobjectionable to the honest foreign Supplier.

(1) Tying clauses

Prohibitions against tying arrangements in international technology transfer transactions have been included in most technology transfer control laws. They are meant to prevent hidden costs for ancillary services and equipment which are 'unneccessary': Suppliers selling technology at a low price should not expect to increase their overall profit margin by secondary means.

It is quite understandable that also the Chinese should be concerned over tying clauses as these clauses may well result in the overcharging of the Recipient by not permitting it to have the advantage of competitive pricing and thus providing a big incentive for the Supplier to transfer the technology.

The TICR require that special approval must be obtained for such a tying clause. Article 10 of the Detailed Rules provides for another safeguard:

'The price of the raw materials, spare parts and components or equipment that the Recipient requests the Supplier to provide and that are necessary for the technology being imported shall not be higher than the price of the same kind of products on the international market.'

While it is not expressly stated as such, it is hoped that internationally comparable prices would be the sole critieria for obtaining the special approval.

One should note in this context that according to Article 8(5) of the Detailed Rules one of the essential terms to be included in the contract is not only 'the price or the total amount of remuneration', but also 'the price of each item', i.e. the price must be broken down or itemized. This makes it easier for the Recipient to check whether the price charged for raw materials, spare parts etc. is not higher than that of similar products in the international market.

The restriction on prices for items sold to the Recipient will, of course, restrict the Supplier's flexibility and may induce him to ask for higher royalty rates/lump sums. To the extent that such higher royalties/lump sums are not acceptable to the Recipient, the restriction may work as a disincentive for the Supplier.

The broad wording of the prohibition on tying arrangements may well lead to the risk of arbitrary interpretation, as the function of the prohibition is to prevent supplementary transactions being used to circumvent the restrictions imposed on the payments derived from the technology transfer. It is, however, frequently not possible for a Supplier to fulfill contractual guarantees that the technology 'can achieve the objectives stipulated in the contract' unless the Recipient agrees to master the necessary technology, accept certain technical services, and use appropriate raw materials and equipment in the course of applying the technology. The Supplier will therefore often require the Recipient to purchase such additional services and material. The tying arrangement may then be necessary to protect the legitimate interests of the Supplier. Aware of these practices, the Chinese legislator prohibited only sales of 'unnecessary' technology, services, and materials. – It is, however, doubtful, whether the approval authorities will accept the judgment of the parties in this respect. If not, the submission of a signed contract to the authorities for approval could be followed by further negotiations.

If Suppliers have no say in the choice of the raw materials or equipment used in applying the technology, they will restrict their guarantees accordingly. The contract must therefore set out in detail the Recipient's requirements and the technical specifications that raw materials, equipment, spare parts, and other inputs must meet in order to achieve the guaranteed objectives and clearly state that any restrictions upon sourcing of such inputs are essential for attaining the contract's objectives and that, if inputs are not sourced according to the Supplier's specifications, it shall not be liable under its guarantee for problems caused by inputs that do not meet the technical specifications.

(2) Restrictions on developments and improvements

Provisions restricting the acquiring parties' research and adaptation of imported technologies to their needs and economic environment have been the objects of broad and generally per se prohibitions under transfer of technology laws in many developing countries and under main antitrust systems. The prohibition in Article 9 of the TICR of restrictions for the Recipient to develop and improve the technology acquired fall in this category as it clearly hinders the Recipient's chances to compete effectively with the Supplier and also runs directly against policies favouring research and innovation.

(3) Restrictions on acquisition or use of competing technology

Article 9(4) TICR allowing a Chinese Recipient to use the foreign Supplier's and simultaneously technology from other sources corresponds to provisions in technology transfer laws of other developing countries limiting the validity of clauses restricting the Recipient's use of competing technology, as they prevent the Recipient from making a reasonable selection of the technology appropriate for its particular needs, are anticompetitive, have a strong negative effect on the Recipient's bargaining power and a limiting impact on its technological development and economic expansion.

The foreign Supplier, however, will normally prefer an exclusive relationship with one Chinese organisation hoping to establish a sound reputation for its technology, and to gain a foothold in the PRC market. It will not want its partner cooperating with its competitors, purchasing their technology, experimenting with the technology acquired from different sources, and even competing directly with the Supplier. Problems, such as the difficulty of maintaining trade secrets, could arise if the Chinese enterprise cooperated with a direct competitor of the foreign Supplier. Careful drafting is essential to afford the Supplier adequate protection in such situations. Where limitations on the use of competing technology are aimed at the use of the Supplier's trademarks in connection with technology it has not itself supplied, a contractual provision enjoining such use will generally be sufficient to protect this legitimate interest without the need for a wider restriction on the Recipient's technology choice.

(4) Exchange of improvements

Article 9(5) TICR prohibiting non-reciprocal terms of exchange of improvements of the acquired technology and thus curtailing the use of grant-back clauses from the Recipient to the Supplier (a provision found in most technology transfer laws), is now supplemented by Article 12 of the Detailed Rules. It provides that:

– the improved technology, including the right to apply for a patent right, shall belong to the improving party;

- the conditions and terms for the Recipient providing improvements to the Supplier shall be the same as when the Supplier provides improvements to the Recipient.

In the absence of a definition, these provisions leave the question open, what constitutes an 'improvement'. Only innovations with respect to the transferred technology? Or will it include new patentable inventions, derived from the concept embodied in the transferred technology?

(5) RESTRICTIONS ON QUANTITY, TYPE AND SALES PRICE OF LICENSED PRODUCTS

To counterbalance foreign investors with a powerful bargaining position, already Article 46(2) of the Joint Venture Law Implementing Regulations provided that 'unless otherwise agreed upon by both parties, the technology exporting party shall not put any restrictions on the quality, price or region of sale of products for export'. Article 9(6) TICR extends this for technology transfer imported to the quantity and type of products manufactured using the imported technology and makes a special approval a requirement for a provision restrictive in this regard.

Similar provisions prohibiting limitations on the scope and volume of production and price fixing are generally contained in technology transfer regulations of developing countries. Restrictions on the type of product to be manufactured are legitimate, if they are field of use restrictions within the specific scope of the industrial property right in question. Price fixing provisions may perform different functions. One of the principal purposes of these clauses is to protect the sales base on which royalties are calculated. This is a relatively frequent practical problem, because royalties are generally fixed as a percentage of net sales. The Supplier may, therefore, have a legitimate interest in stipulating (reasonable) minimum (or maximum) prices to be charged by the Recipient.

(6) RESTRICTIONS ON EXPORT MARKETS

Article 9(7) reflects the Chinese desire to obtain their own export markets. In practice, a restriction may be 'unreasonable' if prohibiting the Recipient from exporting to a market where the foreign Supplier has no presence. Under Article 46(2) of the Joint Venture Law Implementing Regulations the parties could arrive at a contrary agreement disallowing Chinese exports, but under the TICR the approval authority has ultimate control.

A possible compromise on exports is to phrase the restriction in a permissive fashion by providing that the Recipient may sell the goods produced with the technology in designated markets that do not greatly concern the licensor, such as countries of the socialist bloc. This solution will, however, only be valid for the duration of the contract or possibly a few more years after expiration of the contract.

Article 14 of the Detailed Rules now somewhat clarifies the scope of the ban on export restrictions by excepting from the requirement of a special approval restrictions to export to countries and regions:

– where the Supplier has already concluded exclusive licensing contracts; and
– where the Supplier has concluded sole agency (and distributor?) contracts,

thus obviously considering these two situations to be *per se* 'reasonable'. These exceptions are in line with exceptions to similar prohibitions on export restrictions in other developing countries.

For the Suppliers that cannot qualify under one of these exceptions, the issue is how easily approval for restrictions on export sales in other cases will be granted. One notes that under the Detailed Rules only 'approval' is required, whereas the TICR require 'special approval'.

(7) POST-TERMINATION USE BAN

Of particular concern to the foreign investor is Article 9(8) TICR which consistent with longstanding Chinese (and other developing countries') policy and the Shenzhen and Xiamen Regulations and the Joint Venture Law Implementing Regulations allows the Recipient to use the technology after the contract has been terminated.

The restriction on a post-termination use ban is reiterated by Article 15 of Detailed Rules which adds that, if 'at the time a contract expires, a patent involved in the imported technology has not expired, the matter shall be handled in accordance with the relevant provisions of the Patent Law' of the PRC, indicating that in that case a renewal/extension of the contract may be negotiated for.

Under these circumstances, the transfer of technology to the Chinese is in effect an outright (installment) sale or, as it is sometimes called, a 'perpetual license'. The approving authority, however, may find it necessary to grant frequent exemptions to this provision in order to attract advanced technology from industrialised nations.

Pricing the Technology and Method of Payment

The Chinese inevitably and understandably prefer low fees and low royalty rates. Price discussions are therefore the main point in technology transfer negotiations in the PRC. They often will go on until the very end of the contract negotiations. Price reductions, even if substantial, will never be considered as sufficient. The result is that some Suppliers have been glad to get a compensation covering at least their direct expenses in connection with the technology transfer. Technical assistance, such as training of the Recipient's personnel, delegation of the Supplier's specialists to the PRC and engineering services, should in any event be included in the compensation fixed in advance in the contract in order to avoid problems later on.

Article 5(3) TICR appears to give the parties broad discretion over the manner in which the Recipient will compensate the Supplier, providing only that the contract must make provisions for 'remuneration, the form of remuneration and the means of payment', which is reiterated by Article 7 (5) of the Detailed Rules with the addition that the price (remuneration) must be broken down.

By contrast, Article 46(1) Joint Venture Law Implementing Regulations requires that fees for the use of technology be 'fair and reasonable', states that royalties 'shall generally be adopted as the form of payment', and provides guidelines for the setting of royalty rates and calculation of royalty payments. If royalties are to be paid, they shall not exceed the 'standard international rate'. Royalties may be calculated on the basis of net sales of products or by other 'reasonable' methods agreed to by the parties.

To allow the Chinese side and the approval authorities easy evaluation of the reasonableness of the price of the technology, Article 7 (5) of the Detailed Rules now requires not only the total price or remuneration to be specified in the contract, but they must be broken down respectively itemized.

Under the Shenzhen and Guangzhou Regulations the Supplier is required to provide the Recipient with copies of earlier license contracts in respect of the same technology.

Reflecting Chinese concern about the overevaluation of technology, Article 23 of the Shenzhen Regulations provides that when technology is capitalized as part of the establishment of a joint venture, the value of the technology may not exceed twenty per cent of the registered capital of the enterprise, and the foreign side must also supply an equivalent amount of 'cash or materials as investment capital'.

All forms of payment for the technology are permitted: lump-sum payments, running royalties, product buyback or a combination of such methods. Each method has advantages and drawbacks. A lump-sum payment avoids the problems that arise in the calculation of royalties. A standard form contract provides for payment of a lump-sum contract price in negotiable instalments, the first being payable after the signing of the contract and receipt of an export license, the second within 30 days after receipt of the technical documentation has been certified, and the third within 30 days after successful completion of the acceptance test has been certified.

In view of the difficulties of paying a larger initial fee the Chinese prefer to make payments out of sales revenue. A variation that can resolve this problem where a lump-sum is payable, is agreement on payment of installments after sales begin.

If running royalties are agreed on, Chinese negotiators will seek to base them on the 'net sales value' of goods produced using the technology, which they define as gross sales revenue minus all costs incurred in the course of marketing and selling the goods, including sales taxes. An appropriate basis must be decided for determining 'gross sales revenue' and the Supplier must have the right to receive periodic reports from the Recipient on sales activity. The Supplier may also want to provide for minimum royalties irrespective of production or sales.

An issue relating to both lump-sum payments and running royalties is access of the Recipient to foreign exchange. In view of their lack of sufficient foreign exchange, Recipients in Socialist countries frequently express a preference for payment to be effected by countertrade, i.e. compensation or product buy-back: In a separate contract, the Supplier undertakes to buy goods manufactured with the licensed technology (buy-back) or other goods not related to the licensed technology (compensation) to mitigate the burden on the Recipient's foreign exchange outlay for the technology. The Chinese have in recent years increasingly expressed an interest in such arrangements, which, in view of the problems involved with such arrangements for the foreign party well-known from other Socialist countries, make technology transfer negotiations even more difficult and time-consuming.[14]

Guarantees

The issue of the 'technology guarantee' lies at the heart of many Chinese technology transfer contract negotiations. Already the Joint Venture Law Implementing Regulations required that technology contributed 'shall be truly advanced and appropriate to China's needs'. They go on to provide that where loss is caused by the provision of outdated technology, compensation must be paid, if the loss is caused by deception on the part of the foreign Supplier. A further general requirement is that the Supplier must specify in the contract the technical characteristics and practical value of the technology.

Under Article 6 TICR the Supplier must guarantee that it is the 'lawful owner' of the technology transferred and that it is correct, complete, effective and capable of achieving the objectives as specified in the contract. Similar provisions appear in the Shenzhen Regulations. Article 9 of the Detailed Rules similarly provides that the Supplier shall guarantee 'that the technology or documents and materials being provided are complete, accurate and effective and the technical objectives stipulated in the contract can be achieved by using the same'. It adds that the 'delivery time of technical documents shall comply with the requirements for the planned schedule of the Recipient's project'. Already before the existence of relevant legislation, Chinese negotiators regularly raised such demands. The second guarantee

---

14. A detailed discussion of Chinese countertrade practice can be found in J. Bell, *The Complete Guide to Countertrade and Offset in South-East Asia, China and the Far East* (COI Publications London 1988), p. 61 *et seq.*

required reflects standard contract practice. The requirement of a guarantee of 'lawful ownership' seemed to cover the question of the Supplier's liability for infringement of third parties' rights. This is now clarified by Article 11 of the Detailed Rules. It reiterates that requirement while providing more detail: The Supplier shall guarantee that it is the lawful owner of the technology being provided or that it has 'the right to transfer or license such technology'. If the Recipient is accused by a third party of an infringement of its rights by producing or selling products with the technology transferred or licensed, it 'shall be responsible for answering the suit' and compensate the Recipient for the losses incurred, if the infringement is established. Although a provision on handling claims of infringement is welcome, the new provision follows the language of standard form technology import contracts and is thus a rather simplistic response to a complex issue.

The most onerous guarantee required, i.e. that the Supplier must guarantee the capability of the technoloy to achieve the objectives stipulated in the contract, is a result of the unsatisfactory experiences the Chinese had in the past in technology transfer dealings with some Western companies. Chinese negotiators often use this statutory base to put forth an even more extreme demand, that the foreign Supplier guarantee the success of the technology transfer. Sometimes the Chinese side goes so far as to demand that a major portion of the technology transfer fee be paid only upon demonstration of the 'success' of the technology transfer, as evidenced for example by the achievement of a certain set of performance standards or production figures. Hence the importance they place on acceptance tests discussed below. Alternatively or in addition (!), requests are sometimes made that the foreign Supplier provide technical assistance – often without limit and at no extra charge – until the specified level of performance has been met.

Article 7(3) of the Detailed Rules now provides that the contract shall contain the standards, term and method for the assessment and examination of whether the imported technology has reached the objective and the bearing of responsibility for risks. The latter seems to mean liablility for the failure of the imported technology to reach the objectives. Such a situation is generally provided for by the standard form technology import contracts that define the responsibilities of the parties for such a situation.

As the scope of such guarantees depends on the manner in which the 'objectives' are defined in the contract, and upon other contractual stipulations requiring the Recipient to apply the technology in a proper manner, the contract must be drafted carefully to ensure that the scope of such guarantees is limited and clearly defined: The objectives of the contract and the results expected from the Recipient's application of the technology must be set forth in the contract as detailed and accurately as possible; adequate means for assuring that the technology transferred is complete and operational in accordance with the contract must be provided for as well as the maintenance of quality standards be ensured by obligating the Recipient to abide by specified quality control procedures and to permit inspection of its premises by the Supplier's technicians.

Documents

Another point of major concern for the Chinese negotiators is the technical documentation, which, like the technology transfer guarantee just discussed, has a statutory base in Article 5 TICR, providing that the parties should make clear provision in the contract for the 'contents, scope and necessary description of the technology to be imported'. This concern is also expressed in the standard form contracts the Chinese entities often use – a significant portion of these contracts often deals with documentation – and by an almost obsessive concern with the details of the documentation and by negotiating for payment of penalties if the documentation is incomplete or inaccurate.

The notion is that by the provision of detailed and accurate documentation the transfer of technology can be effected in a straightforward and relatively simple fashion, which is, of course, not true. Documentation by itself is (relatively) worthless and the technology transfer can only succeed with the active cooperation of both parties, i.e. between their technical and other relevant personnel.

Acceptance Tests

A major problem area in the negotiation of technology transfer contracts are the clauses on acceptance tests, which are required in order that the Supplier ensure the Recipient's ability to use the technology properly and that he be capable of manufacturing the product.

One aspect of the Recipient's attitudes toward these transactions is to treat the transaction like the sale of a bundle of documents intended to ensure that the Recipient, after using the instructions contained in the documents, will produce a product which meets the contract specifications. Yet the standard contract clauses do not contain language which requires the Recipient to follow the Supplier's instructions strictly, although Recipients will agree to insert such a requirement if the Suppliers insist.

Chinese standard form contracts are similar in the organization and language of the clauses on acceptance tests: They usually provide that the tests shall be conducted in China in the presence of the Supplier's technicians with test methods and other technical aspects provided in detail in the appendix to the contract. If the acceptance test demonstrates that the product conforms to the specifications agreed on in advance, then the parties are required to sign an acceptance certificate.

If, however, the product fails to pass the acceptance test, the clauses, first of all, require both parties to consult together and analyse the causes. In addition the Chinese side will want the contract to reflect agreement that the two parties will together work out and resolve any difficulties that may arise, conduct another acceptance test, and clarify the responsiblity. The clauses may also require that in such an event, the period for which the Supplier is

269

required to keep his technicians in China may be extended for an agreed time.

If responsibility for the failure is determined by the parties to lie with the Recipient, then the parties shall sign a certification of acceptance test 'termination', but the Supplier may be required to assist the Recipient in trying to eliminate the defects. If responsibility lies with the Supplier, it will have to supply the Recipient with the correct documentation and assist it in taking measures to eliminate the defects. If the defect cannot be remedied within an extended time period agreed by the parties, then the Supplier usually has to pay a penalty under the penalty clause in the contract.

In any event, the parties should agree at the outset on a precise definition of the test methods which will be used, and on the standards that will be employed to measure conformity of the tested sample or prototype with contract specifications. The beneficial feature of these acceptance tests must be impressed upon the Chinese party during the negotiations, linking the success of the product in export markets to maintaining its quality which is associated with the Supplier's trade name. If the end-user representatives are technically competent, it should not be too difficult to reach agreement with them on these matters, which are normally the subject of a detailed appendix.

Training and Technical Assistance

Both the Shenzhen and Xiamen Regulations require the foreign transferor to train Chinese personnel so the Chinese side can master the technology provided. The Xiamen Regulations call for training in such areas as technology, design, management and marketing.

The TICR, however, do not obligate the Supplier to train the Recipient's personnel so as to ensure that the Recipient will be able to completely master the technology. The issue of training is left to the discretion of the parties to the contract.

Because of the emphasis placed in practice on training and technical assistance, it is of considerable importance for the contract to provide in detail for it and for which party will bear the expense, the more so as often more technical assistance is to be given than expected, also with regard to a continuous quality control and marketing.

However, although the Chinese side wants to receive training and technical assistance, it is reluctant to pay more than a small fee for the Supplier's services and frequently requests that such charges be included in the technology fee and that they should not be separately identified in the contract. It remains to be seen, whether this practice will continue in view of Article 7(5) of the Detailed Rules requiring the price or remuneration to be broken down/itemized. Standard Chinese documentation on training requires insertion of the details of the person/days to be spent in either country by the personnel of the other side. Responsibility for international travel and for living expenses is negotiable, although it is both common and reasonable to adjust the scale of living of foreign personnel in China to local levels.

Quite apart from the inclusion of appropriate language on financial responsibility for such costs, it is essential to include language on the living and working conditions of foreign personnel in China, the more so, as they are unaccustomed to China's lower standard of living. This is especially important because the precise conditions under which foreign personnel (and, in some cases, their dependents) will live are often not studied carefully by the Chinese side or discussed in detail by the two sides at the time the contract is negotiated.

Within the context of a joint venture contract, these training expenses are usually borne solely by the joint venture company. When technology is being licensed separately, on the other hand, the Supplier is often expected to bear the cost of training. The respective responsibilities of the parties should be negotiated: living quarters, entry and re-entry visas, availability of transportation to and from work, medical care, interpreters, work clothing and security. The Chinese usually expect a long-term relationship with respect to the Supplier rendering the necessary technical assistance.

Confidentiality

A key issue and point of major concern in every technology transaction is the problem of protecting the Supplier's proprietary information. Unless confidentiality can be maintained, the Supplier may lose substantial revenue by having the Recipient subsequently resell the transferred technology to numerous entities throughout China.

In contrast to other laws and regulations relating to the transfer of technology and discussed in the following, the Joint Venture Law and its Implementing Regulations do not specify any requirement as to confidentiality. It is therefore imperative to provide for confidentiality expressly in the joint venture contract where know-how is transferred as part of a foreign party's contribution to the capital of a joint venture.

Article 7 TICR provides as to confidentiality that the Recipient shall undertake to keep confidential that part of the technology that is secret and has not been made public in accordance with the scope and period agreed upon by the parties. The scope and lenght of time the Recipient will be bound by the confidentiality obligation were left entirely for the parties to decide. The period needed not be limited to the term of the contract which was of concern to certain foreign investors with very advanced and specialised technology, where a ten year confidentiality period would be insufficient. Thus, although a foreign Supplier was generally required to 'sell', rather than give a temporary license for its technology, it was at least able to negotiate a confidentiality period longer than the maximum ten year term of the technology transfer contract.

Article 13 of the Detailed Rules however, now sets clear limits on the confidentiality obligations:

first, it stipulates that the confidentiality period must generally not exceed the effective term of the contract and that a special approval will be required if the Supplier desires such longer period. In that case, the period shall be specified in the contract and the reason therefore be stated when applying for approval;

second, Article 13 allows an extension of the period of confidentiality if the Supplier is under an obligation to provide improvements, but in that case the confidentiality period begins on the date the improvement is provided and may not extend for a term longer than the original term of the contract;

third, Article 13 provides in correspondence with international practice, that if the technology is made public during the confidentiality period through no fault of the Recipient, its confidentiality obligation terminates.

The limitation on confidentiality periods in the Detailed Rules may not present a problem in the – in any event rare – case of a 'pure' patent license. Most times, however, technology is transferred/licensed either in 'hybrid' contracts combining a patent license and know-how transfer or a 'pure' know-how contract. In such cases, a clause providing for the confidentiality obligation to survive the expiration of the term of the contract is of paramount importance to the Supplier. It remains to be seen whether the Chinese authorities will acknowledge the legitimate interests of the Supplier in their treatment of an application for the special approval.

The Shenzhen and Xiamen Regulations go a step further than the TICR and the Detailed Rules in not only providing the parties to the contract are bound by confidentiality obligations, but also that any Chinese personnel who have access to confidential technology must not disclose or use such technology without authorization. The Xiamen Regulations also specify that, in the event of an unauthorized disclosure, the Supplier has the right to 'take back' the relevant information, terminate the contract and demand compensation for losses in accordance with the stipulations of the contract.

In the absence of such a provision in the TICR and the Detailed Rules or any civil or common law on trade secrets or unfair competition, foreign Suppliers have recourse for unauthorized disclosure only against the Recipient that is a party to the relevant contract. Therefore the remedies for breach of the confidentiality obligation by the Chinese Recipient or its personnel should be clearly specified in the contract. Although damages for breach of contract may, pursuant to the FECL, be recoverable against a contractual Recipient that discloses confidential information, injunctive relief against unauthorized use by third parties may be difficult to obtain.

Those involved on the Chinese side, from the Recipient to the approving authority, usually acknowledge the Supplier's need to maintain the confidentiality of at least some portion of the technology being transferred. Of course, most Chinese negotiators are unwilling to accept a blanket obligation to unconditionally maintain the confidentiality of the Supplier's technology and usually press for limits on both the portion of technology to be kept confidential and the length of time the Recipient will be bound by the confidentiality obligation. One feels, however, uncomfortable when the confidentiality issue is more often than not a relatively uncontroversial subject during negotiations. This gives the impression that a Recipient's willingness to accept a confidentiality obligation in the contract is less a reflection of its willingness to be bound by this obligation, but rather of the sense that breaching it may not lead to any sanctions and that therefore there seems to be little cost in agreeing to include a confidentiality obligation in the contract. Even if the Recipient is making an effort to protect the confidentiality, the success of such an attempt may be dubious: In the Chinese bureaucratic system, enterprises are not independent and it is not unlikely that other enterprises and administrative organs, such as the department in charge and the approval authority gain access to the Supplier's confidential technical information.

The new Detailed Rules restricting the duration of the confidentiality obligation is, however, an indication that the authorities are treating this issue seriously and it is to be hoped that this attitude will filter down.

In this connection, it must be kept in mind that in the PRC, as in the state economy countries of the Eastern bloc, the contractual partner of the Supplier of technology frequently is not the end-user of the technology, but a foreign trade corporation which acts in close cooperation with the end-user. Its negotiators often resist attempts to limit disclosure to the end-user with which negotiations have been carried out. Recently, however, there seems to be more willingness to limit disclosure or use of the 'licensed' know-how, e.g. to a named plant or factory. The language of Article 7 TICR seems to permit such limitations which is rather important: Under the new Detailed Rules the obligation of confidentiality runs only to the Recipient. The end-user of the technology, strictly speaking, not being the Recipient, the end-user might want to argue it was not bound by this provision.

In order to protect the Supplier's interests first of all the confidential information should be defined as broadly and as clearly as possible and the Chinese partner be clearly obliged not to disclose or duplicate the technology or other proprietary information without the Supplier's written authorization. This obligation should survive the termination of the contract. The contract should then provide that disclosure of confidential information to employees shall only be on a need-to-know basis and that each employee to whom such information is disclosed should be required to sign an individual confidentiality agreement with the Recipient (and preferably also with the Supplier), precautions, which, with the increased mobility of labor in China, are of even greater importance now than they used to be.

Illustrative of such a situation is a dispute between a US corporation and a Chinese enterprise over the divulgance of confidential information by a former employee of the latter.[15] It was resolved exclusively by administrative means, as the main antagonist in the dispute, the employee, was beyond

15. *CDI Corporation* v. *Shenyang Stochastic Instruments Factory*, reported in: *China Law and Practice*, Vol. 1, No. 7, 24 August 1987, p. 17.

the reach of legal remedies, there being no privity of contract between him and the US corporation. Similarly, the new employer was beyond the legal range of the US corporation.

The lesson to be learned from this case is that a supplier of technology should:

– execute a confidentiality agreement with all individuals who may come in contact with its technology in the normal course of their employment or at least require the Recipient so to do;
– use a provision in the technology transfer contract with the Recipient providing that it is liable for breach of confidentiality by key personnel.

For foreigners who transfer their latest, previously unpatented techniques to China, the Chinese patent law may provide some reassurance. Even if a technology transfer contract lasts only five to ten years, the foreign company will enjoy fifteen years protection against unauthorized use of its technology if it has a patent registered in China.

Duration of Contract

Most laws regulating international technology transfer transactions include provisions against unduly long duration conditions. Already prior to such legislation in the PRC Chinese Recipients have been reluctant to enter into agreements that obligate them to make payments over long periods of time. A period of five years had been common, although longer periods were possible. The contract duration desired by the Supplier depends in part on whether payment is by lump-sum or running royalty. The Supplier must, however, realize that in many cases PRC law makes a license contract an installment sale by linking duration restrictions with limitations on post-termination royalties, restrictions on the Recipient's use of the technology at the end of the contract and other post-termination obligations imposed on the Recipient.

The length of the contract should allow an adequate time for the Recipient to master the imported technology but may not exceed 10 years: From the Chinese point of view, the main purpose of the technology import is the successful exploitation of a technology in production and not simply the carrying out of a business transaction, as foreign parties often see it. Whereas foreign Suppliers view a technology transfer contract as an alternative marketing strategy and therefore as a method of earning royalty revenue for as long a time as possible, the Chinese look upon the same contract as a means of mastering a technical innovation.

Consequently, Article 8 TICR provides that the term of the contract shall be as long as the Recipient needs to absorb the technology transferred, but not longer than ten years without a special approval by the approval authority. The Shenzhen Regulations are more strict, their Article 19 making five years the normal limit, subject to possible extension and, unless the technology is contributed as part of the capital of a joint venture, the term of contracts involving patented technology is not to go beyond the expiration date of the patent concerned. The Joint Venture Law Implementing Regulations limit the term of a technology transfer to a joint venture to ten years. The Xiamen Regulations do not contain any provisions concerning the contract term.

A term that exceeds these limits must either have special approval or be effected by renewal of the contract at the end of the original period, with such renewal also subject to approval by the original approval authority. In practice, however, special approval for an extended term is usually difficult to obtain. Article 21 of the new Detailed Rules, however, now offers the parties the opportunity to explain in detail the reasons why the contract term should exceed ten years.

The usual maximum duration of ten years together with the unrestricted use of the technology after expiration of the contract will in particular for products with high technical standing often be unacceptable: Since it may be quite a number of years until the Recipient's start up of production and as sales may grow slower than originally expected, the Supplier would then only receive royalties during a few remaining years.

Language

According to Article 12 FECL contracts should normally contain a provision concerning the languages used in the contract and their effectiveness, thus leaving the solution of the issue of language to the parties. The parties to technology transfer contracts often agree to sign only an English text, although in practice a Chinese translation will be prepared for internal review purposes. To avoid ambiguities and misunderstandings, it must be ensured that the Chinese text, even if not signed, is an accurate translation of the foreign language text. If both the Chinese and the foreign language text are to be signed, the contract should provide that they are equally authoritative, unless the parties agree that, in case of discrepancies, one text prevails over the other. In both instances, it is of great importance to ascertain whether the Chinese terminology has the same or a similar meaning to the corresponding English terminology, which, in fact, often meets certain obstacles.

Settlement of Disputes

PRC legislation generally requires each foreign-related contract to have a dispute resolution clause.[16] No special rules apply to licensing: According to

---

16. As to 'The Role of Arbitration in Economic Co-operation with China' *see* J.A. Cohen, in: M.J. Moser, *Foreign Trade* ... (above note 1), pp. 508–531. *See also* E. Lee, *Commercial Disputes Settlement in China* (Lloyd's of London Press 1985).

Article 8(7) of the Detailed Rules, the contract shall provide for 'the method for the settlement of disputes'. Details are left to the parties. During negotiations, however, the Chinese normally press for an arbitration clause to follow the ubiquitous clause calling for 'friendly consultation' between the parties as a first choice. Similar to the Japanese, the Chinese prefer negotiation to arbitration to resolve disputes and there is a strong preference for arbitration over litigation if some form of dispute settlement should prove necessary.

Clauses providing for third-country arbitration are permitted under Article 37 FECL and are often accepted. The most popular foreign choice to date is arbitration under the auspices of the Institute of Arbitration of the Chamber of Commerce in Stockholm, although Zurich (Chamber of Commerce) or London (London Court of International Arbitration) are occasionally agreed to. It is often accepted to use the UNCITRAL Arbitration Rules under the administration of the said Arbitration Institute. Hongkong's current effort to become an arbitration center has Chinese support: Clauses providing for arbitration pursuant to the rules of the International Arbitration Centre in Hongkong are more and more frequently found. Chinese parties sometimes suggest arbitration in the country of the defendant as a compromise.

ICC arbitration has been unacceptable to Chinese parties until the very recent past because of Taiwan's participation in the ICC. This situation seems to be changing, as very recently clauses providing for ICC arbitration have been suggested by Chinese parties themselves.

Another solution might be to provide for arbitration within China by an ad hoc body in accordance with the UNCITRAL Arbitration Rules, which are familiar to a foreign party. They contain detailed provisions as to procedure and an equitable selection of arbitrators. The award rendered by such an arbitral panel may also prove easier to enforce in China than that of a foreign panel, although the enforcement of foreign awards in the PRC has been simplified by its accession to the 1958 New York Convention on the Recognition and Enforcement of Foreign Arbitral Awards.

Contract Approval

The contract for the transfer of technology must be in writing and be submitted by the Recipient within 30 days from the date of signature to the MOFERT or local authorities ('approval authorities'; Article 4 TICR, Articles 5 and 17 of the Detailed Rules) together with an appropriate application for approval, a copy of the contract with a Chinese translation and documents evidencing the legal status of the parties to the contract (Article 10 TICR).

Article 6 of the Detailed Rules provides in great detail for examination and approval 'at different levels' and adds to the documents to be submitted under the TICR the approved feasibility study and details concerning financing. Their Article 8 requires the specification of the numbers of patents/

trademarks or of the applications therefore, if the technology import contract involves the transfer or licensing of Chinese patents/trademarks. The approval authority shall approve the contract or deny approval within 60 days from the date of receipt of the application. If it fails to make a decision within that period, the contract shall be deemed approved and becomes effective automatically (Article 4 TICR, Article 19 of the Detailed Rules).

Even though a time limit has been imposed on the authorities regarding when they will have to decide whether to approve or reject a contract, this can nevertheless develop into a long and drawn out process if they require frequent amendments and revisions of the contract terms. The Supplier should therefore urge the Recipient to take advantage of the new provision in the TICR authorizing it to consult with and seek pre-examination from the authorities during the negotiations.

One problem arising in connection with deemed approval is whether a contract that contains clauses requiring 'special approval', i.e. unfair restrictive clauses listed in Article 9 TICR, can be approved in such fashion. Another problem in this context is that Article 24 of the Detailed Rules requires that the 'Approval Certificate for Technology Import Contract' must be presented when going through such processes as acquiring bank guarantees, letters of credit, payment, account clearance, Customs declaration and tax payment. Officials from MOFERT have, however, indicated that a deemed approval will be fully effective and that an approval certificate will be issued on such basis.

Article 18 TICR provides that if the contract contains any of the following provisions and is not amended within the time limit specified by the approval authority, the contract will not be approved:

- the contract violates the current laws or regulations and/or is detrimental to the public interest;
- the contract is detrimental to state sovereignty;
- the contents of the contract are inconsistent with the approved feasibility study of the project;
- the basic terms and contents of the contract are incomplete;
- the contract does not contain clear and reasonable provisions on liabilities in the event of a dispute over property rights in the transferred or licensed technology and other disputes arising during the performance of the contract and the method of resolving such a dispute;
- the contract does not contain reasonable provisions for the technical level and the economic benefits that the transferred or licensed technology should attain, including a warranty concerning the quality of the products produced with such technology;
- the price of the imported technology and the method of payment for it are unreasonable;
- the provisions for the rights, liabilities and obligations of the parties to the contract are not sufficiently clear, reciprocal or reasonable;
- the contract contains provisions promising preferential tax treatment which the state tax authorities have not agreed to.

277

The Detailed Rules repeat the provisions on effects of approval or disapproval of a contract that are set forth in the TICR and the FECL, providing that contracts only become effective upon approval and that the effective date is that of the approval. They allow for the amendment and resubmission of a disapproved contract.

PRC Taxation

Before signing a contract, it is advisable to seek a written ruling on the tax consequences of any transaction in the PRC and to include it as an appendix to the contract.[17] Unfortunately, in the past it was difficult to obtain one. In Beijing, the municipal tax bureau has informed MOFERT officials that it will only give rulings after a contract has been signed. The contract should therefore spell out the anticipated tax treatment for the transaction, obligate the Chinese party to assist the foreign party in obtaining available tax reductions or exemptions, and tie the contract's effectiveness to official approval of the desired tax treatment. Attempts to put the entire burden for the payment of taxes on the Chinese party have been consistently rejected by the Ministry of Finance.

Some local tax bureaux and the Ministry of Finance, although they are unwilling to give written opinions, are increasingly willing to provide informal advice prior to the signing of contracts if they are given the opportunity to review the complete contracts with the appendices after the parties have initialled them.

Suppliers having an 'establishment' in the PRC will be taxed under the Foreign Enterprise Income Tax Law ('FEITL') on net royalty income with a source in the PRC at progressive rates between twenty and 40 percent, while others will be subject to a flat twenty percent withholding tax on the gross income. In addition, a local income tax of ten percent of the amount of taxable income is levied, making the overall tax burden 30 percent to 50 percent. Generally, foreign enterprises earning fees for the use within the PRC of proprietary technology have been taxed on the withholding basis. The withholding tax applies to fees for the use of proprietary rights within the PRC, technical training, technical services (whether conducted within or outside of China), and technical documentation provided in connection with a transfer of technology.

When fees for a technology transfer are subject to a withholding tax, it

---

17. For an overview on the Chinese tax system, *see* T.A. Gelatt and R.D. Pomp, 'China's Tax System: An Overview and Transactional Analysis', in: M.J. Moser (ed.), *Foreign Trade* ... (above note 1), pp. 42–89. For a more detailed introduction, *see* T.A. Gelatt and Ta-Kuang Chang, *Corporate and Individual Taxation in the People's Republic of China* (Hongkong: Longman Group 1985), and E. Jehle, *Investment and Taxation in the People's Republic of China* (5th edn.) (Amsterdam: International Bureau of Fiscal Documentation, 1985).

may be reduced to ten percent or a total exemption may be granted for royalties in some fields of advanced technology under two circulars issued by the Ministry of Finance in May 1982 and January 1983 providing more detail on Article 27 of the Implementing Rules to the FEITL. A reduction to ten percent normally requires approval by the local tax authorities, but if the Recipient is located in one of the SEZs or the fourteen open coastal cities the rate of withholding tax has been reduced to 10 percent across the board.[18] The local authorities may grant further reductions or a complete exemption from tax if the transferred technology is considered 'advanced' or offered on 'preferential' terms. For transfer to Recipients outside such areas, total exemption from withholding tax must be approved by the Ministry of Finance itself and will be available only if the technology is 'advanced' and the terms of the transfer are 'preferential'.

The PRC has signed or prepared to sign bilateral agreements for the avoidance of double taxation with respect to taxes on income with a number of countries. Most of these agreements have taken the 1977 OECD Model Agreement on Avoidance of Double Taxation as well as the United Nations model for developed and developing countries as a reference. The main content of these agreements is therefore very similar.

---

18. As to tax and other incentives offered in the Special Economic Zones and the 14 Open Coastal Cities, *see* E. Pow and M.J. Moser, 'Law and Investment in China's Special Investment Areas', in: M.J. Moser (ed.), *Foreign Trade* ... (above note 1), pp. 199–269.

Chapter 12
Negotiation and Establishment of Joint Ventures in the People's Republic of China

by Stefan Messmann

Senior Counsel, Volkswagen AG
Wolfsburg, Germany

Introduction

The Chinese often pretend that a contract is nothing else but an indication of mutual distrust. But in the same time the contract seems to be, nevertheless, a useful instrument to implement the economic aspects of the open door-policy. The following figures prove that clearly: the contracted foreign investments, since China had opened its doors to the outside world in 1979, total more than US$21.9-billion from nearly 30 countries, more than US$ 8.47-billion of which had been actually invested. So far, from 1979 up to the end of 1987, 10,000 joint venture contracts have been signed. More than 4,000 joint ventures have begun operations.[1]

About 60 per cent of the total foreign investments came from Hong Kong, followed by investors from Japan (10.5 per cent), the United States (8.7 per

---

1. *See China Daily*, 23 Jan 1988.

cent) and the EEC countries. From the EEC countries the most investments came from the United Kingdom (2.6 per cent), followed by France (2.4 per cent) and Germany (1.2 per cent). Most of the money has gone into light industry, textiles and the hotel business. Little of it has gone into high technology, energy and transport projects, which are what China would like to develop. There is no surprise in it: four times as many foreign investors believe in the profitability of service joint ventures than in the profitability of manufacturing joint ventures.[2] However, according to a recently published survey, enterprises involved in production accounted for 85 per cent of the newly approved joint enterprises, compared with 76 per cent in 1986.[3]

After the conclusion of more than 10,000 joint venture contracts and several years of operation of some of them, the time is mature to outline the first experiences.

My personal experience is based on negotiations on the Volkswagen Joint Venture Contract. The negotiations on this Joint Venture Contract lasted five years. We have had, during this period of time, close contacts with a multitude of foreign investors and councellors and, of course, exchanged experiences with them. Therefore, I will not only mention my own experiences but also relate to the experiences of and solutions found by some other foreign investors.

After this short introduction, I would like to relate to some chosen problems, such as the Chinese negotiating style and the working language, the legal framework of the Chinese foreign economic legislation, the financial constitution as well as the organizational structure of joint ventures.

Negotiation and Establishment of Joint Ventures

I already stated that the negotiations for the conclusion of the Joint Venture Contract of Volkswagen lasted long. As far as I know, that is not an exception. Negotiations with Chinese partners last usually longer than with partners from other countries. The reasons therefore lay merely in the Chinese negotiating style as well as the language difficulties the foreign partner meet in China (and *vice versa*).

In the following I will deal first with the problems just mentioned.

---

2. Only ten per cent of Japanese firms engaged or interested in doing business with China agree that manufacturing firms with equity joint ventures are likely to make acceptable returns. The portion is higher for American firms (seventeen per cent) and higher still for Europeans (28 per cent). The reluctance of the Japanese to make equity investments again comes out in the results on service where they are less bullish than American or European firms. *See* Campbell, *China Strategies: The Inside Story*, University of Manchester/ University of Hong Kong 1986, p. 30.
3. *See China Daily*, 23 Jan 1988.

Negotiations with Chinese partners

Chinese negotiating style

The Chinese negotiating style may be characterized[4] by:

- opening moves;
- period of assessment;
- end game and;
- implementation.

In the opening moves, Chinese will make efforts to establish a sympathetic counterpart as an interlocutor in order to cultivate personal relationship or even 'friendship' with him. The period of assessment is then characterized by:

- facilitating maneuvers like sightseeing, toasts etc.;
- pressure tactics; and
- endless patience exercises.

The end of game usually comes unexpected, often combined with a political event, such as a visit of high ranking politicians from the foreign partner's country, and no matter whether the principles stressed early in a negotiation had been observed or not. The end of game thus played is usually followed by pressures for implementation giving the impression that contracts are never quite final.

Vis-à-vis such negotiating behavior, the following guidelines may be useful for foreigners negotiating with Chinese partners:

- know the substantive issues;
- master the past negotiating records;
- know your own bottom line;
- present your position in a broad framework;
- be patient;
- avoid time deadlines; and
- minimize media pressures.

---

4. *See* Solomon, *Chinese Political Negotiating Behaviour*, January 1983 (unpublished). Although Solomon described the Chinese **political** negotiating style, it appeared that there is no substantial difference between the Chinese political and commercial negotiating behaviours. The essential of the cited paper is therefore also valid for negotiation on joint venture or technology transfer contracts. *See also* Pye, 'The Chinese Trade: Making the Deal,' in: *Harvard Business Review*, No. 4, July/August 1986.

Working language

The language to be used in joint venture contracts is the second reason for long negotiations. Although it is not prescribed in any regulation, the Chinese authorities regularly ask for the Chinese version of joint venture contracts for approval. However, foreign partners seldom accept to sign a contract in Chinese only. Therefore, the most of joint venture contracts are negotiated and signed both in Chinese as well as in a foreign language. The most frequently language used in joint venture contracts is English, even when the foreign partner is not originated from an English speaking country. Many may object that contracts having two original versions may be subject to frequent disputes on interpretation. That is, in principle, true. Therefore, in many cases the contracting parties determine one sole working language to be used exclusively.

However, even without the determination of the working language, problems of interpretation of bilingual Sino-foreign joint venture contracts might not be greater than such in multi-language countries like Switzerland where every legislative act on federal level is mandatorily promulgated in three languages.

LEGAL FRAMEWORK OF CHINESE FOREIGN LEGISLATION

It may be a common place for lawyers but it should, nevertheless, be mentioned that in each international contract the applicable law should be determined first because the most subsequent solutions can only be made in dependence of the applicable law.

According to Article 5, paragraph 2, of the Foreign Economic Contract Law,[5] joint venture contracts can only be governed by Chinese law. This very clear provision generates several problems for the foreign partner. The main question is: How acceptable is the Chinese law for foreign investment[6] and could a foreign arbitral tribunal make use of it? For an answer to this question, the starting point is the examination of the status of the Chinese economic reform.

In the actual stage of the reforms of the economic system, the aims are now described as 'planned commodity economy' because according to the Marxist ideology, products traded on the market are called 'commodities'. In contrast to this formula, before the reforms of the economic system, plans were imperative and set concrete goals, e.g. the amount of certain

---

5. The Foreign Economic Contract Law of the P. R. of China of 21 March 1985; for an English translation *see China Economic News*, Beijing, 1 April 1985, hereafter cited as 'CEN'.
6. The Law of the P. R. of China on Joint Ventures Using Chinese and Foreign Investment of 1 July 1979; hereafter cited as 'the Joint Venture Law'; for an English translation *see*: *Victor E. S.* Sit (ed.), *Commercial Laws & Business Regulations of the P. R. of China*, hereafter cited as 'CLBR', Hong Kong 1983, pp. 326–328.

items to be produced by enterprises determined by the state plan and to be delivered to certain other enterprises for prices determined by authorities in charge of such enterprises. Actually, in the new 'planned commodity economy' system—imperative plans are replaced by indicative plans setting only general instructions as guidelines for the economic policy of the state which itself tends to withdraw from the direct economic operations. Thus far, however, several questions remain unclear. It is especially not yet definitively settled how the state intends to withdraw from economic activities, however, simultaneously maintaining property in the means of production in state-owned enterprises, whereas such state-owned enterprises shall, on the other hand, exercise proprietary rights in their means of production. In this context, questions such as these become corner-stone problems not only in China but also in other socialist countries envisaging economic and legal reforms.

The Chinese economy is developing and likely to develop further to a mixed system using macro-economic indicators elaborated upon by the State Planning Commission and having an increasing number of market elements. These economic reforms, which slow some parallel features to those existing in Hungary and Poland, generate on the other hand legal reform.

To date, decisions of state courts and arbitral tribunals do not play any important role at the interpretation of laws. The quality of awards is still low and in general they are not quoted in legal literature. That practice may also change in the future, but it is not certain whether it will become more authoritative than the legal doctrine.[8]

The importance of economic law is often emphasized by top party and government leaders. For example, in a letter to the Economic Legislation Research Centre of the State Council and the China Economic Law Research Society, party and government leader Zhao Ziyang wrote that economic legislation was required for the development of the 'planned commodity economy'.[9]

Furthermore, economic tribunals have been set-up at 3,300 higher, intermediate and basic courts all over the country.[10]

The legal development in China has been remarkable: On the one hand, in 1981 China enacted the Economic Law[11] and in 1986 the Principles of

---

7. See Münzel, in: *Gutachten zu Fragen des chinesischen Wirtschaftsrechts*, 1983 (unpublished), but also *see* Weggel, 'Gesetzgebung und Rechtspraxis im nachmaoistischen China,' *China aktuell*, August 1986, p. 522.
8. See Münzel, *op. cit.*, note 7 above. However, foreign-Sino commercial cases seem to go now more frequently to arbitration. Thus, according to *China Daily*, dated 29 October 1987, the Foreign Economic and Trade Arbitration Commission has accepted 130 cases involving foreign partners from dozens of countries, including the United States, Japan, Germany, Italy, Poland, Czechoslovakia and Hong Kong since the beginning of 1987 and arbitrated 30 of them.
9. *See China Daily*, 21 July 1987.
10. Idem, but also *see China Daily*, 20 August 1987.
11. The Economic Contract Law of the P. R. of China of 13 December 1981; for an English translation *see CLBR*, note 6, pp. 300–308.

Civil Law[12] as the corner-stones of the internal legal regulations. Further-more, it developed the typification of enterprises by different rules[13] and enacted a very controversial and hotly debated bankruptcy law[14] which, however, will only come into effect after a comprehensive company law has been passed. The difficulties to put such a law into effect are political: it may lead to an increase of latent unemployment without backing it by adequate social insurances.

On the other hand, it probably developed foreign economic legislation even more: The Joint Venture Law of 1979[15] was soon followed by the Joint Venture Income Tax Law,[16] the Foreign Enterprises Income Tax Law,[17] the Statute on Industrial Relations,[18] and the Implementation Regulations on the Joint Venture Law.[19] The following years have seen the promulgation of the Foreign Economic Contract Law[20] and the Technology Import Regul-

---

12. General Principles of Civil Law of the People's Republic of China', *Renmin Ribao* (overseas edn.), 17 April 1986.
13. *See* for references Münzel, 'A Law in Development: The Company Law of the P. R. of China: a Branch of Law in the Process of Development', *Chinese Economic Law International Symposium* in Lausanne, 5 and 6 December 1986, Zürich 1987, hereafter cited as 'Lausanne Symposium', pp. 19–57.
14. For a rough translation of the Chinese bankruptcy law *see Summary of World Broadcasts* FE/8435/C1/6 December 1986. *See also* Liu Xiaoxing, 'Zur Einführung der Institution des Konkurses für unsere chinesischen Unternehmen (mit Vorbemerkungen von Münzel)', *RabelsZ* 49 (1985), pp. 347–357, Münzel, 'Kartellrecht in China', *RIW* 4/1987, pp. 261–276, Chang Ta-Kuang, 'The Making of the Chinese Bankruptcy Law: A Study in the Chinese Legislative Process', 28 *Harvard Int. L. I.* (1987), pp. 333–372, and Peng Xiaohua, 'Characteristics of China's First Bankruptcy Law', *loc. cit.*, pp. 373–384.
15. *See* note 6 above. Subsequently, the central government established so-called 'special economic zones and open cities' (Dalian, Qinhuangdao, Tianjin, Yantai, Qingdao, Lianyungang, Nantong, Shanghai, Ningbo, Wenzhou, Fouzhou, Guangzhou, Zhangjiang, Beihai, Hainan) allowing them to enact special investment legislations. *See*, e. g., Regulations of the P. R. of China on Special Economic Zones in Guangdong Province, approved on 26 August 1980; reprinted in: *China Laws for Foreign Business* (CCH Austl. Ltd.), hereafter 'China Laws', 70–800; Regulations of Shenzhen Special Economic Zone on Foreign Economic Contracts, approved on 11 January 1984, reprinted in: *China Laws*, 73–505; Regulations for the Administration of the Tianjin Economic and Technological Development Zone, adapted on 20 July 1985, reprinted in: *China Laws*, 92–003. *See also The Law of the P. R. of China on Enterprises Operating Exclusively with Foreign Capital*; for an English translation *see China Law Reporter* 1987, Vol. IV, No. 1, pp. 63–65. For commentaries *see* Oborne, 'China's Special Economic Zones', *Development Centre Studies of OECD*, Paris 1986.
16. The Income Tax Law of the P. R. of China concerning Joint Ventures with Chinese and Foreign Investment of 10 September 1980; for an English translation *see* CLBR, note 6 above, pp. 178–179.
17. The Income Tax Law for Foreign Enterprises of the P. R. of China of 13 December 1981; for an English translation *see* CLBR, not 6 above, pp. 186–187.
18. Regulations on Labor Management in Joint Ventures Using Chinese and Foreign Investment of 26 July 1980; for an English translation *see* CLBR, note 6 above, pp. 331–332.
19. Regulations for the Implementation of the Law of the P. R. of China on Joint Ventures Using Chinese and Foreign Investment of 20 September 1983, hereafter cited as 'the Implementation Regulation'; for an English translation see: *Law and Regulations of the P. R. of China*, vol. 2, Hong Kong 1984, pp. 71–87.
20. *See* note 5 above.

ations,[21] two enactments which, along with the legislation governing joint ventures, now form the corner-stones of the legal regime regulating foreign business activity in China.

In addition to these laws, some others of comfort to foreign partners should be mentioned. There are such laws as the Trademark Law[22] and the Patent Law.[23] Thus far, China has promulgated nearly 60 laws and regulations dealing with foreign economic activities, including seventeen issued by the National People's Congress and more than fourteen by the State Council. In addition, ministries and commissions under the State Council have also promulgated over 30 rules and regulations, and the various localities have introduced by-laws and statutes to encourage foreign investment.[24]

Furthermore, numerous international conventions regulating investment protection and avoidance of double taxation have been concluded between the government of the People's Republic of China and some other countries. Thus, between 1982 and 1986, the Chinese government concluded investment protection treaties (also called investment promotion treaties) with Sweden, Romania, Germany, France, the Belgium-Luxemburg Economic Federation, Finland, Norway, Austria, Thailand, Italy, the Netherlands, Kuwait, Sri Lanka, Singapore, Switzerland, the United Kingdom and Denmark.[25] Although the investment promotion treaty concluded in 1982 between China and Germany may be considered to be a 'trendsetter', the main trading partners of China, namely the United States and Japan, are not content with the guarantees provided in the German investment promotion treaty and have been negotiating, without success, for many years on their own treaties.

In addition, the government of China negotiates very actively on treaties for the avoidance of double taxation. It has already concluded such agreements with Belgium, France, Germany, Japan, Malaysia, Norway, the United Kingdom and the United States. For all these treaties the model treaty of the OECD (1977) served as a basis.[26]

China has also joined, on 22 January 1987, the UN Convention on Recognition and Enforcement of Foreign Arbitral Awards.

---

21. Regulations of the P. R. of China on Technology Import Contract Administration of 24 May 1985; for an English translation *see* CEN, not 5 above, 17 June 1985. *See also:* Detailed Rules and Regulations for the Implementation of the Regulations on Administration of Technology Import Contracts of the P. R. of China of 20 January 1988; for an English translation *see China Economic News* 8 February 1988.
22. The Trademark Law of the P. R. of China of 23 August 1982; for an English translation *see* CEN, note 5 above, Supp. No. 5, 1983.
23. The Patent Law of the P. R. of China of 12 March 1984; for an English translation *see* CEN, notes 5 above, Supp. No. 2, 1985.
24. *See Beijing Review*, No. 7, 16 February 1987.
25. *Idem*, but *See also* Johnston, 'Checklist of International Agreements Signed in 1985 and 1986 by the P. R. of China', *China Law Reporter* 1987, Vol. IV, No. 1, pp. 41–62.
26. *See* for references and more detail: Hoorn, 'China's Entry into the Tax Treaty Network – Definitional Problems', *Information Bulletin of the European Association for Chinese Law*, No. 3, Vol. II, September 1986, p. 7–11.

Despite these developments, many potential foreign investors still believe, however, that China's legal framework is not yet adequate to safeguard foreign investment.[27]

However, the development of the Chinese economic law encounters several problems. The main problems are the creation of a legal duality, the harmonization of economic laws and such concerning legal definitions.

Since 1980, the Chinese legal system is factured and two separate legal régimes are undergoing parallel develoment.[28] The consequences of this legal policy are somewhat disturbing. For example, a Chinese joint venture contract is governed by the Foreign Economic Contract Law, but a sales contract between such a joint venture (which is a Chinese legal entity) and a Chinese supplier or purchaser is governed by the Domestic Economic Contract Law. Similarily, transfers of technology from a foreign party to a joint venture and from the joint venture to a Chinese entity, even to another joint venture, are governed by different regulations.

What are the consequences of this legal duality?

Joint ventures doing business with state-owned enterprises in China must coordinate their activities with state plans. The result is a convergence in the economic environment in which Chinese and foreign enterprises operate in China. Nevertheless, they are subject to differential legal treatment. This situation may rather act as a deterrent to both increased foreign investment and the successful absorption of such investment into Chinese economy. As foreign business expands its activities in China and becomes subject with greater frequency to domestic legislation, foreign business, Chinese economic entities and Chinese lawyers and judges may be confused by parallel legal régimes that cover the same type of economic activity and are based on similar principles, but have differences in emphasis or application. Moreover, as both domestic and Chinese-foreign laws proliferate, unless greater effort is made to delineate which set of laws applies in particular situations, conflicts will arise with increasing frequency.

Another problem is that on harmonization of economic laws. This problem is generated by changes in internal economic relations.[29]

Accordingly, there exist actually vertical and horizontal relations. The horizontal ones are regulated by Civil Law, whereas the vertical relations are regulated by Economic Law. A harmony between horizontal and vertical regulation in Chinese domestic laws is required. This harmony, however, has not yet been reached in all legal fields.

Thus, the position of the state-owned enterprises, very important as suppliers and sales partners of joint ventures, is determined by the General

---

27. *See* Campbell, *op. cit.*, note 2 above, p. 91.
28. Macneil, 'China Needs only one Legal System', *The Wall Street Journal*, 6 December 1985.
29. Hu Yuanxiang, 'On Harmonization of Economic Laws', *Lausanne Symposium*, note 13 above, pp. 157–166.

Principles of Civil Law. However, their provisions do not regulate the question how these enterprises may achieve managerial rights and the right of using land. The future Company Law is to solve such problems. In addition, the Five-year Plans, even if the government renounced to run enterprises directly, will not free the enterprises completely of the control by the government or other administrative organizations.

Furthermore, there are definition problems in many of recently enacted laws.

In the tax law, e.g., definitional problems emanate from the fact that in tax treaties terms are being used which have no basis in internal Chinese law or what might be considered an insufficient basis. This applies, e.g., to dividends, a concept which is by itself generally understood in the framework of company law while there is still no Chinese company law at present.[30]

However, the absence of company law generates another definitional problem, too. As Article 4, paragraph 1 of the Joint Venture Law provides that a joint venture shall take the for of a limited liability company, the question arises to know which elements such a limited liability company contains. Does it contain elements universally known in this form of company, or does it contain some other elements leading toward another legal form?

In examining this question, we find that in most legal systems regulating the limited liability company there are very strict provisions on the external responsibility of associates.[31]

Summarizing such examination, it is the responsibility of associates which distinguishes the limited liability company from other forms of company.

In Chinese law, however, Article 19, paragraph 2 of the Implementation Regulations stipulates that 'each side to the joint venture is liable to the joint venture within the limit of the capital subscribed by it'. It does not mention neither here nor elsewhere any further responsibility of associates, nor may Article 4 of the Joint Venture Law stipulating that 'risks and losses of a joint venture shall be shared by the parties to the venture in proportion to their contributions to the registered capital' be interpreted in the above-mentioned sense.

Thus, there are no elements of extended responsibility of associates in a Chinese limited liability company like in other legal systems knowing such a form of company. Therefore, the limited-liability company according to the Chinese Joint Venture Law having:

– a registered fixed capital;
– decision making organs; as well as
– legal personality,

---

30. *See* Hoorn, *op. cit.*, note 26 above.
31. *See*, e. g., for the Swiss Law: Code des obligations, Article 802; for the German Law: GmbH-Gesetz, 27 and following and for the American Law: Henn, *Handbook of the Law of Corporations and other Business Enterprises*, St. Paul, Minn. 1970, 2nd ed., p. 96.

appears rather to be a company *sui generis*. It seems, however, to be more than a 'partnership' as suggested by some authors.[32]

These examples demonstrate clearly the difficulties met by the Chinese legislator: starting from a legal vacuum after the Cultural Revolution, he often inserts notions into laws without caring whether such notions may really cover the situations to be regulated. But it is true, however, the intention of the Chinese legislator is, in doing so, to recomfort the potential foreign partner by offering him legal notions to which he is accustomed.[33]

In any event, the Chinese economic law may be used with some skill and may therefore be considered as a useful basis for awards of foreign arbitral tribunals as well as prior conciliation negotiations.

After this presentation of the legal framework of the Chinese foreign economic legislation and of some of its problems, selected problems of joint venture contracts shall be examined.

Joint ventures once were established in the P. R. of China, as well as in other socialist countries having enacted joint venture legislations, by investment agreements, also called joint venture contracts. Actually three forms of joint ventures are known in China:

– the equity joint venture regulated by the Joint Venture Law;
– the contractual joint venture, the impact of which is regulated by tax laws; and
– the wholly foreign-owned venture.[34]

The following concerns only equity joint ventures and will neglect the other forms mentioned above.

FINANCIAL CONSTITUTION OF JOINT VENTURES

I understand 'financial constitution' to embrace the whole financial scheme of a joint venture, such as the amount of the equity capital, the participation ratio, the structure of investments and their evaluation, the determination of profit and the retransfer of the capital invested.

I shall briefly deal with each of these questions.

---

32. *See* Horsley, 'Investing in China in 1985', Theroux, E. (ed.), *Legal Aspects of Doing Business with China 1985*, New York 1985, p. 156.
33. *See* Messmann, 'La norme juridique et la réalité dans la législation chinoise sur les sociétés mixtes', *Lausanne Symposium*, note 13 above, pp. 225–238.
34. To be regulated by the Law of the P. R. of China on Enterprises Operated Exclusively with Foreign Capital of 12 April 1986; for an English translation *see* CEN, note 5 above, 21 April 1986. However, the existing wholly foreign-owned ventures have been established prior to the enactment of this law.

Amount of the equity capital

In my introduction I mentioned that from 1979 to the end of 1987 10,000 Sino-foreign contracts for establishment of equity joint ventures were signed. Roughly 3,000 of them are equity joint ventures. Nevertheless, in examining the amounts invested according to these joint venture contracts, I have to put them in correct economic perspective: 63 per cent of joint ventures have an investment amount of below US$1-million, 25 per cent have an investment between US$1 and 5-million, five per cent between US$5 and 10-million, four per cent between US$10 and 30-million, and only 1.7 per cent have an investment amount higher than US$30-million.

In other words even if the number of joint venture contracts signed is encouraging, the total amount of investments according to such joint venture contracts hardly satisfy the Chinese expectations.

The Chinese legislation for joint ventures provides a minimum participation ration of 25 per cent for the foreign partner,[35] but there is no minimum amount in absolute figures for the foreign partner's participation.

By enacting a participation limit of 25 per cent, the Chinese legislator argued that an efficient participation of the foreign partner in the management of the joint venture can only be expected if the foreign partner is really willing to contribute to a minimum extent to the equity capital of the joint venture.

This minimum contribution is considered by the Chinese to be at 25 per cent. On the other hand, China sees in this amount the underlimit to reach its macro-economic targets by absorbing foreign capital.

Originally, neither the Joint Venture Law nor its Implementation Regulations provide the ratio between the equity capital of the joint venture and the loans. It appears, however, that many joint ventures were undercapitalized having a ratio between the equity capital and loans as bad as 1:10. As a reaction to this phenomenon, the Chinese legislator modified Article 21 of the Implementation Regulations, stipulating that in cases where the total amount of investments do not reach US$3-million, no loan will be granted to the joint venture.

At investments between US$3 and 10-million, the registered capital has to reach the half of the total investments and at least, US$3-million. At investments between US$10 and 30-million, the ratio between equity capital and loans has to be 1:3 and the registered capital at least US$5-million. At investments higher than US$ 30-million, the ratio has to be 1:4 at a minimum registered capital of US$10-million.[36]

---

35. Joint Venture Law, Article 4 paragraph 2.
36. *See* Provisional Regulations Governing the Proportion of Registered Capital to total Investment of Sino-Foreign Joint Ventures of 1 March 1987; for an English translation *see* *FBIS Daily Pub.*, PRC, 2 March 1987.

Until now, joint venture partners were free to fix the deadlines for capital contribution payments. However, the new Investment Regulations for the Partners of Sino-Foreign Joint Ventures which entered into effect on 1 March 1988 state that investment deadlines should be clearly defined in joint venture contracts. If the contract requires the investment be made in one lump sum, payment must be made within six months after the joint venture contract is approved. A joint venture will be automatically disbanded if the partners fail to make investments on time as required under the contract.[37]

Structure of capital contributions and their evaluation

Capital contributions may be made, according to the Joint Venture Law, in cash as well as in kind.[38] Contributions in kind are above all property rights and know-how, right to use of land, buildings, plants, equipment, and trade-marks.

Accordingly, the contributions in kind may be divided into two categories:

– in such containing transfer of technology; and
– in such relating to equipment, right to use of land, buildings, and plants.

The Chinese legislator has a broad understanding of the notion of technology transfer. His understanding is not only limited to the transfer of documents necessary for the manufacture of a product, but much more.

The demand to obtain as much technology as possible is explicitly contained in the demand for automatic transfer of even future know-how of the transferor. The transfer of technology implies, besides the transfer of drawings and plans, especially the training of personnel both in China as well as abroad and the corresponding consecutive transfer of know-how for manufacturing, quality assurance, after-sales and management.

Article 44 of the Implementation Regulations stipulates the modality of the technology transfer when made as a contribution in kind of the foreign partner. It states that the technology acquired by the joint venture shall be appropriate and advanced and enable the product to reach conspicuous economic results domestically or to be competitive on the international market.

But China did not set universally valid standards to determine in which cases the technology to be transferred is appropriate and advanced. These notions may only be validated casuistically by comparison with other products and manufacturing methods by taking into consideration the following conditions:

---

37. *See* Provisions on the Contribution of Capital by parties to Joint Ventures Using Chinese and Foreign Capital of 1 March 1988 (to be published in English).
38. Joint Venture Law, Article 5.

- China should eagerly need the product to be manufactured or it should be qualified for export;
- the product in question should contain considerable improvements in quality in comparison with products already manufactured as well as cause higher productivity in manufacturing process; and last but not least
- it should lead to considerable saving of raw materials and energy.

The provisions of the Regulations on Administration of Technology Import Contracts of the P. R. of China from 24 May 1985[39] are some-what more explicit but in principle the before-said remains valid.

Problems of evaluation relating to equipment, right to use of land, buildings and plants arise mainly from the Chinese economic system itself.

In substance, it is essential to mention that often the depreciation methods used by Chinese state enterprises are not easily understandable because either exact figures are not available or they cannot be made transparent enough for the purposes of the foreign partner.

Apart from this, Chinese use rather low depreciation rates, in comparision with international practice, like most socialist countries.

However, in a concern to make investments for foreigners more attractive, many regions (but not the whole country uniformally) enacted, *inter alia*, new rules on depreciation rates. Thus, e.g., in Dalian the depreciation rates are fixed for:

- buildings at fifteen per cent;
- machinery and equipment at twenty per cent; and
- vehicles, electronical and measuring instruments between 30 and 40 per cent.[40]

The reform of state enterprises may also change the situation just described in so far. In the future, state enterprises running with profit shall be evaluated according to the use of their production means: i.e. the Chinese machinery and equipment to be contributed in kind by the Chinese side shall be evaluated by taking into consideration the average profit of the last three years of the enterprise concerned.

Not less problematic is the evaluation of premises. Until now Chinese partners indicated rates which were far higher than those for comparable items in the countries of the east and south-east Asian region.

Chinese officials explained such figures with the argument that they also contain the compensation of costs for infrastructure to be established parallely.

In order to encourage foreign investors, the State Council uniformized in November 1986 the site-use fees. Acordingly, site-use fees for export-

---

39. *See* note 21 above.
40. *See* Nachrichten für Außenhandel, 31 October 1986.

oriented or technologically advanced enterprises, except for those located in busy urban sectors of large cities, shall be computed and charged according to the following standards:

- five to twenty Yuan per square meter per year in areas where the development fee and the site use fee are computed and charged together; and
- not more than three Yuan in site areas where the development fee is computed and charged on a one-time basis or areas which are developed by the joint ventures themselves.[41]

Determination of the profit

The joint ventures form in the Chinese economy an extraneous body comparable, for example, with the situation of joint ventures in Rumania. Therefore joint ventures are mainly regulated by special legislation which is not applicable to Chinese enterprises without foreign capital. According to these specific regulations Chinese joint ventures may, unlike purely Chinese enterprises, fix their sales prices autonomously, i.e. without approval by competent Chinese authorities. Joint ventures shall only submit the prices fixed by themselves to the authorities for the record.

By this, we are reaching one of the most important points of an equity engagement in the People's Republic of China at all. That is to say that in a country regulating directly or indirectly each business activity of a joint venture, it would not be advisable to take any engagement if a joint venture could not fix its sales prices freely and influence by this the formation of profits. This being guaranteed by the legislation, it remains a matter of agreement how to construct a reasonable guaranty-like provision in negotiating the contract.

Politically somewhat delicate is the answer to the question which amount of profit the Chinese may consider as reasonable. The answer will certainly differ from one economic branch to other and the profit rate may also depend on the amount invested as well as on the duration of the joint venture. In most cases, however, the profit is determined in certain percentage of the turnover or the registered capital.

It is interesting to notice in this regard that, according to Chinese sources, more than 90 per cent of the joint ventures already operating are making profits. Only few joint ventures closed or have serious problems.

Retransfer of capital

The problem of capital retransfer emerges from the Joint Venture Law itself. Namely the law does not answer the question whether the foreign

---

41. Provisions of the State Council of the P. R. of China for the Encouragement of Foreign Investment on 11 October 1986, Article 4; for an English translation *see Shanghai Economic News*, 15 November 1986.

partner may retransfer the value effectively invested, i.e. the genuine or historical value, or the re-valorized value, i.e. the effective value of the assets of the joint venture at the liquidation in a proportion of the registered capital.

Though the Joint Venture Law does not answer this question, the practice shows that joint venture contracts may foresee the retransfer of the effective value of assets of the joint venture due to the foreign partner at the liquidation even taking into consideration the ongoing concern principle. It seems to be important to mention in this context that in case of litigations on liquidations the foreign partner may submit such litigations to a foreign arbitral tribunal even against Chinese authorities. This seems to be of particular importance because the Chinese partners and authorities usually avoid, according to current experiences, litigation during the terms of joint venture contracts but this attitude may change radically at the liquidation of a joint venture.

ORGANS OF JOINT VENTURES

There is still no company law in China regulating joint venture companies. The Joint Venture Law and its Implementation Regulations only present a frame of a probably future company law.[42] Therefore it must be the task of the joint venture contract to regulate the organization of joint ventures and especially to determine the competences of their organs.

The practice knows in this context various solutions. These solutions conform in many cases to the company law of the foreign partner. In most cases, however, joint ventures adopted the Anglo-American system of the board as the only organ having both supervisory and management functions.

Beside this system, the dual system is often adopted. In the Volkswagen joint venture this last mentioned system has been chosen. Accordingly, this joint venture has beside the board of directors as a supervisory organ a management board as a separate organ called executive management committee.[43]

Board of directors

The Joint Venture Law stipulates that the board of directors is the highest organ of the joint venture. According to the law,[44] the chairman shall be nominated by the Chinese partner while the vice chairman may also be nominated by the foreign partner. Despite this clear regulation exceptions

---

42. *See* Münzel, *op. cit.*, note 13 above.
43. *See* Messmann, *op. cit.*, note 33 above, as well as idem, Chinesische Gesetzgebung über Investitionen und Technologietransfer – bisherige Erfahrungen der Praxis, BfA Rechtsinformation Nr. 194, 1985.
44. Joint Venture Law, Article 6 paragraph 1.

from this rule are frequent. These exceptions often arise from the desire of the Chinese partners themselves to transfer the charge of management of the joint venture to the foreign partner especially at the start-up phase because they probably think that the foreign partner is more experienced to run the company in some special cases.

In the Volkswagen joint venture, the board of directors consists of ten members five of which are nominated by Volkswagen. The chairman and the second vice chairman are nominated by our Chinese partners while the first vice chairman shall, according to the articles of association, always be nominated by the foreign partner.

The board of directors shall deliberate and decide all important questions in connection with the business activities of the joint venture. These are especially:

- nomination of executive managers and cadres;
- establishment of expansion and development plans;
- establishment of production and business programs;
- budgets;
- determination and repartition of profits;
- termination of the business activity; and
- all other questions the contracting parties may determine.

In most joint ventures, the board of directors convenes at least once a year for a meeting. A second or third meeting is rather an exception because board meetings often last several days or even a week. Of course, this shall not be generalized. For example, the board meetings of the Volkswagen joint venture generally do not last more than two or three hours. The board meetings usually take place at the business place of the joint venture, which solution is, however, not compulsory but desired by the Chinese board members.

The long duration of most board meetings and the fact that they usually take place in China are very time-consuming. The foreign partner therefore faces the problem whom to nominate as a board member. Should the foreign partner nominate his top managers who cannot afford to consecrate too much time to Chinese affairs, he will be well advised to foresee alternates for regular board members. It is equally possible to foresee in articles of association, in addition or alternately to the just mentioned solution, that board members may also exercise their prerogatives by proxies. In consideration of these various solutions the foreign partner shall, however, have in mind that continuity and personal contacts play a very important role in business relations with Chinese partners.

Executive management committee

The executive management committee in the Volkswagen joint venture has day-to-day managerial duties, i. e. the duties of the Vorstand of a company organized under German law. It consists of four members, the Chinese side having the right to nominate the managing director, who is in the same time also a member of the board of directors, as well as the personnel and administrative director, while Volkswagen has the permanent right to nominate the production director and the commercial director. The commercial direction comprises all financial, sales and purchase activities.

It appears from the aforesaid that the partners to the Volkswagen joint venture opted for a double parity: In the board of directors as well as in the executive management committee.

A specific problem in both organs may be the regulation of the right to represent the joint venture both in and out of court. Chinese partners often argue that the chairman of the board being the legal representative of the joint venture according to the Joint Venture Law, shall be the only legal representative of the joint venture. They further use to argue that the chairman of the board may transmit his representation competences to other persons at his choice. The fear of the foreign partner of potential abuses emanating from such a solution may appear justified. In my opinion, too, this solution for a joint venture with equal foreign participation is not quite satisfactory.

Under these circumstances, one of the solutions might be that the Chinese chairman of the board of directors shall indeed be the legal representative of the joint venture but may only represent the joint venture both in and out of court together with the first vice chairman or another board member nominated by the foreign partner.

In the executive management committee, the Volkswagen joint venture also adopted the principle of double representation according to the German company law. This principle, which does not exist in other legal systems, foresees that all important engagements have to be signed by two executive managers nominated by the Chinese and foreign side respectively.

At the regulation of the working method of the executive management committee one should focus his attention especially at stale-mates in this organ. I think that in the board of directors for strategical reasons solutions will always be reached even if deliberations there may be time-consuming. This, however, may be different in the executive management committee facing day-to-day management problems. Long deliberations and failing in decision-making in this organ may have more far-reaching consequences than similar situations in the board. Therefore, in the Volkswagen joint venture in cases no decision is reached in the executive management committee, the matter will be subject for decision by unanimous vote of the chairman and the two vice chairmen. Should this restraint board also fail to reach a decision, the entire board shall decide.

DURATION OF JOINT VENTURES

The Chinese investment law previously did not foresee neither a minimum nor a maximum period of duration for joint ventures. For Chinese authorities the only important point of view so far is that the foreign capital should not remain permanently present in the Chinese economy. This somewhat ideologically colored requirement is not specific to China. We can find it in all other socialist countries permitting and regulating foreign investments.

Only the Implementation Regulations have stipulated a duration from ten to 30 years for joint ventures. This provision changed, however, some time ago and stipulates actually a maximum duration for joint ventures of 50 years.

Outlook

Although the Joint Venture Law was enacted as early as mid-1979, it lasted a quite long period of time until foreign partners in greater number decided on equity engagements in China. From 1984 to the beginning of 1986, it seemed that the break-even point for foreign investment was reached. The first semester of 1986 indicated, however, a clear cut-down of foreign investment of twenty per cent in comparison with the same period of 1985.[45] The reasons for such a development may be found above all in:

– the contradiction in the economic reform itself (causing especially distorted price structures and engendering thus a hardly controlable economic framework;[46]
– the deterioration of China's investment climate as a result of such economic development;
– the lack of skilled staff and workers as well as of experienced managers; as well as
– the development of the local supply industry for manufacturing joint ventures.

The Chinese leadership rightly assessed the thus created situation and reacted promptly: the promulgation of the Provisions of the State Council of the P. R. of China for Encouragement of Foreign Investment[47] was the first step to improve the investment climate. These provisions apply to all enterprises set up in China with foreign investment:

---

45. *See Handelsblatt*, 7 October 1986.
46. *See* Hiemenz and Bo Li, 'Die Volksrepublik China – Absatzmarkt und Investitionsstandort der Zukunft?', *Kiel Discussion Papers of the Institut für Weltwirtschaft Kiel*, December 1986.
47. The so-called 'Twenty-two Clauses'. These provisions were completed by regional measures. Furthermore, a complete set of rules and regulations has been formulated by the Ministers and Departments under the State Council in order to implement the 'Twenty-two Clauses'. They are all published with English translation, i.e., in the Collection of the Laws and Regulations for the Encouragement of Foreign Investment in Beijing in May 1987 by the Department of Treaties and Law of the Ministry of Foreign Economic Relations and Trade.

- they are allowed to trade foreign exchange with Renminbi among themselves, instead of having to go through a bank;
- if foreign investors reinvest their profits in China, the tax paid on profit is refunded if such reinvestment lasts at least five years;
- they are exempt from paying the consolidated industrial and commercial tax (a kind of sales tax) levied on goods to be exported (except for crude oil and a few other items);
- procedures for imports of machinery and raw materials and exports of end products are simplified;
- the autonomy of joint ventures is reaffirmed. Thus they have the authority to set production plans, hire or dismiss employees, set wages and manage their enterprises 'with international advanced scientific methods'.

Some other regional measures include furthermore the following incentives:

- fees for use of Chinese land have been reduced to the minimum rate charged in municipal regulations for the particular type of land in question;
- joint ventures pay the same rates as state-owned enterprises for electricity, gas, water and heating instead of higher rates charged previously,
- joint ventures are charged by only twenty per cent of the total amount of wages and salaries of their staff and workers;
- housing and commuting subsidies that investors have to pay their staff and workers are reduced; and
- exemption from local taxes is extended from two to seven years after a joint venture becomes profitable.

As the result of such measures, as early as 1987 2,230 enterprises with foreign investment, with a total contract volume of US$3.68-billion, had been approved. It represented an increase of 30 per cent over 1986.[48]

Of course, the effect of these new incentives are not yet palpable. But they might contribute perhaps to a more realistical approach of the foreign partners to the Chinese market[49] and to put the expectations of the potential investors and the real possibilities in China in a commensurate relation.

The remaining part to be contributed by the foreign partner to the successful business of a joint venture is, however, a great one. One of the most important tasks of the foreign partner is to enable the personnel of the joint venture to achieve its work. The labor skill of Chinese staff and workers has been largely neglected during the Cultural Revolution. Thus, most joint ventures lack skilled labor forces as well as experienced local

---

48. *See China Daily*, 23 January 1988.
49. The American Counsel General in Hong Kong, Mr. Burton Levi, is of the opinion that many foreign investors are rather careless in doing business with China. *See* Ausländische Investoren in China sind oft leichtsinnig', *Blick durch die Wirtschaft*, 11 June 1986.

managers. However, it is both difficult to dismiss unable labor force and to recruit more capable ones from other localities than the seat of the joint ventures.

As a matter of fact:

- the dismissal of staff and workers would create politically and economically intolerable unemployment; and
- the more skilled labor force often meets bureaucratical and economic burdens.

In such a situation, joint ventures cannot but give incentives to and to train the existing labor potential at place.

At the Volkswagen joint venture, this target is envisaged by the introduction of two substantial measures:

- a new salary and wages system; and
- a training program.

Soon after its establishment, the Volkswagen joint venture abandoned the state stipulated uniform wages and salary system replacing it by a new incentive system. The introduction of the new wages and salary system serves the following aims:

- more fairness through remuneration related to job requirements;
- performance incentive for all employees through a performance bonus linked to the productivity of the joint venture; and
- motivation of all employees through appropriate development and promotion possibilities to more demanding and thus higher paid positions.

The new wages and salary system consists in:

- basic salary and wages depending on the requirements of the posts;
- subsidies as stipulated by the state; and
- premium depending on the production output.

Really new in this system is the premium to be calculated on the basis of the production volume. It means that the premium will be given when the annual production volume reaches 85 per cent of the planned volume or more and will be calculated in proportion to the production volume in excess. The calculation of the premium takes place individually and is based on the performance appraised by the respective superiors. The appraisal takes place every six months.

The joint venture also introduced a traning program. It consists of:

- an apprentice training for graduates from junior middle schools; and
- a development/management training.

All the apprentices in the first year, independent of the later professions, will have the same elemental training. After this period, they shall be trained in their specialized fields. In the last year of apprenticeship, the apprentices will be sent into the factory for a professional on-the-job training.

The development/management training aims, on the other hand, to qualify the staff and workers of all sections to higher performance consisting in in-plant and outside training.

More sensitive, because it is out of the control of joint ventures, is the development of the local supply industry for the purposes of manufacturing joint ventures.

The difficulties of the Chinese supply industry are multiple:

– on the one hand they are comparable with the difficulties of the joint ventures themselves as far as they concern the labor force;
– on the other hand they are different (and additional) as far as they concern the availability of foreign exchange for imports of raw materials and technology as well as other elements like energy supply and additional investments in order to satisfy the requirements of joint ventures.

However, the Chinese authorities concerned are well aware of the problems of the supply industry as outlined above. They are therefore undertaking sincere efforts in order to remedy the actual difficulties. It will certainly take time to overcome them, but the continuation of the actual political and economical reforms may be considered as an encouraging sign of success.